EN6GW

FREUD AND FUTURE RELIGIOUS
EXPERIENCE

FREUD
AND FUTURE
RELIGIOUS
EXPERIENCE

Anthony J. De Luca, Ph.D.

Philosophical Library
New York

This head of Christ [Titian's "Maundy Money"], . . . , is the only one that enables even people like ourselves to imagine that such a person did exist. Indeed, it seemed that I was compelled to believe in the eminence of this man because the figure is so convincingly presented. And nothing divine about it, just a noble countenance, far from beautiful yet full of seriousness, intensity, profound thought, and deep inner passion; . . . I would love to have gone away with it, but there were too many people about . . .

Sigmund Freud, "Letter to Martha Bernays,"
December 20, 1883.

CONTENTS

Preface   xiii

Acknowledgments   xv

Introduction   1

Chapter I   Development of Person (Ontogeny):
            Genetic and Teleological Influences,   19
    A. The Evolutionary Thinkers: Darwin, Haeckel,
       Lamarck, Jackson,   20
    B. Freud's Composite Evolutionary Model: Genetic,
       Phylogenetic, Adaptive, Teleological,   22
    C. Phylogenetic and Genetic Influences on
       Ontogeny of Person,   24
       1. Growth,   24
       2. Regression,   26
    D. Adaptive and Teleological Influences on
       Ontogeny of Person,   28
       1. Growth,   28
       2. Regression,   33
    E. Philosophical Analysis of the Evolutionary Model,   34
       1. Nature and Proper Use of Model,   34
       2. Changeability of Biological Models,   35
       3. Genetic Model: Insufficient,   36
       4. Phylogenetic Model: Meaningless,   38
       5. Teleological Model: Insufficient,   40
    F. Philosophy of Genesis and Telos,   41
       1. Notions of Genesis, Telos, Reductionism, Dialectic,   41
       2. Extension of Our Notions to Freud's Thought,   43

Chapter II   Psychoanalytic Concepts Descriptive of Person:
      Genesis and Telos,   55
  A. Philosophical Analysis of Psychoanalytic Concepts,   56
    1. Concepts Borrowed from Other Sciences to Describe
      Human Psyche,   56
    2. Relation of Concepts and Structures to Observables,   58
    3. Concepts Reformulated as Observables,   60
    4. Confirmability: Verification and Falsification,   62
      a. Oedipus Complex,   62
      b. Topological and Structural Concepts,   63
      c. Unconscious,   65
  B. Dialectic of Genesis and Telos in the Psychoanalytic
    Concepts,   69
    1. Conscious and Unconscious,   70
    2. Ego, Id, Superego,   72
    3. Identification,   72
    4. Sublimation,   73

Chapter III   The Religious Neurosis: Genesis and Telos,   81
  A. Exposition of Cases Dealing with Religious Phenomena:
    Genesis,   83
    1. Paraphrenias,   83
      a. Dementia Praecox,   83
        1. Mechanism,   83
        2. The American Physician,   84
      b. Paranoia,   85
        1. Mechanism,   85
        2. Schreiber Case,   86
    2. Obsessions,   91
      a. Mechanism,   91
      b. Obsessions and Religious Practices,   93
      c. "Rat Man,"   95
      d. "Wolf Man,"   97
    3. Hysterias,   102

a. Anxiety Phobia, 102
1. Mechanism, 102
2. "Little Hans," 104
3. "Wolf Man," 105
b. Conversion Hysteria, 106
1. Mechanism, 106
2. Haizmann Case, 108
3. Dostoevsky Case, 112
4. "Un-neurotic"—Leonardo, 114
B. Philosophical Critique of the Methodology Employed, 117
1. Experimental Setting: Interview, 118
2. Scientific Status of Interpretation (Hypothesis), 120
a. Clinical Inference, 120
b. "Causal" Relationships: Similarity, Contiguity, Frequency, 121
c. Prediction and Postdiction, 122
d. Overdetermination, 124
e. Refutability, 125
1. Control, 126
2. Lack of data, 127
3. Not Public, 127
3. Non-experimental Setting of Cases, 128
a. Absent Patient, 128
b. Overdetermination, 129
c. Inaccurate Historical Data, 130
4. Conclusion, 132
C. Reductive Analysis of Religious Phenomena in the Cases Allows for Possible Emergence of Sacred: Telos, 133
1. Exploration of the Notions of Symbol, Sacred, "Wholly Other", Religion and Faith, 133
2. Religious Neuroses: Sign of Sublimation, Identification and Archaic Symbol of the Sacred, 136
3. Religious Symbol, 144
4. Sacred Symbol, 145
5. Evolution in Awareness of "Wholly Other" as Other, 148

Chapter IV   The Origins of Religion: Genesis and Telos,   159
  A. Analogy of the Development of Neurosis (Individual) and
    Religion (Race),   160
    1. The Analogy,   160
      a. Trauma,   160
      b. Latency,   161
      c. Return of the Repressed,   161
    2. Difficulties in the Analogy,   162
  B. Exposition of the Evolution of Religion from Its Origins:
    Genesis,   164
    1. Animism,   165
      a. Pre-animism,   166
      b. Animism Proper,   166
    2. Taboo,   169
      a. Taboo Analogous to Obsessional Neurotic and
        Anal Stage,   169
      b. Comparison of Taboo and Obsessional
        Prohibition,   170
    3. Gods and Their Surrogates,   173
      a. Totemism,   173
      b. Monotheism,   176
    4. Conclusion: Gradual "Return of the Repressed,"   182
  C. Philosophical Critique of the Reductive Analysis of the
    Origins of Religion,   183
    1. Methodology Employed,   183
      a. Use of Analogy,   183
      b. Field Work,   184
      c. Primal Crime as Historical,   184
      d. Archaic Heritage,   185
    2. Underlying Principles Involved,   186
      a. Causes,   186
      b. Genetic Explanation,   188
      c. Evolution and Unilinear View,   189
      d. Monocausality,   191
      e. Methodological Individualism,   192
  D. Reductive Analysis of Religious Phenomena in Culture
    Allows for Possible Emergence of Sacred: Telos,   194

1. Evolution in Awareness of "Wholly Other" as Other,   195
2. Religious Forms Seen as Symbols of "Wholly Other,"   198

Chapter V Contemporary Religious Experience:
             Genesis and Telos,   207
A. Exposition of Contemporary Religion: Genesis,   208
   1. Religious Ideas and Infantile Foundations,   208
      a. Illusions,   208
      b. Consolation,   209
      c. Accusation,   212
   2. Reason for Religious Beliefs,   216
      a. Tradition,   216
      b. "Credo Quia Absurdum,"   217
      c. Act "As If,"   219
      d. Philosophy   219
   3. Religionless Education,   220
      a. Science,   223
      b. Psychoanalysis,   226
B. Critique of Freud's Position,   227
   1. Religious Person as Dependent,   227
   2. Future Consolation,   227
   3. Value of Individual Religious Experience,   228
   4. "Purpose" in the World,   229
   5. "Scientism", Philosophy and Religion,   229
C. Emergence of a Religion Beyond Accusation and
   Consolation: Telos,   232
D. Freud's Contribution to Contemporary Philosophy of
   Religion,   235
   1. Abandonment of Naïveté,   235
   2. Commitment to the World,   235
   3. Purification,   237
E. Summary,   240

Bibliography,   251

Index,   263

Freud and Future Religious Experience
PREFACE

I would like to consider this work in the long tradition of *theologia negativa* or simply what God is not—his unknowability. Dionysius, while dependent on those before him, brings into focus the *via negativa* which all subsequent thinkers have modified and elaborated upon; some were consciously aware of what they were doing as Aquinas and others perhaps unconsciously like Freud. I am not alone in linking Freud to this tradition. My work has been long in process and others were sympathetically perceiving the same thing.[1]

As Dionysius said long ago the mind begins by denying of God those things which are most removed from Him and proceeds upwards gradually denying of God the qualities of creatures till it attains "the super-essential Darkness." Man is inclined to anthropomorphic conceptions of God and it is necessary to take away these human ideas *(via remotionis)*. When the mind has freed itself from thinking of God incorrectly i.e. in the human way, it enters the "Darkness of Unknowing," or the realm of mysticism.

My work is a cerebral excursion—by that I mean it places emphasis upon ideas, thoughts, and intellect rather than upon feelings, desires and affect. So it sounds more philosophical than mystical. However, it is only a beginning. Hopefully, at a later time this schizophrenia will be healed through another work.

---

[1]Fromm, Erich, "Letters to Dr. DeLuca," June 14, 1973; June 27, 1973, Feb. 10, 1975. "Some Post Marxian and Post Freudian Thoughts on Religion and Religiousness," *Concilium* (New York: Paulist Press, 1972) pp. 146-154.

ACKNOWLEDGMENTS

The author and publishers wish to thank the following for permission to quote from their various works:

Duquesne University Press, Pittsburgh (*Phenomenology of Atheism,* by William A. Luijpen, copyright 1964 by Duquesne University Press);

New York University Press, New York ("Psychoanalysis and its Discontents," by Ernest Van den Haag in *Psychoanalysis, Scientific Method, and Philosophy,* edited by Sidney Hook, copyright 1959 by New York University Press);

Yale University Press, New Haven (*Freud and Philosophy* by Paul Ricoeur and translated by Denis Savage, copyright 1970 by Yale University Press).

Allen and Unwin Ltd., London, from the *Introductory Lectures* in *The Standard Edition of the Complete Psychological Works of Sigmund Freud,* edited by James Strachey, published by Allen and Unwin Ltd., by arrangement with The Hogarth Press, Ltd., the Institute of Psycho-Analysis and Sigmund Freud Copyrights Ltd.

Basic Books, Inc., New York, from "A Seventeenth Century Demonological Neurosis," in *Collected Papers of Sigmund Freud,* Vol. 4 and from "Notes upon a Case of Obsessional Neurosis," in *Collected Papers of Sigmund Freud,* Vol. 3, both edited by James Strachey, published by Basic Books, Inc., by arrangement with The Hogarth Press, Ltd., the Institute of Psycho-Analysis and Sigmund Freud Copyrights Ltd.

FREUD AND FUTURE RELIGIOUS EXPERIENCE

Introduction

We are approaching the passing of the second millenium; and whatever our world view may be, it undoubtedly has been influenced by the religious traditions that stand before and after the pivotal point which marks the common era. The views which religious traditions, theologians and philosophers have given us of the "Wholly Other," God, or Supreme Being, are in constant need of modification due to the simple fact that they are communicated in a process universe; world views change and as a result concepts of the "Wholly Other" evolve too. Man has no odyssey unless there is a succession of moments; and the journey to the "Wholly Other" is marked by steps which are subject to the erosion of time; thus the path is always more or less obscure.

When we look to history in considering man's religious odyssey, we find the believer for the most part employing a guide to help on that journey. Strangely, the guide does not always seem to be a believer of the same persuasion. The Bishop of Hippo selected the pagan Plotinus; Dante called upon Virgil to help on the trip to the Beatific Vision; Aquinas needed Plato and Aristotle—two good pagan Greeks—for his five ways to God and the divine names. Could there have been the mystic poet Teilhard without Darwin who unfortunately was not a member of the "true faith?"

It seems that man has not given up on the impulse or desire to speak about or even relate to the ground of being—the "Wholly Other." And now the eve of the third millenium: whom do we take as a guide for our sophisticated believer who presently enjoys a heightened state of consciousness which ancient man could never have dreamed of? When we search our century, which some have called the analytical century, we realize the guide would have to be one who has plumbed

1

the depths of the human psyche in a way no man has ever done before. The guide will be the unbeliever Sigmund Freud (1856-1939).

In our work on Freud's theory of religion and contribution to the philosophy of religion, we take the position that his reductionism of religious manifestation to wish fulfillment has validity but is not exhaustive. His reductionism is a necessary step to appreciating an implicit teleology[1] discoverable to us. For we believe that besides reductionism there is also an implicit teleology in Freud's thought. The presence of this teleology allows *us* to further develop this side of Freud with reference to a philosophy of religion. The significance for the field of philosophy of religion is that reductionism destroys "religion" with the result that the implicit teleology, we discover, points to faith. The "religion" which we refer to as passing away is "*negative religion*" which has become irrelevant because of its cultural limitations. This type of "religion" is not a viable form in helping man reach out to God or the "Wholly Other." We are not speaking of religion which, for example, William James speaks of in the *Varieties of Religious Experience*. By faith, we mean man's act of belief or assent to a world which is revelatory and which points to an ultimate. These positions will be discussed in the following pages.

We will consider first Freud's *theory of religion*; he speaks about the God man has made. Freud concedes that it is possible that there might be a God and even one corresponding to the ideas man has of Him. However, he considers the expression of man's relation to God—religion—as man made: the forms which religion has taken grew out of the culture of the time or the particular psychological disposition of the individual person. Thus religion is *man's* attempt to relate or communicate with another being whom he calls God. In speaking of God most men have similar ideas about Him; He is considered all powerful and as Creator.

Freud makes use of the psychoanalytic method to investigate any phenomenon which involves man as an individual or as a group; psychoanalysis was devised in order to understand the human mind. He considered analysis as a branch of empirical psychology and therefore scientific; the psychoanalytic hypotheses and theories arrived at by him were derived from observations of the behavior of his patients. In order to gain scientific respectability for psychoanalysis, Freud tried to model his methodology after the other sciences. Thus he allowed room for the falsification of his generalizations, as seen in the modifications in his theories over the course of his writings. In addition, he generalized from his neurotic patients because he assumed only a quantitative and not a qualitative difference between the neurotic and the "normal."

Since Freud used psychoanalysis to understand man, he felt the method was applicable to man as manifesting religious behavior. For religious behavior merely shows man engaged in one human activity among his many others. Analysis, by definition, is reductionistic; i.e., it breaks down an observed psychological phenomenon into its components. Freud analyzed religious behavior (the manifest) and found that there was a correspondence with unconscious conflicts or wish fulfillments (the latent). Thus he considered that religious behavior was a neurotic manifestation or at least an answer to unconscious wishes. Religion was an *illusion* because it was an answer to all our wish fulfillments and promised all those things which we most longed for.

For Freud, religion was an infantile manifestation because religious people showed the same longings, fears, and desires which the little child displayed toward his father; the religious man feared, desired and longed for God the Father. It was especially clear that the neurotic used religion as a repressive force against the unconscious impulses which he feared.

Freud points out that not only did the *individual* use religion as a way of manifesting neurotic conflicts and wish fulfillment, but religion as practiced by *mankind* was a manifestation of the same thing. Just as the neurotic is faced with his unresolved Oedipal conflict, so the race has never forgotten the primal crime; humanity is still guilty over this primordial incident. Mankind, like the neurotic who desires his own father, still longs for the primal father.

While Freud reduces religious experience (both of the individual and of the group) to unconscious conflicts and wish fulfillments, he nevertheless looks forward to the time of the passing of religion. On the analogy of an individual neurotic who outgrows or is helped to overcome his conflict, mankind will outgrow its neurosis—religion. When a child reaches maturity, he puts away the infantile things and

3

so the race as it matures will give up its infantile desires. There is the gradual exchange of the "pleasure principle" (the way we would like things to be) for the "reality principle" (the way things are). For Freud, the demise of religion will bring the liberation of man from the gods he has created. No longer will a god of morality stand over man accusing him. At the same time, man must come to realize that there is no god of consolation which he found as a child in his own father. With the passing of illusions, man is better equipped to stand in the presence of the universe and comprehend it. At present, man makes use of Science which is the best instrument so far for revealing the world as it really is.

Let us now consider the relationship of Freud's theory of religion to the *philosophy of religion*. Philosophy of religion is usually taken to mean a philosophical discipline in which the thinker engages in reflective thinking about man's religious experience or worship. When we consider philosophy of religion we are thinking primarily about the examination of *man's* experience. Freud is not usually considered a philosopher and he did not engage in anything resembling a natural theology; his treatment of the epistemological value of religious experience is very limited.

Freud did examine religious manifestation—man's expression of his relationship with God. However, he studies the phenomenon not as a philosopher, but as a psychoanalyst. From his studies he concluded that religion was a "universal obsessional neurosis." This statement could be taken to mean that religion, which is traditionally taken to be the manifestation or expression of man's relation to the Divine, or God, or the "Wholly Other," is interpreted as wish fulfillment. This statement has immediate philosophical implications. For, if correct, it would appear to destroy all previous and future attempts of philosophers to maintain that there is anything more than neurosis or the infantile involved in religious manifestation. Thus Freud does make a philosophical statement about religion. The ramifications are seen in the fact that philosophers of religion can hardly proceed without reflecting upon Freud's position.

Let us first consider Freud's method of investigation. We believe that if psychoanalysis is competent to investigate man (and religion is one of the activities of man), then psychoanalysis may be able to say something meaningful about his religious activities. The question that

4

the philosopher would be drawn to discuss in this matter would be the competency of psychoanalysis to investigate man completely. Since Freud proposes psychoanalysis as a science, the thought arises as to whether its methodology is satisfactory according to the norms of philosophy of science. Philosophy of science concerns itself with the meaningfulness of concepts and the proper formation of hypotheses. It shows that Freud used the concepts properly and arrived at hypotheses validly on the clinical level. Philosophy of science also shows that there is some degree of probability in the Freudian hypothesis that religious manifestation was an indication of wish fulfillment and/or neurosis. However, philosophy of science indicates that Freud does not give us anything conclusive because of lack of data. While Freud gains some support from philosophy of science on the clinical level, he does not do that well on the cultural level because his use of anthropological data was not in total accord with good methodology.

However, in spite of the limitations indicated by the philosophical critique made from the vantage point of the philosophy of science, there is some degree of support for Freud's conclusions. What is apparent is that Freud's investigation of religious phenomenon from the *genetic* aspect seems to be correct. Philosophy of science would point out that as far as a *reductionism* goes Freud's methodology was sound. Thus what has been revealed about "religion"—its neurotic and illusory side—we believe must be taken seriously. However, we maintain that a genetic analysis is not exhaustive in accounting for a phenomenon and here we believe this holds true for the religious phenomenon.

However, we wish to emphasize again that what has been revealed by the reductive analysis is true as far as it goes. Because we say our discovery is incomplete, we do not wish that what has been discovered be minimized. To minimize the results of the reductionism would mean that there has been no progress made in the development of the philosophy of religion. We want the philosopher of religion to *reflect* over the results of the reductionism, or the moment of negation or alienation. Too frequently, Freud has been dismissed as having a materialistic orientation and thus the philosopher of religion was tempted to ignore his conclusions. Philosophy of religion does itself a disservice with this attitude.

Thus we wish to reflect on the meaning of this moment of the reduction of religious experience. We reflect in a way analogous to the mystic who contemplates the darkness in order to better comprehend the emerging trace of light. It is only when we see the negative moment that we are better able to appreciate the elusive positive moment.

If evidence shows that Freud's conclusions are probably correct, then the philosopher has to re-examine his attitude toward religious experience. He must look to the *possibility* of the infantile at the root of his experience and may either abandon the evidence of psychoanalysis or accept the reductionism. The first option would be to ignore a portion of reality. The second option is a challenge. We would have to admit that a reductive interpretation points to the infantile basis of religion. This evidence would force us to look at religious manifestation without our previous naïveté.

Thus in Freud's analysis of religious manifestation the neurotic, the infantile and wish fulfillment have been revealed. The philosopher of religion has always been interested in purifying the religious experience. Before the time of psychoanalysis, the great mystics suffered with the problem of removing the projection of self from the "Wholly Other." Religion which has at its root solely the neurotic, the infantile and wish fulfillment we might call "*negative religion.*" Freud thus provides, through his reductionism (psychoanalysis), an instrument for the further purification of religious experience and the destruction of "negative religion." Psychoanalysis is particularly oriented toward the discovery and the removal of the neurotic from human behavior. Religious experience is part of the behavior of man. Thus analysis is of service in the removal of the neurotic at the foundation of the religious experience or in discovering the neurotic when it is intermingled with the religious experience.

"Negative religion" is not only manifested on the individual level but is also a cultural phenomenon. For religious forms which the community employs may no longer be meaningful—they may not have the capacity to bring man to an encounter with the "Wholly Other." Religious forms may once have been viable but presently they may take man further away from reality. Freud's analysis does much in removing the archaic forms of religion.

6

Thus far we have given emphasis to the reductive side of Freud's theory of religion. When we accept the validity of the Freudian reductionism, with its explanation by means of genesis, then the philosophical question may still arise as to whether a reductive explanation has *fully* accounted for the religious phenomenon under question. We may grant that the reductionism has revealed a great deal; e.g., the infantile dimension at the basis of religion. But a phenomenon is not totally explained by considering its genesis *alone.*

We believe that there is an *implicit* teleology to be found in Freud's thought. However, it is to be admitted that Freud does not speak of *teleology* in his writings; it is probable too that he was not aware of the teleological direction of his thought. Since we are dealing with psychic phenomenon, we will define teleology in terms of man. By teleology we mean direction or purpose—the employment of means to achieve an end. There is something *intrinsic* to man by which he moves to an end. The mind seems to have within itself a dynamism by which it stretches out to grasp more and more of reality; man grows in consciousness; mankind also grows and tends toward a more heightened consciousness. This movement or direction to a more and more heightened consciousness we view as teleological. We have teleology when we are able to see a direction emerge whether it be a movement from neurosis to health, the arrival at a more heightened consciousness, a greater grasp of reality, the victory of the "reality principle" over the "pleasure principle" or the emergence of a less and less distorted view of the "Wholly Other."

When a phenomenon under Freud's investigation is seen from *both* his explicit reductionism and the implicit teleology, it is more clearly understood. However, because the teleology is implicit, it is often necessary that we draw it out ourselves. This we believe can be done by setting up a dialectic between genesis and telos.[2] Thus in the process of reducing to genesis we are aware of our descent from the phenomenon under investigation. The descending steps of the genesis implicitly point to another factor which must be present to enable us to distinguish the lower steps from the higher; this we call *telos.*

We believe that a better understanding of Freud is achieved by the involvement of a dialectic in which we see a phenomenon negated by a reduction to genesis which in turn makes apparent a telos. We therefore believe that if we employ this dialectical approach to his analysis of religion, we will be able to have a deeper understanding of his contribution to the philosophy of religion.

Genesis and telos are two poles of a phenomenon; and there is a dialectic in Freud's thought between genesis and telos. Hence, the deeper significance of genesis is not realized unless it is seen by contrast with the emerging telos. For teleology is not completely understood without genesis. Thus Freudian reductionism or the descent to the genetic is a preparation for the ascent of the telos. With this orientation we can understand the reductionism to genesis and the implicit teleology in Freud's analysis of ontogeny of person. We believe that where he makes a reduction of person, a way opens up for the emergence of a teleological dimension of person. For while man may suffer from neurosis there is something intrinsic to his very being by which he attempts to integrate the aberration and move on to health.

A deeper philosophical insight into the psychoanalytic concepts describing person is seen when we explore their dialectic with each other: the concepts have their genetic side and their teleological side. In a way the id and superego look toward the past. Yet when id and superego are involved in a dialectic with the ego, which is in contact with the present, there is a forward movement. The unconscious seems to be in the sphere of the primordial; consciousness represents the here and now. But when impulses become conscious we have a forward movement. Repression seems to be an annihilation of the freedom of the ego but in the end the ego may emerge more liberated. In transference there is a struggle between self-alienation and recognition. Sublimation above all shows the person dying to himself and in the same moment the emergence of a new creativity.

There is a deeper philosophical meaning beyond the apparent reductionism of the religious neurosis. For even in the neuroses, there is a forward movement. The repressed, which was buried in the deep past, *finally* comes to full consciousness. At this point, the person is given a second opportunity to overcome or work through the neurosis; he is given an invitation to be reborn. There has been a continuous dialectic going on between the past and the present and between the unconscious and the conscious. With the ''return of the repressed'' to consciousness, past and present meet in one moment. The next moment determines whether a forward telos will emerge or whether there will be a descent into the past.

In any event, the dialectic continues: in "becoming conscious" the telos appears more readily; the new person is prepared to confront and struggle with reality anew on a plane of more heightened consciousness; where a person fails to come to grips with the returning-past-repressed he may appear to be defeated. But it is to be remembered that the struggle was not one taking place in the past but rather in the present moment. It is distinct from the past, thus allowing us to contrast the past moment with the present moment. Only the contrasting of the moments in the process enables us to determine a movement of "becoming conscious." Finally, it is only when we reduce the present to its genesis that a history of a struggle emerges. The religious neurosis is reduced to a symbol pointing to a struggle of the person trying to grasp reality and the present symbol cannot be reduced.

The religious symptom may be reduced to a symbol which also points beyond itself and which is also here in the present moment in the religious manifestation. But the symbol points in two directions: into the past and into the future. The symbol points to a past struggle of the ego trying to grasp reality but also being too threatened by it; the genesis of the neurosis holds this past history. Genesis consists of a series of steps—but one step at a time. Genesis does not distinguish the past from the present and does not reveal the future. Telos gives meaning to genesis and is the forward aspect of symbol. Telos does not reveal how things happened in each step of the struggle of the ego and reality, but it reveals the meaning of what has happened. Telos does not reveal one step. Telos only reveals that there are succeeding steps and indicates that we have moved.

Thus the reduction of the religious symptom to its genesis (the Oedipus drama) still allows for the emergence of symbol. The particular, varied, distorted religious symptom was not the significant factor. The significant factor emerges after the reductionism has taken place. We believe that religious experience, after it has been subjected to a reductive interpretation, emerges as a symbol of a person's continuous struggle to grasp reality. This endeavor to grasp reality ever more fully we regard as teleological. Religious experience thus bears

9

witness to the person's endeavor to see ever more fully reality as it reveals itself. For the person stands in time before the revealing cosmos; he asks questions about the meaning of reality; he asks questions about ultimate reality and his relation to the latter. The expression of this relationship or religion changes with time. But the quest is the same: a symbol of man trying to grasp the ultimate. Through an analysis of the various neuroses we are able to see an evolution in awareness of *other*. This forward movement in the evolution in awareness of other is viewed as teleological. In the religious neuroses, we may trace an evolution in awareness of the *"Wholly Other"*: there is a less distorted view of the "Wholly Other" which is seen to emerge. In examining the religious neuroses, we are involved in a negative theology.

The "Wholly Other" is the Transcendent. In our thinking we endeavor to prevent inadequate notions from being applied to this Being. We can have an awareness that there *is* a "Wholly Other" who is the ultimate source of meaning and being of the cosmos but we cannot know *what* the "Wholly Other" is. Our work is not concerned with the problem of the existence of the "Wholly Other." The philosopher of religion may accept the existence of the "Wholly Other." (Freud, too, allows for the possibility of a God). But the philosopher is also concerned with saying some things about this Being even though inadequately. Here Freud's treatment of the religious neuroses and our further development provide a journey in which the emergence of less distorted views of the "Wholly Other" appear. This movement forward in less distorted views or, positively speaking, this direction toward a more and more adequate vision, we see as teleological.

The religious experience of mankind has been a reaction to the primal crime which evoked guilt, fear and longing. In this respect, mankind has been reacting to an Oedipal drama on a cultural level. It is likely that there was no *historical* primal crime; the crime was committed within the precincts of the individual psyche. The origins of religion may thus reveal the history of a cultural reaction to a common feeling of guilt, fear and longing which each individual experienced. Thus if we take all the religious forms manifested through the culture and engage in a reductionism, we find that we are again involved in a struggle between the past and present.

In each period in the evolution of man's consciousness we see a forward step in the comprehending of reality the way it *is* and not the way man imagined it to be. It is the influence of man's past (with its inadequate grasp of reality) in confrontation with the present which culminates in a product which may suffer from distortion. Religious manifestation in a way is a history of distorted views of reality; genesis records this to be so. Since it is bound to time, the religious manifestation of man is always inadequate; mankind can only grasp that much of reality which the human psyche is capable of understanding at that particular moment. The evolution of mankind has been an odyssey in the understanding of the other as other. Thus the notions of the "Wholly Other" suffer because of historical limitation. But reality continues to reveal and Telos reveals a movement forward. The distortion grows less and less in the dialectic of past experience and present revelation. Thus a reduction of the religious manifestation of man reveals a symbol. It is a symbol which points in two directions: the past and the future. Genesis is a series showing man with his limited consciousness and with the burden of fear, guilt and longing in confrontation with a present moment. Genesis reveals that a confrontation has taken place; genesis does not reveal the meaning but telos does; telos by means of symbol reveals the mind opening up to infinity.

Telos reveals the movement from moment to moment; telos reveals the gradual victory of the "reality principle" over the "pleasure principle." Telos reveals man "becoming conscious." Only from the perspective of telos can we see something emerging. The influences of the past are being diminished: the moment of annihilation, in a way, has been overcome. Telos, while it cannot reveal to us the future, points to it with promise. Thus religious forms in culture, when reduced to genesis, reveal a telos. When the religious forms are interpreted symbolically, they begin to bear witness to a new future. We do not linger over the dead symbols of the past; we rise above these to see the meaning of the emerging movement between, but also above, the symbols. The new emerging symbol is at its height of meaning in its present moment. Thus mankind, in time, begins to behold a less and less distorted view of the "Wholly Other."

There is the gradual victory of the "reality principle" over the "pleasure principle." Therefore, reality or being is known more and

11

more; that which was concealed has now been revealed. This forward movement we see as teleological. If the world is the manifestation of God, then man is moving to a greater and greater depth of understanding of that world or reality. But God is the fullness of reality or being. At least, man is moving toward an idea of the "Wholly Other" which suffers less from our projection. The "Wholly Other" or the fullness of being is seen to approach more and more as distorted views of being are removed. The movement of Freud's thought is a revealing of reality the way it is. We take this thought further and say the fullness of reality or the "Wholly Other" also becomes more manifest.

In his reductionism of contemporary religious experience, Freud points out the great amount of wish-fulfillment that may enter into religious experience; this would make the experience merely an illusion. Freud indicates all of the infantile features underlying present religious experience, such as looking for the God of "accusation" and "consolation." This God must be unmasked and destroyed; the God of morals which man constructed became our source of accusation; the father of our fears must be put away. The God of "consolation" must also be at an end; we must no longer strive after a father satisfying all our desires. Thus we will see that Freud's reductionism and unmasking lead to the destruction of the God man has made and the destruction of "negative religion."

Freud, like Moses, demands that man give up his idols. For man has created a god who enslaves, annihilates, and who takes us away from our commitment to the world and our fellow human beings. With the destruction of the old idols man must be careful not to reconstruct new ones. After the Freudian reductionism, accomplished by means of unveiling the genesis of our gods, is there anything that emerges? We still have man in confrontation with the world before him. The basic dynamism intrinsic to man is revealed: the drive to know being in all its depth and richness; the desire to know *completely*. Man's history shows that he has made shrines in memory of the thing he sought to know. At the moment of the desire to know we have faith; when that moment goes into the past or becomes memory, we have "religion." It is not the stages in the genesis that are important; it is the movement that emerges over the stages.

Man in trying to come to the "Wholly Other" makes use of

"religion" which treats the sacred as being in the sphere of objects. The objectification of the sacred makes it an object along with the other objects of culture. We are left with sacred *objects* and not *signs* of the sacred. Thus religion reifies and alienates faith. Freud, through his reductionism, brings about the death of the religious object. On the other hand, faith is of the realm of the symbolic which points beyond but which always runs the risk of being objectified. Where objectification takes place an idol is born; accordingly faith is always a precarious experience.

In the course of our work, we shall see that the philosopher will move from "religion" to faith by means of atheism; this atheism puts an end to "negative religion." In the process our narcissism will be lost and reality will reveal itself all the more fully. In the moment of the losing of the self we are resigned. But resignation must give birth to consent. Having died to the old order we say "yes" to the new creation.

Freud's reductive interpretation gives us an insight into current feelings about the absence of God as man moves to the time of a radically new philosophy of religion. After the Freudian reductionism, we are still left with man in confrontation with a reality revealing ever new. And man is impelled to meet reality with faith.

Having seen the problematic, we will endeavor to carry out our proposal in the following manner. We will embark on the task of first trying to find the underlying ideas in Freud's thought which will perhaps provide a key to the organization of his religious thought. We will show that Ernst Haeckel's model[3] provided a means for organizing Freud's ideas; and that an interesting schema appears when we, following Freud's lead, substitute psychological and cultural phenomena in place of the biological data which Haeckel originally used the model to explain. Freud's ideas will begin to take their place in the schema and things which seem to be isolated will now become an integrated part of the whole. This schema is expressed in the outline on page 14.

A. Ontogenetic Development of the Person	B. Regression (Religious Neuroses)	C. Phylogenetic Development of Religion

1. Oral
   a. autoerotism
 	
   b. primary
     narcissism
	1. Paraphrenias
	   Dementia
	   Praecox
	   (American
	   Physician)
	   b. Paranoid
	   Dementia
	   (Schreber)
		1. Animism
		   Pre-animism
		
		   b. Animism
		   Proper

2. Anal-Sadistic	2. Obsessions
	   (Rat Man; Wolf
	   Man)
		2. Taboo

3. Phallic	3. Hysteria
	
	   a. anxiety-phobia
	   (Little Hans)
	   b. conversion
	   hysteria
	   (Dostoevsky,
	   Haizmann)
		3. Gods and
		   Surrogates
		   a. Totemism
		   b. Monotheism

4. Genital	4. The Un-Neurotic (Leonardo)	4. Science

The schema indicates the general divisions that will be adopted in our work in order to understand Freud's theory of religion. These general divisions are (A) the ontogeny of person, (B) the person as religious, and (C) phylogeny of religion. We will show that for every type of neurosis (regression) discovered, Freud also has a case study illustrating that neurosis but with a *religious* theme as the symptomatology. For when man regresses he is repeating ontogeny and phylogeny. For Freud, in the development of race, man's evolving religious practices resemble the private religions (the neuroses). There is the dependence of *present* phenomena upon a *past* genesis. For this reason we believe that Freud's theory has a basic deterministic component. There are two types of determinism in Freud: one in which the person is determined by his own past (ontogeny) and a second in which the person is determined by the past of the race (phylogeny).

We shall endeavor to show that a certain teleology or purpose can be found in the schema. In development and change there was a breaking out of the dependency upon the past. The individual person in virtue of a dynamism intrinsic to his own being moves toward maturity and as long as he does not fall victim to regression (neurosis or unresolved father-conflict), then he escapes from "religion" (Leonardo). The race, too, is growing in maturity and it soon will have resolved its Oedipal complex (the murder of the primal father) as seen in the disappearance of "religion" and the advent of the scientific age. Both the individual and the race are moving toward a greater grasp of the "reality principle" (the way reality is), and away from the "pleasure principle" (the way we would like reality to be).

Seeing this combination of a marked determinism with a reliance not only upon a past ontogeny but also a past phylogeny *and* at the same time an implicit teleology, we will be interested in seeing how Freud came to arrive at this model. He was influenced by the evolutionary biologists, some of whom were deterministically oriented and others who allowed for some teleology.

We will examine Freud's analysis of the ontogeny of person involving growth and regression. (We believe it is necessary to understand Freud's analysis of person qua person before we can handle person as religious.) We will see that he followed the biological model giving emphasis in this study to definite phylogenetic and ontogenetic influences on the behavior of the person, but at the same time we will see teleological influence. Accordingly, we will examine the meaning of a phylogenetic, genetic and teleological explanation. An analysis of cause and explanation shows that biogenetic explanations do not account for the entire phenomenon under investigation; they tend to be reductionistic. And a teleological explanation alone is incomplete. We will proceed to obtain a deeper philosophical insight into Freud's *reductionism* of the ontogeny of person by contrasting it with teleology. We will discover that the person is better able to comprehend other

15

as other, as he strives to break out of the influences of the past. (This growth in understanding other will have relevance when we come to discuss the "Wholly Other.") The individual struggles to give victory to the "reality principle" over the "pleasure principle."

In Chapter II we will continue our analysis of person. However, this time we will be interested in the psychoanalytic *concepts* which will have a bearing upon the explanation of person as religious. These concepts will be examined with reference to their meaningfulness as analyzed from the perspective of philosophy of science. Having been assured of their meaningfulness, we will go on to see their reductionistic and teleological polarity.

Having understood more deeply the Freudian analysis of person, we will be prepared to understand his analysis of person as religious (Chapter III). Freud maintains the *hypothesis* that religious experience is the manifestation of the latent Oedipus complex. We will make an analysis of the method of arriving at the hypothesis according to the norms of the philosophy of science. Assured of the probable validity of the hypothesis, we will attempt to derive a deeper understanding of the religious neuroses by means of the dialectic of genesis and telos. We will see man's struggle to grasp the ultimate meaning of reality hidden beneath the religious symptom. An evolution in awareness of the "Wholly Other" as other will also be seen.

What we traced on the neurotic level we will try to do on the phylogenetic level in our examination of the *origins* of religion (Chapter IV). For Freud, in the beginning was the primal crime—the murder of the father. Mankind has never forgiven itself for this crime. According to the psychic development of the race at any particular time, man manifested his reaction to the crime by corresponding religious practices from pre-animism (earliest) to monotheism (latest). Philosophy of social science indicates that Freud's interpretations explaining the origins of religion are out of harmony with the established body of scientific knowledge. Since Freud has basically the genetic approach, he handles cultural phenomena in the same way as the psychological, i.e. looking for one cause as totally explanatory. The Freudian explanation of the origins of religion seems to be oblivious of other causes such as environment, history and anthropology. We will contrast the reductionism involved in the Freudian critique of the origins of religion with an implicit teleology;

and a deeper philosophical insight is seen with regard to the religious cultural forms. We will see that the latter are symbols of man's striving to grasp reality the way it is. For the fullness of reality—the "Wholly Other"—is only approached by stages. There is an evolution in less distorted views of the "Wholly Other" revealed through man's religious history.

After analyzing the origins of religion, it is logical to consider Freud's treatment of the role of religion in contemporary civilization (Chapter V). Contemporary religion offers man a God of consolation and accusation. This God must be given up as He is an idol. Freud's reductionism destroys the idol in order to reveal man's perennial quest to comprehend the revealing cosmos. Science, in a way, shares the same goal as religion: to understand the cosmos as it reveals itself. Man, in searching for the "Wholly Other" as revealed through the world, comes closer to his goal because he is less influenced by the "pleasure principle" which distorts reality.

NOTES

[1]The theory of purpose, ends, goals, final causes; as opposed to reductionism which explains the present and the future in terms of the past, teleology explains the past and the present in terms of the future.

[2]The terms "genesis" and "telos" and the idea of a dialectic between the two has been suggested by the writings of Paul Ricoeur. However, these concepts and the dialectic are seen as a perennial problem over the course of the history of philosophy; therefore, these notions are not unique to Ricoeur. We attempt in the course of this work to develop this notion of dialectic with regard to Freud's treatment of the religious phenomenon.

[3]Morton Beckner, *The Biological Way of Thought* (New York: Columbia University Press, 1959), p. 97.

Chapter I

Development of Person (Ontogeny): Genetic and Teleological Influences

In this first chapter we will consider the ontogeny of person; we will examine the influence of evolutionary thought on Freud's particular orientation toward reality. We believe that Freud accounts for a phenomenon by both a phylogenetic and an ontogenetic past, but at the same time, and to a lesser extent, teleology is responsible for a phenomenon. A known *model* is frequently employed by a scientist in the work of discovery in order to shed light on some unknown phenomenon which bears some resemblance to the known model. We will first investigate the evolutionary models available to Freud: these biological models were both of a genetic and teleological type. From these Freud formed a composite model which was ambivalent since it was primarily genetic but allowed for some teleology.

We will then examine Freud's extension of the composite model to explain the ontogeny of person with its growth and regression. We first discuss the phylogenetic and genetic factors operative in ontogeny; and then we go on to what we believe to be the teleology implicit in Freud's discussion of ontogeny. We conclude that both the genetic and teleological are present in Freud, although he may not have been totally aware of the teleological presence.

Since Freud considered psychoanalysis to be a science, we will first make an analysis (from the perspective of the philosophy of science; i.e., principles of sound methodology) of his employment of the composite biological model. Then we will analyze the nature of phylogenetic, ontogenetic and teleological explanations in order to see how well they account for a phenomenon. A genetic explanation is concerned with the origins or beginnings of the phenomenon while a teleological explanation deals with the purpose or direction of the phenomenon. We will see that neither a genetic nor teleological explanation *alone* can completely explain a phenomenon under study. Rather one points to the other. We will then engage in a philosophical discussion of the dialectic of genesis and telos. A reductionism of a phenomenon to its genesis only reveals its telos. Teleology is only appreciated by seeing genesis. It is only Freud's reductionism which allows us to see a teleology emerging in his thought. If the teleological element is excluded, the very effort to explain a phenomenon in terms of the purely genetic reveals the inadequacy of the explanation. An understanding of the telos can only be made with reference to a reduction to genesis. We conclude that Freud's exposition of the ontogeny of person is fully understood by considering his reductionism as a movement toward the revealing of a telos. This chapter will thus prepare us for a deeper understanding of the psychoanalytic concepts bearing on the religious. For when a dialectic is seen between the concepts, a teleological aspect emerges (Chapter II). In the analysis of person as religious a reduction of the religious behavior to its genesis will reveal a telos (Chapter III).

A. *The Evolutionary Thinkers: Darwin, Haeckel, Lamarck, Jackson*
    Freud, as we will show, was much influenced by the evolutionary climate of his times; and so the thought came to him that the psychological make-up of man could be investigated in the same way as other living beings. He used the evolutionary models that were available to him for this investigation.[1] "Freud depended on the biological frame of reference for his own scientific 'security.' "[2] In our study of the evolutionary thinkers we will find some of them to be genetically oriented and others with a teleological outlook. However, it will be impossible in this study to explore the separate and distinct influences of such thinkers as Jean Lamarck (1744-1829), Charles Darwin (1809-1882), Ernst Haeckel (1834-1919), and John Hughlings Jackson (1835-1911).[3] Freud took from these thinkers what he believed would be useful to him for understanding the psychological data he was working on. He is shy in mentioning the names of those to whom he was indebted. What Freud came up with was a composite model which borrows something from each of these

20

thinkers.[4] Because diverse ideas went into the making of the composite model, it is not surprising that it has a certain inner tension.

In Freud's autobiographical study we find the following statement: '. . . the theories of Darwin, which were then of topical interest strongly attracted me, for they hold out hopes of an extraordinary advance in our understanding of the world.''[5] Darwinian theory seemed to have been able to order so much world data which appeared to be unrelated. Man, too, had his place in the evolutionary scale; he could be considered biologically as a product of nature. Freud made use of the Darwinian model which pointed to the fact that the development of the individual (ontogeny) was in accordance with inborn laws.[6] Thus, Darwin's thought tends to a genetic orientation.

When Freud combined the Darwinian model with Haeckel's biogenetic law (''ontogeny recapitulates phylogeny'') and with Lamarck's ideas, he arrived at a composite model which led him to views which have been challenged seriously by scientists.[7] Haeckel saw the phylogeny as having an effect on ontogeny. ''. . . Haeckel postulated a special faculty of protoplasm, the 'mneme' of the nuclei of the germ cells, to account for recapitulation . . .'' The ''mneme'' was a record of memory of the events of the phylogeny.[8]

Lamarck's model, which allows for the inheritance of acquired characteristics, made Freud aware of the processes of adaptation which Darwin's theory (genetic model) did not always emphasize.[9] ''Our intention is to base Lamarck's ideas completely on our own theories and to show that his concept of 'need,' which creates and modifies organs, is nothing else than the power unconscious ideas have over the body . . .''[10]

Freud also made use of the studies of John Hughlings Jackson on neuropathology. In the Jacksonian model, the nervous system is made up of a hierarchy of systems in which the higher ones control the lower.[11] The schema of nervous forms is not arranged chronologically (the higher forms evolving out of the lower) but hierarchically (the higher forms regulating the lower). In the hierarchical forms of the nervous system there are the most general to the most special, the most indefinite to the most complex, and the most autocratic to the most voluntary.[12] When there is functional retrogression, we find the regression resembles *earlier* stages of the structural organization of the individual.[13] Yet Jackson considered regression as an indication of the inner dynamism of the person directing toward integration in the face of an obstacle.[14] Thus a teleological orientation becomes apparent through what would seem to be an "apparent" regression.

It should become apparent how, for example, the various models come into play with Freud's treatment of *regression.* The idea that nervous function passes through evolutionary stages which represent and recapitulate those of lower and extinct species has the thought of Darwin[15] and Haeckel behind it. Darwin claimed that the stages of earlier evolution may reappear when some disturbance ("lesion") occurs in the ordinary development of the individual. He falls back to a more primitive or ancestral behavior. This latter process Darwin called "reversion." Thus, in the *Descent of Man,* we find Darwin looking at the brain of a "microcephalous idiot," considering it as resembling an ape, and as an example of what happens to a normal brain after pathology. Darwin also considered gross and serious defects in character in certain families as a "reversion" to the savage state from which man is not really very distant.[16]

It is further to be pointed out that the concept of "regression" is hardly to be distinguished from "dissolution," a term used by Herbert Spencer and later by John Hughlings Jackson whose thought Freud respected. For Freud, libidinal development along with its possible neuroses (regression) is a history of functioning and not *only* chronology. Jackson also saw reversal in the levels of normal functioning in the nervous system as regression, dissolution and dedifferentiation.[17] However, there is a dynamism in the living thing which allows it, through over-activity in another area, to compensate for the deficiency (regression). Freud, with a certain *ambivalence,* saw the neurosis as a regression to the past but at the same time saw the symptom to be at the service of the individual as a whole. There is the attempt at adaptation (Lamarck), unification and further growth thus indicating a *telos.*[18] Thus, neither genesis nor telos alone completely explains the phenomenon.

B. *Freud's Composite Evolutionary Model: Genetic, Phylogenetic, Adaptive, Teleological*

In the composite model, we have the following models contained: genetic, phylogenetic, adaptive and teleological. Each model in its own unique way can explain growth, fixation and regression; it will be our task to see how adequate each is alone.

In the *genetic* model, causes of the ontogenetic development will be sought in terms of traits in the individual already present at birth. A corresponding implication for libido theory will be to understand development in terms of innate predispositions characteristic of the person. According to the genetic model, fixation and regression in the individual are explained as a return to an earlier stage in biological development. The corresponding application for libido theory will be to understand fixation and regression (neurosis) as going back to an earlier stage which the person went through on the way to personality development.

The *phylogenetic* model thus explains causes for ontogenetic development with reference to phylogeny. A corresponding application for the libidinal theory of development would be to view its causes as bound to the history of the race. In the phylogenetic model we will explore fixation and regression in the individual as a going back to an earlier stage of the phylogeny; and the corresponding application for the libidinal theory is to see fixation and regression (neuroses) as a return to a more primitive time in the history of mankind.

In the *adaptive* model causes of ontogenetic development will be sought in terms of confrontation with the environment. With regard to libido theory, one would then understand development in terms of a give and take with the environment. Fixation and regression in the adaptive model are seen to be inabilities for further growth because of an unfavorable environment. So, too, in libido theory, fixation and regression are seen as a stand-still in growth because the environment prevents further growth.

With reference to the *teleological* model we will look for causes of ontogenetic development in terms of an inner dynamism which is directive toward growth. In libido theory, we see a movement from the immature toward the mature. Fixation and regression in the teleological model are seen as interruptions which must be integrated so as to allow the inner dynamism of the being to maintain its unity. So, too, in libido theory, fixation and regression are seen as the ego's attempt to bring unity to disoriented drives.

While these models separately appear to be very different, Freud brought all of them together in his thought. For the most part, he is

23

genetically oriented but there is an implicit teleology. Sometimes we find him bringing together both the genetic and teleological aspects.

C. *Phylogenetic and Genetic Influences on Ontogeny of Person*

Having seen the formation of the composite model, we will see its application in the full development of the person's ontogeny. For Freud, the ordinary growth and regression of the person (ontogeny) are influenced by *past* phylogenetic and ontogenetic factors. These represent the more predominant non-teleological factors in Freud's thought. However, Freud is ambivalent throughout his writings as to which of the *past* factors is operative viz. in our discussion we will discover that phylogenetic and genetic causes entwine. We consider first the influence of past factors on *growth.*[19]

1. *Growth*

The order in which the instincts appear seems to be phylogenetically determined and the length of duration of the instinct before repression seems to be determined in similar fashion.[20] Those things which act upon sexual development, e.g., disgust, shame and morality, are "historical precipitates" of the prohibitions imposed externally during the "psychogenesis" of the race. In the growth of the individual, these inhibitions come into play spontaneously when activated by outside influence.[21] A *comparison* can be drawn between the individual's libidinal development and the evolution of mankind's view of the universe: the person moves from narcissism to maturity, as the race moved from animism and omnipotence of its own thoughts to science. Thus an exchange of the pleasure principle for the reality principle is made.[22]

Freud is taken up with the phenomenon of the same phantasies with the same content on the same type of occasion being reported by persons who have not had experiences from which the phantasy could be derived.[23] He believes that "primal phantasies" are a phylogenetic bequest i.e. where the person's own experiences have been inadequate or incomplete, he draws from beyond experience to "primaeval experience." ". . . children, in their phantasies, are simply filling in the gaps in individual truth with prehistoric truth."[24] He compares the "phylogenetically inherited schemata" to the categories of philosophers: the schemata place in proper order the "impressions" coming from experience; the "phylogenetically inherited schemata" are "precipitates" from the whole story of civilization e.g. the Oedipus complex. Thus, when experiences diverge from the schemata, they are "remodelled" in the mind to conform. This theory Freud confirmed in a case which "seemed" to be an inverted Oedipus complex but worked itself out as the classical Oedipus complex.[25]

Freud does leave room for the "accidental" factors of life. "There is room for the ontogenetic view side by side with the more far-reaching phylogenetic one."[26] In later writings, he maintains that the person's archaic heritage does not only consist in dispositions but "subject matter" or "memory-traces" of the earlier experiences of mankind.[27] For in the psychic life of children today, we can perceive the same archaic characteristics which were at the beginnings of civilization.[28]

Freud believes that dreams show us an early stage of man's mental life. Thus, he is happy with the dream description of Havelock Ellis as "the return of the mind in dreams to an embryonic point of view . . ."[29] During sleep, the mind is free to engage in primitive modes of thinking.[30] Dreams, like the neurosis, display a regression to the time of childhood; they use the methods of expression available then.[31] Through an analysis of dreams, one can arrive at man's "archaic heritage"—or the material which is "psychically innate." In dreams are preserved a wealth of antiquities.[32] The dream-work brings us back to the person's childhood and ". . . in so far as each individual somehow recapitulates in an abbreviated form the entire development of the human race, into phylogenetic prehistory, too."[33]

Having accepted the biogenetic model, Freud was inevitably faced with the methodological problem of determining whether the ontogenetic factor *or* the phylogenetic factor was the influencing cause of a particular behavior.[34] Freud maintains that one cannot determine what the influence of the primaeval period of one's ancestors (heredity) is, until the influence of childhood experiences have been examined.[35] At another time, he says, ". . . not a few of the child's new experiences will be intensified because they are repetitions of some primaeval phylogenetic experience."[36] He was aware of the possibility that what he postulated in analysis as forgotten experiences of childhood (infantile sexuality) might have been phantasies created in later life. Where the after effects of such postulated infantile impressions were seen in the analysis, then the cause

25

was assumed to be either a constitutional factor or disposition phylogenetically related. This dilemma of causes held Freud back from publishing. Yet, in view of the evidence from his cases, he maintained this "more difficult and more improbable view," i.e., the person really had the sexual experiences in early childhood.[37] Thus we see the ambivalence in Freud's thought with regard to locating, in time, the true cause for present behavior.

2 Regression (Neurosis)

We have been concerned with the ontogeny of person under the aspect of normal development and have seen the person develop in confrontation with the world. However, this confrontation takes place in the shadow of past influences both genetic and phylogenetic. Where normal growth is disturbed, we have *regression* i.e. the person has not been able to face reality. The neurosis represents a compromise: a portion of reality is sacrificed but the personality still moves to integrate itself. At the same time, Freud sees regression as a victory of the forces of the past (genetic and phylogenetic). Again, we will see the appearance of telos and genesis.[38] In all stages of sexual development, it is possible for some portions of sexual drive to remain behind at an earlier stage. ". . . we propose to describe the lagging behind of a past trend at an earlier stage as a *fixation*—a fixation, that is, of the instincts."[39] Freud points out, many times throughout his writings, that in development, fixations may be left behind.[40]

Freud looks now to the second danger in development— *regression.* It is possible that where advancement has been made and also a serious obstacle encountered there may be a return to earlier stages. The stronger the fixations might have been on the path of development, the easier it would be to return to them in the face of difficulty in advancement.[41] At another time, Freud tells us that it is difficult to find anything that can be compared to the mind in its development. For in the mind all the earlier stages persist alongside the later stages which have arisen from the earlier. The earlier stages have to be present someplace in order to explain the capacity for regression.[42]

The sexual constitution of the neurotic along with accidental influences has disturbed the normal development of sexuality.[43] Further, regression may also take place when normal lines of satisfaction are no longer satisfying.[44] There may be *fixation* to a particular time

26

when obstacles to satisfaction were presented; this period becomes a weak spot where there may be a return, if later problems of frustration present themselves.[45] Thus, the particular choice of neurosis will be contingent upon the place of development of the ego and the libido when it was disturbed.[46] In the case of frustration, there may be escape from reality into phantasy along with a revival of earlier phantasies. The life of phantasy is exempt from reality-testing and is infantile.[47]

The neuroses show us that some degree of regression or return to an earlier stage has taken place. Paranoia shows the greatest degree of regression, obsessional neurosis less, and hysteria little or none.[48] "There is a dictum in general pathology, Gentlemen, which asserts that every developmental process carries with it the seed of a pathological disposition, in so far as that process may be inhibited, delayed, or may run its course incompletely." This is true in the development of sexual function as it may leave behind it abnormalities or predispositions to illness along the way of regression. In neurosis, all the complex of instincts fail to come under the genital primacy.[49]

Where a person does develop a neurosis, Freud sees phylogenetic forces operative. Yet, at times, he will mention that the phylogenetic influence is an "inference." Thus Freud indicates some degree of ambivalence in determining causal factors. In his analysis of "An Infantile Neurosis," Freud pointed to the fact that there were no threats or hints of castration made by the boy's father. Yet, it turned out that he feared castration from the father. "At this point the boy had to fit into a phylogenetic pattern . . ." Heredity, therefore, took the lead over "accidental experience." For it was the father who, in the primal past, castrated the sons.[50] Freud also looks at the neurotics as ones who ". . . have inherited an archaic constitution as an atavistic vestige . . ."[51] Those that undergo libidinal regression may have been predetermined to this by heredity.[52] In any event, the neurotic turns more easily from the reality principle to the pleasure principle. ". . . they set an internal act in place of an external one, an adaptation in place of an action—once again, something that corresponds, phylogenetically, to a highly significant regression."[53]

Freud frequently wrote of a phylogenetic factor as playing a part in the causation of neuroses.[54] At one point, he mentions that the influence of a phylogenetic factor is "based only upon inference." The diphasic development of libido makes one infer that something

27

must have happened to the human species which has been left behind—an "historical precipitate"—an interruption in sexual development. For the neurotic, the dangers met in developing are experienced as more threatening than in the ordinary person.[55] Freud mentions in *Three Essays on Sexuality* that more attention is given to the "accidental" (experienced) factors influencing a person's development than the "dispositional" (inherited) ones. The "accidental" factors are the ones that come more under the influence of psychoanalysis while the "dispositional" factors are seen to be activated as a result of the experience of the person.[56] Further, Freud considers it unimportant whether phantasies of the primal scene (seduction, castration) were derived from the phylogenetic heritage or by personal experience. Both are possible. In the "pre-history" of neuroses, the child fills in phylogenetically what is missing ontogenetically.[57]

Thus, while Freud claims (by inference) that the neurotic may fall victim to the influences of the race's past, they are not clearly distinguished from the influences of the individual's own past. It is evident that the past factors determine neurotic activity. Yet, it is also to be seen that the person was in *confrontation* with some aspect of reality which caused the regression to take place. Further, as a result of the confrontation, the person moves to keep as much of reality as his psyche will allow.

D. *Adaptive and Teleological Influences on Ontogeny of Person*

In the development of person, we will observe the influence of an implicit teleology. As the person develops, there is a movement toward greater awareness of the other as other i.e. as a being distinct from himself. As the individual becomes more a person, he has, at the same time, further recognized the other. In fact, the dialectic of self and other is necessary for this growth. There is also a forward movement seen in the dialectic of the "reality principle" and the "pleasure principle." Thus growth and maturity bring a fuller realization of the world the way it is.

1. *Growth*

We will trace the ordinary development of the person, giving specific attention to libidinal *object* (the object to which libido is directed: self, others) and libidinal *aim* (the way in which libido is satisfied: oral, anal, phallic, genital). These forementioned stages also parallel advances in the greater awareness of reality. (On the basis of the biological models Freud employed, this examination of ontogenetic development would shed light upon the development of the race. Also, since neurotic behavior is regressive to the various stages of early libidinal development, this present study would give insight into the neuroses. The neuroses as regressive would shed light on the early origins of the race's development.) The ontogenetic development seems to have a certain direction to it for as the child develops, there is an increasing awareness of the ''reality principle'' and a diminution of the ''pleasure principle.'' This process of transition is what we call growth.

Oral Stage. The first stage in the libidinal development of the child is the oral phase as pleasure is experienced especially in the mouth. Sexual activity is bound up with the taking in of food: the object of both activities is identical—the mother's breast[58] which is the first object of the sexual instinct.[59] In this oral phase, object-cathexis and identification cannot be distinguished from each other, i.e., the child does not see the objects as distinct from himself.[60] All reality appears as one.

Thumb sucking would show the sexual aim minus the nutritive one.[61] In addition, the sucking instinct is not directed toward other people but is satisfied from the subject's own body.[62] The child prefers his own skin because it provides him with a second erotogenic zone, and thus he achieves satisfaction independently of the external world which he is not able to control.[63] This is the auto-erotic phase; the instincts, independently of each other, look for the fulfillment of satisfaction in the infant's own body.[64] ''The sexual instincts behave auto-erotically at first; they obtain their satisfaction in the subject's own body and, therefore, do not find themselves in the situation of frustration which was what necessitated the institution of the reality principle.''[65]

So far, the activities of the child have been auto-erotic without distinguishing any outside objects. When satisfactions were missing, he merely hallucinated them. With time, the child perceives himself as an entity. In the earliest life of the child, there is the narcissistic cathexis of the ego, which factor presupposes that there is some degree of organization: the libidinal cathexis is concentrated on the ego rather than being directed to outside objects.[66] In the ego, the whole quota of available libido is stored up.[67] In this "primary narcissism" the ego is taken as object with extreme hypo-cathexis of objects in the environment as distinct from himself.[68] At this stage, while there is not yet an awareness of external reality, there is at least the awareness that the being of the person is somewhat distinct from other surrounding objects.

The condition of primary narcissism gives way to *secondary narcissism*: the ego begins to cathect the ideas of objects with libido and thus transforms narcissistic libido into object libido.[69] However, these objects are loved because they so closely resemble the infant that they are scarcely distinguishable from himself.[70] The oral stage is divided into the first sub-stage where there is only oral incorporation with no ambivalence toward the mother's breast and the second sub-stage where there is biting activity ("oral-sadistic" or "cannibalistic pregenital organization").[71] Thus, in this second sub-stage, there is ambivalence which will become very obvious in the anal-sadistic phase.[72]

Anal Stage. Following the oral stage, the anal zone in the infant becomes highly erogenous; there are two drives operative: active and passive. Activity for mastery is carried out by muscular development while the organ designed for a passive sexual aim is the erotogenic mucous membrane of the anus. The objects for these drives are not identical;[73] i.e., activity is directed to an outside object and passivity is directed to the self.[74] Here we have a sexual polarity and an extraneous object. In addition, there is no organization or subordination to the reproductive function.[75] The component instincts which dominate this pre-genital organization are the anal-erotic and sadistic ones.[76] Here the significance for the person is that there is an awareness of himself as a separate entity and of an outside object apart from himself to which he is also drawn. Thus awareness is being extended to the outside world; the external world must be accounted for; this outside world is in confrontation with the person and thus defines his limits. Here the "pleasure principle" must be sacrificed a little more to the "reality principle."

We now consider the active side of the anal stage or anal sadistic: satisfaction is looked for in aggression and in the excretory process.[77] As the person strives after the attainment of the object (the other person), his strivings appear as a desire for mastery. It is not important whether the object is annihilated or injured in the process. "Love in this form and at this preliminary stage is hardly to be distinguished from hate in its attitude towards the object. Not until the genital organization is established does love become the opposite of hate."[78]

In considering the passive side of the anal stage, we see that children derive pleasure from the bowel movement. In the giving of faeces they are complying with reality; when they retain them they are in defiance of reality.[79] Defaecation is the first occasion on which the child decides between a narcissistic and an object loving attitude. He may give; or he may retain for auto-erotic satisfaction. Thus defiance represents a narcissistic clinging to anal erotism.[80] In the course of the anal stage there is a movement from a destructive to a friendly attitude toward objects. "It is in the middle of this phase, therefore, that consideration for the object makes its first appearance as a precursor of a later erotic cathexis."[81] The anal stage thus marks an advancement in the person's orientation or turning to the other as other.

Phallic Stage. The child moves from an emphasis given to the anal zone to a concentration on the phallus as a source of pleasure; this phase is called the phallic stage which coincides roughly in time with the Oedipal phase. According to Freud, there is a concern with the genitals but only that of the boy's as the girl's still remain unknown. In the phallic phase sexuality of early childhood reaches its height[82] along with the beginnings of organization and the subordination of other impulses to the primacy of the genitals. There is also the beginning of the coordination of the general urge to pleasure with the sexual function.[83] In addition, the phallic phase differs from the genital phase in that the former only knows one genital—the male.[84] The boy, in the phallic stage, feels pleasurable sensations in the penis. At this same time, he becomes his mother's lover for he would like to possess her like his father does. The father is both envied and admired because of his unique position, authority, and physical strength. Seeing the father as his rival the child wants him to go away.[85] The mother understands that the son's sexual stimulation has reference to her. Thus she may forbid him to touch the penis and may also threaten that the father will take it away. This threat is taken more seriously if the boy sees the female genitals and fears the same may happen to him.

With the repression of the desires for the mother there begins the latency stage.[86] It is to be added that this whole drama may be taking place on the unconscious level. With the demolition of the Oedipus complex the boy's object-cathexis of his mother may be given up. In place of this he may either identify with the mother or increase his identification with the father. The latter process is more normal and allows an affectionate relationship with the mother to continue and simultaneously the boy's masculinity is consolidated.[87]

Thus in the phallic stage the person has more of an integrated personality and a very clear ability to take an outside object as one to be loved. The teleological direction is also apparent in the identification with the father which is an overcoming of a desire to possess in order to identify with. This process shows the integration of component drives in order to relate to the other more fully.

Genital Stage. "The final outcome of sexual development lies in what is known as the normal sexual life of the adult, in which the pursuit of pleasure comes under the sway of the reproductive function and in which the component instincts, under the primacy of a single erotogenic zone, forms a firm organization directed towards a sexual aim attached to some extraneous sexual object."[88] With puberty infantile sexuality takes its final shape. Where the sexual instinct was auto-erotic, it now clearly takes an object. In early development there were various instincts and several erotogenic zones which were not unified but sought their own pleasure independently of each other. However in the genital phase, there is a new sexual aim and all instincts come together to achieve it. The various erotogenic zones become subordinate to the genital zone. At the same time affectionate and sexual feelings are combined in their direction toward the sexual object and aim.[89] "We have defined the concept of libido as a quantitatively variable force which could serve as a measure of processes and transformation occurring in the field of sexual excitation." When we speak of "quantity of libido," we mean the libido at the service of the ego, or "ego-libido." Thus when we say the ego cathects sexual objects, we mean the libido, at the service of the ego, is sent out to a particular object. In the latter case "ego-libido" has become "object-libido": the libido is concentrated on objects rather than the ego; it fixes on an object or abandons it for another object.[90] "Ego-libido" being transformed into "object-libido" is a sign of growth or normal development and forward movement is revealed.

Thus in the genital stage of development some previous libidinal cathexes are still present, and others are made preparatory to genital satisfaction. Some desires are removed from the genital organization by repression or by sublimation[91] which shows the ego engaged in a teleological movement of transforming libido to serve a new aim. The sexual instinct becomes subordinated to the reproductive function; it becomes "altruistic."[92]

Thus under normal conditions, the person is fulfilled or reaches maturity in a genital orientation. Here he is completely aware of the other as other and has the ability to love altruistically. We have been involved in a forward moving dialectic in which the person through confrontation rises to a higher stage of consciousness. He extends himself to the outside world and thus deflates his own egoism which was the original hindrance to a complete grasp of the world. In other words, we have seen in the movement toward maturity an exchange of the "pleasure principle" for the "reality principle."

2. Regression (Neurosis)

We have traced the ontogeny of person illustrating normal growth; we believe there is a certain forward movement revealed. We turn now to the situation where normal growth is interfered with; i.e., when we have the occurrence of regression or neurosis. We wish to demonstrate that Freud sees regression as the person's attempt at recovery and reintegration. This inner dynamism or movement toward recovery we consider as teleological. The very use of the concept of growth or regression indicates a teleological model; the concepts would be meaningless if there were no direction implied.

The whole experience of the neurotic has been an attempt at recovery as the symptom indicates the person's continued effort at integration. Freud, from his earliest writings, has shown that in the neuroses the ego, in order to continue its confrontation with reality, may have to sacrifice a portion of it. In every defense there is some gain in that intolerable anxiety is warded off.[93] *"The delusional formation, which we take to be the pathological product, is in reality an attempt at recovery, a process of reconstruction."*[94] When libido is withdrawn from external objects, it may return to the ego; the ego again sends out the libido in order to reconstruct a world which the ego may find tolerable. This new world, although delusional to an extent, makes reality tolerable for the ego.

He [paraphrenic] seems really to have withdrawn libido from people and things in the external world, without replacing them by others in phantasy. When he *does* so replace them, the process seems to be a secondary one and to be part of an attempt at recovery, designed to lead the libido back to objects.[95]

We have seen the extension of the evolutionary model (genetic and teleological) to Freud's exposition of the ontogeny of person under the aspects of growth and regression. It is obvious that the ontogeny of person was very much influenced by the past, not only by the ontogenetic past but also the phylogenetic past. At the same time there seems to be an implicit teleology as the individual is in contact with *present* reality and continually must take account of it by integrating the past experiences with the new. The two factors of genesis and teleology are present in Freud and we believe that one cannot be understood without the other.

E. *Philosophical Analysis of the Evolutionary Model*
1. *Nature and Proper Use of Model*

We must now examine from the perspective of philosophy of science the proper use of a model which we have seen Freud construct and employ. How sound is the field of biology for providing a model for another discipline? Do the evolutionary models themselves adequately explain biological growth, fixation and regression? If they do not, how does this affect their extension to Freud's psychological theory? Let us consider Freud's employment of the composite model. ". . . *a model for a theory* consists of an alternative interpretation of the same calculus of which the theory itself is an interpretation."[96] Thus Freud's composite *biological* model is an alternative interpretation of the different stages of development the person goes through on the way to maturity and the theory of libidinal development is another interpretation. A model is employed in order to aid in discovery rather than for validation i.e. it acts as a heuristic device.[97]

When Freud was doing his pioneering work in psychology, there were not available any "traditional methodological models" to be of aid to him.[98] What Freud had were the evolutionary models in vogue at the time he began his work and from these he constructed a composite model. Initially this model would have been more *familiar* and more concrete than the complex subject matter of personality development. With the empirical model there is "heuristic efficacy" because of the supposed ease of seeing the data which the model accounts for. "When the model relationship does obtain, we are, so to speak, guaranteed that implications of the model have corresponding implications in the theory of concern."[99] The thought here is that since model and theory have been able to provide interpretations of the same data, the model (about which we initially know more) may be suggestive of further information about the data. We feel secure with the model because it was able to provide an interpretation of the data.[100]

Besides the great value of a model, it has its unique dangers and risks.[101] Freud should have realized in his early work that where one has only a vague idea of the theory of libidinal development as an interpretation of psychological data then one cannot know certainly that the composite model will have the same structure as the psychological theory. There is danger especially where it is not demonstrated that the model and the theory are both interpretations of the data.

2. *Changeability of Biological Models*

It should be recalled that Freud's model is a composite which he constructed from the evolutionary thinkers of his own time; he cannot be considered to have proceeded illogically by combining Darwinian and Lamarckian models which today would be considered incompatible. Nor can he be blamed for the employment of the biogenetic law which biologists today do not support. What we will criticize, however, is his falling victim to the use of a model which he should have realized was based upon biology and thus offered good possibility of changing with further biological discovery. Also, in the last decade of his life when biological thought considered the inheritance of acquired characteristics as suspect he should have realized that his model was also in question. Perhaps he did realize this eventuality and therefore all the more vehemently upheld the inheritance of acquired characteristics.[102]

There are, of course, inherent dangers in using biology as a yardstick, in that concepts in biology change as more data become available or that the concept and model may be wrong.

35

Illustrative of this is the fact that Haeckel's biogenetic law, coupled with a Darwinian model and a curious Lamarckian view of evolution, indubitably had an influence on Freud's thinking in the area of human development and on his formulation of the "genetic" principle. [103]

3. Genetic Model: Insufficient

Although the *genetic* model or explanation has deficiencies, it tells us something. ". . . they [genetic explanations] can be generalized, yield laws, and can thus be made the basis for ordinary causal explanation, limited to the relations of dependence between parts that are manifested in normal development."[104] A genetic explanation will attempt to understand a present activity in terms of the major events that the being went through in its past development. These past events in some way are seen to produce and influence the present. But not all past events are taken to account for the present. Thus, there is a danger that there might be a tacit assumption involved in the selection of certain past events as having an influence on the present behavior.[105] Further, in a genetic explanation, the premises employed do not account completely for the present fact under consideration; the premises state *some* conditions necessary for the present phenomenon. Therefore a genetic explanation might be considered probabilistic.[106] "In short, a genetic explanation of a particular event is in general analyzable into a sequence of probabilistic explanations whose instantial premises refer to events that happen at different times rather than concurrently, and that are at best only some of the necessary conditions rather than a full complement of sufficient ones for the occurrences which those premises help to explain."[107]

To hold that *all* ontogenetic development is predetermined by hereditary traits would seem to be unverifiable and unfalsifiable.

. . . biologists today consider the genotype as consisting of a collection of potentialities. The phenotype consists of all the characteristics—elicited potentialities—that an organism may develop, depending on those specific circumstances under which he may happen to grow up. Any one genotype may in a different

environment give rise, within certain limits, to different pheno-
types.[108]

We have seen how the *genetic* model has some empirical and
philosophical meaning in explaining development. Let us proceed to
Freud's extending the genetic model to explain the other aspects of
ontogeny namely, *fixation* and *regression*. In attempting to find a
biological model (in the framework of genetic determination) for
psychological fixation, he mentions that in biology all preparatory
phases are not successfully overcome and some functions are held
back at an earlier stage. This statement is followed by the example of
the Ammocoetes which is supposed to illustrate fixation in development. But what Ammocoetes shows is that it is in a transitional stage between a lower vertebrate and a higher vertebrate.[109] In terms
of its own development there is no fixation i.e. it developed into what
it was determined to develop into. This example cannot serve as a
model for psychological fixation, simply because it does not illustrate
fixation for the individual in the biological order. If Freud meant the
Ammocoetes to illustrate a species below a higher one and therefore
fixated because of a more primitive evolution, then again there would
be no bearing on psychological fixation. Where fixation is involved in
man it is in terms of the person himself and not in terms of a form
higher than himself.

Another difficulty is that Freud actually cannot find a biological
model to aid in understanding psychological fixation. This is so
because in the libidinal theory the mind contains the earlier stages
alongside the later stages which have arisen from the earlier; this
allows for regression. In the biological model it would be impossible
for organs to persist in all stages of development ready to come into
operation when development was inhibited. Freud was dimly aware of
the difficulty of finding a biological model for this psychological
phenomenon.[110]

In the libidinal theory of development fixation and *regression* are
intimately bound up together. One would therefore be inclined to
suspect that the biological model being employed to explain fixation
would also be used as an explanation of regression. This is not what
happens. Freud must have realized that there really was no biological
model to be found; thus when he continues with the matter of regres-

sion, he compares it to people on a journey who return to a previous stop off place.[111] Freud should have realized that reductionism in terms of a past genesis does not account for the entire phenomenon.

The significance of this discussion of fixation and regression is that biology has no genetic model for Freud's psychological view of these two phenomena. This should have been an indication to him that a person's having passed through certain stages would not mean that he would return to those exact stages. On the contrary, the new behavior, albeit regressive, would be the resultant of the person in confrontation with reality here and now. The individual does not regress to the original past stage of infantile development. Rather his regression is a later development; it comes later in the genesis of his own history. In one respect the behavior is regressive, but at the same time there is a movement forward. Freud's attempt to explain the phenomena of fixation and regression by means of a reduction to *genesis* serves as a means for revealing a *teleology* in the individual. Moreover, the very attempt to explain by a reductionism shows a telos; for the concept of regression is unintelligible unless teleology is considered.

Thus we would have to conclude that the genetic model has some value in providing explanation: certain major phases of development are seen to be genetically predetermined and it is possible that some causal link may be determined between the present and past. When the genetic model is extended to account for fixation and regression, we find that there is no empirical evidence to show that fixation takes place the way Freud thought it did in biology. Therefore he had an invalid model for fixation and no model for regression. Logically, we can be suspicious about their extension to psychological theory; we have seen their limitation. In an attempt to reduce a biological phenomenon to its genesis, a complete reductionism is seen to be impossible; in the process a telos is seen. With Freud's extension of the biological model to ontogeny of person we might suspect that a reduction to genesis will reveal a teleology there, too.

4. *Phylogenetic Model: Meaningless*

In examining the phylogenetic model, we find it to be challenged both on empirical and logical grounds. Evidence from embryology shows that the early stages of ontogeny bear only a superficial resemblance to the adult ancestors and fetal membranes have nothing corresponding to them in the adult. There are some kinds of recapitulation but not on the scale proposed by Haeckel.[112] Noted also are reversals in the order of the appearance of organs in ontogeny as compared with the appearance in phylogeny;[113] in mammalian development, the embryo really resembles the fish embryo rather than the adult fish;[114] the way in which embryonic stages are reached differs from the ancestors.[115] There are also many stages that were passed through in the phylogenetic development which are omitted in the ontogeny. In addition *modifications* arise in the embryo which enable it to live in surroundings which change over the course of time.[116]

We turn now to a logical critique of the phylogenetic model. Haeckel held that phylogeny is a mechanical cause of ontogeny. This is impossible because the changes which took place in adults over several generations cannot be said to be a *cause* of ontogenetic development at least in the ordinary way *cause* is used.[117] Haeckel, probably realizing that a causal connection was not really existent between ontogeny and phylogeny, introduced ". . . a special faculty of protoplasm, the 'mneme' of the nuclei of the germ cells to account for recapitulation . . ."[118] Here we have the introduction of an *ad hoc* hypothesis to save the major hypothesis. "Mnemic causation" holds that if we have reason to believe that an historical event took place in the past then we have evidence for a "hypothetical" trace existing in the present. It could be objected that there is no way of proving that mnemic causation actually occurs; further, biology has been able to operate without the assumption of "mnemic causation."[119]

In an historical explanation a present phenomenon is seen to be understood in terms of the sequence of past events[120] i.e. an attempt is made to establish a connection between a series of past events and the present event. Haeckel saw in matter a mnemic function: "It seemed, for example, to Haeckel that the unicellular radiolaria which he studied could construct their delicate and complex tests only if they 'remembered' the necessary sequence of activities employed by their ancestors. Haeckel and others applied the same concept in an attempt to understand the phenomena of recapitulation."[121] As soon as one saw the phenomenon of recapitulation, it became apparent that there was not only relevance between phylogeny and ontogeny but that the sequence of events in phylogeny determined the sequence of events in ontogeny. Yet it is most difficult to establish a cause-effect relationship between the two because we do not see the constant conjunction of the events of phylogeny and the events of ontogeny in recapitulation. Rather we have "... a parallelism of sequences of events that occur at times which may be separated by geological time intervals."[122]

Thus it is seen that we cannot establish a cause-effect relationship between ontogeny and phylogeny. And the employment of "mneme" as an explanation cannot be proved. Thus from the start, Freud was involved in a model which was empirically and logically unsound. His extension of the phylogenetic model to ontogeny of person leads to an over-dependency on the past to the neglect of present influences. Before a model is employed for heuristic purposes, it must be shown to be an alternate interpretation of the same data that the libidinal theory explains. However, if the phylogenetic model cannot account for the data with which it is primarily concerned, namely, biological phenomenon, then the proposal to extend it to account for psychological data is dangerous from the start.

5. *Teleological Model: Insufficient*

At times there appears to be a *teleology* in Freud's thought. There seems to be some direction or purpose in the phenomena of growth and development. However, what we consider telos, Freud merely observes as ontogeny recapitulating phylogeny; i.e., development is already set in view of the phylogenetic law and genetic principles. A thing is merely fulfilling what it was already destined to be. Thus the apparent goal and purpose is reduced to origin: "... The more general fallacy that the origin of a thing determines its end."[123] Freud's thought seems to have a certain ambivalence as we discover processes which reveal themselves as teleological but which he does not advert to as such. He does not advert directly to telos probably because of his view that for a theory to be scientifically respectable it has to be deterministic and reducible to a set of components. And Freud, above all things, wished his thought to be considered scientific.[124]

Just as a genetic explanation *alone* is incomplete, a teleological explanation *alone* does not give a full accounting of a phenomenon. Given a present phenomenon, it is not sufficient to explain it by merely pointing to the aim it serves which may only be descriptive; it may not get to the underlying causes or factors which are responsible for the phenomenon having that apparent purpose or aim.[125] To account for its present aim in terms of *only* a genetic explanation would be inadequate for the reasons already indicated; i.e., it does not account for present causes. Teleological explanations tend to cause difficulty because they appear to be satisfied with apparent relationships or *a priori* patterns which have not been scrutinized. The point is that a particular limited orientation in viewing a phenomenon may lead to the inability to give a full accounting of that phenomenon as it reveals itself. Freud was caught in this tension.

Thus we are brought to the point where we must deal with the theoretical concepts involved; these concepts must be understood in themselves.

F. *Philosophy of Genesis and Telos*
1. *Notions of Genesis, Telos, Reductionism, Dialectic*

To obtain a deeper meaning of Freud's thought we will engage in the exploration of the nature of genesis and telos. Then we will extend our study to Freud's ideas. Reality reveals itself under two aspects— the genetic and the teleological. We find teleology throughout the organic world and in conscious activity. Below the animate world we find causation more explained in terms of mechanism or determinism. Teleology and mechanism seem to be opposite poles. But in all living things which appear to be teleological, there may lie beneath their movement a determinism. Mechanism and determinism allow for no teleology only when it is assumed that the entire world is material.

Genesis or origin shows the past history of telos. Genesis marks the place where telos once was. Telos represents a forward movement or purpose in the world. It can only manifest itself through the world; when its manifestation is recorded it becomes part of genesis. Genesis and telos are complementary ideas; yet genesis may be considered the anti-thesis of telos. The genetic side of reality stands over against the teleological dimension. Because of their polarity they highlight each other. They are intimately connected for when telos becomes past time it becomes part of genesis. One concept is thus seen as generating or passing into its opposite. We cannot really think about the genetic without relating it to the teleological. We may make an attempt to take a phenomenon and see only its genetic side. We may try to divorce ourselves from any teleological orientation; i.e., we engage in a reductionism. When we make a reduction we go backward in our dialectic. We take the synthesis and reduce it to the thesis. However, when reductionism explains the synthesis only in terms of the genesis, an error is committed. The fact is that between thesis and synthesis there is the moment of confrontation or anti-thesis. Only by the realization of the *three* moments of the dialectic can we escape from a blatant reductionism. We discover that the genetic aspect does not account for the phenomenon under investigation. In fact, the reduction only makes us more aware that something is missing. The missing aspect or telos is seen therefore to be something above and beyond the genetic. In the process of viewing a phenomenon from the genetic side, the mind seems to be forced to grasp for more; for the genetic in its inadequacy implies the teleological. Genesis or telos taken alone shows us only a one-sided view; when a dialectic is set up between the two concepts the one-sidedness disappears in the synthesis. Genesis and telos are involved in a conflict of opposed concepts. The resolution of the conflict takes place in a synthesis which itself gives rise to another conflict. The dialectic is taken to mean the positing of the thesis, an opposition to the thesis or anti-thesis, and a resolution arising from a synthesis. Thus telos is opposed by genesis; and out of the opposition we have the two synthesized into the present moment of experience. There is a forward movement in that the synthesis of the present moment becomes the thesis of the next process. This continuous dialectic resembles the operation of the mind in its search for truth; with its state of consciousness derived from the past, it confronts the present moment only to rise to a more heightened state of consciousness.

With man becoming more self-conscious, the teleological aspect of reality becomes more manifest. The world is a necessary precondition for telos being seen; and telos manifests itself best through the human mind. Man's mind shows most clearly the two-fold aspect of reality; in the mind's record of past experience we have the genetic and in the mind's present moment of awareness we have the teleological.

The ideas of genesis and telos both arise from the same source— human consciousness. The person in understanding himself knows that his actions have their genesis in himself; he knows at the same time that the action was for a purpose. In genesis, the mind looks back and in teleology the mind looks forward. Genesis and teleology both make themselves felt upon human consciousness. The person can only comprehend the cosmos through the use of both genesis and telos. Progress unfolds to us a long series of causes and past relationships. One phenomenon is explained in terms of another which itself demands an explanation. Genesis alone does not give a complete explanation but implies a teleology.

A subject does not arrive at self-consciousness merely by a reflection upon the originating causes that go into psychic development. He must realize the significance of the *teleology* that has been uncovered in his movement toward "becoming conscious." On the other hand, we are not aware of the teleological aspect of the process of "becoming conscious" unless there is the necessary dispossession or reductionism. Unless we make the reductionism, the telos does not emerge.

Self and other show an extension of this dialectic of genesis and telos. The self is in confrontation with the world of objects and other selves. To become self-conscious the self must recognize the other. The self sees the other as identical with and different from itself. The self in confrontation with the other affirms first its own identity. In the beginning the self would destroy the other so as to affirm its own self-hood. The self learns not to destroy the other for the other becomes the source of the self becoming self-conscious.

2. *Extension of Our Notions to Freud's Thought*

We will attempt now to extend these ideas of genesis, telos, dialectic and reductionism to the thought of Freud which we have considered in this chapter. The dialectic of the forces of genesis and telos is seen most clearly as operative in the human mind. We believe that Freud is involved in the problem of time which is best perceived through the mind's operation (*distentio animae*). The mind is pulled in two directions: by the past (genesis) and by the future (telos).

One aspect of Freud's thought reveals the dependency of the present upon the past: Here growth is seen merely as an acting out of what was determined by the past. We grow in awareness not because of our confrontation with the world here and now but rather because past factors have so determined our growth. The reality that reveals itself will be a repetition of the past; or so it will seem to us. There is no need to look for novelty, for there is none. The past is merely being played out again and again. It is like the eternal return; we are not yet in time and there can be no progress. This is a stifling world for the person; he can do nothing else than be resigned to the Fates. The past

43

determines completely the present; and this would make the past and the present the same. However, in the Freudian ontogeny of person there is the struggle between genesis and teleology. For Freud the movement toward greater awareness of reality and self appears as a re-enactment of what happened in the phylogenetic past and the person's own past history. The teleological movement which is seen as a "becoming conscious" seems to be viewed in relation to what was determined by the past.

If we follow Freud at this stage we have both a genesis and a telos. However, the telos tends to be reduced to genesis. And thus the dialectic has not progressed to the point of showing the telos as revealing more than genesis. At this point, however, we can show that the Freudian reductionism only places in greater relief the teleological dimension. Telos goes beyond the past. Telos is only appreciated when one sees what one has moved through by means of reducing the present to the past. If "becoming conscious" is reduced to past stages, the *telos* of the whole process still emerges.[126] For we have person in confrontation with a present full of novelty and variability. Person cannot be totally dependent upon the past for he does not come prepared with a blueprint to confront the present moment. The present moment which the person confronts is like nothing that has been seen in the past; past and present are not the same.

Freud's ontogeny of person must from a logical viewpoint make a clear break with the phylogenetic past. We believe that we do find this break in Freud. The person lives in the present and the dialectic with present reality brings him to a sense of awareness which the past could not have had. Thus the person does escape the past determinism because reality reveals itself ever new. When person is truly aware of the present as distinct from the past, he is immediately aware of genesis and telos. Both flow onward together.

In the dialectic of growth the person has been better equipped "to know." Thus reality is revealed with greater depth. The person comes to see the world in a new way because of his heightened consciousness. There is the expectation that the process of growth will be continuous thus indicating a movement to an ever-widening grasp of reality. Expectation of the new comes about when the person realizes not only the operation of genetic forces but sees them as denials or reductions which work to reveal a telos. It is when we reduce the

44

present phenomenon to its genesis that we become conscious of movement and teleology. For the past origins in contrast to the present moment reveal movement. Movement indicates that we are in time.

The ontogeny of person shows the gradual deflation of the ego. The brilliance of reality in confrontation with the self makes the ego shrink back. We could consider a dialectic of "ego" and "non-ego," for when the ego thought of itself as all things, it was at its lowest state of consciousness. Only through a series of negations does person grow in consciousness. Having "become conscious" it is not enough for the subject to look back at each of the earlier stages of the dialectic to understand one's present state; it is also necessary to see the dialectic and the forward movement that has emerged (telos).

There is a movement of cathexis being attached to the ego, then to those resembling the ego and finally those different from it. There is a loss of egotism and a gradual turning to more and more awareness of the outside world. There seems to be in the person an inner dynamism which moves toward reality and an ever fuller grasping of it. The ego-libido gradually becomes object-libido. In a way there is a moment of annihilation of the self through confrontation with the world, only to recover the self at a more heightened consciousness and a correspondingly greater awareness of reality. The *hope* for a still greater depth view of reality is engendered both when one sees the *past* struggle and *present* teleology.

The ontogeny of person moving through the oral, anal, phallic on to the genital stage represents a negation of the past. To move forward (telos) there must be a giving up or denial of the past stage (genesis). In the movement forward there is a statement of telos (thesis) which is negated by genesis (anti-thesis); the synthesis is achieved in the higher stage of development. When we engage in a reductionism to see the origins of the mature stage, there is a dialectic revealed. It is the ego bearing the past in confrontation with the present world; out of this confrontation a new stage emerges. A full appreciation of one's arriving at a stage where one can relate more fully to the other is not obtained without a reductionism of the present stage. For genesis reveals the struggle—a losing and a receiving, a growing and an annihilation. Genesis, at the same time, reveals a teleology which we enjoy at the present moment and which gives greater promise in the future.

45

The struggle between the "reality principle" and the "pleasure principle" can be further considered. In a way reality must negate pure pleasure which seeks to escape into illusion; in the negation growth takes place. The new stage arrived at displays a fuller grasp of reality; in time, a confrontation with present experience allows for further reflection and deeper penetration of reality. The new stage emerging thus manifests a still greater predominance of the reality principle and a corresponding lessening of the pleasure principle.

Person strives to allow the reality principle to predominate. When he is unsuccessful, it might seem that victory has been given to the past as in regression or neurosis. However, when a reduction is made, it is revealed that person has not really moved back into the past. The person remains in the present using a defense which *resembles* the past. The person's genesis shows much development has taken place from the time of the past to the present moment of confrontation. The genesis of the person reveals a series of moments but they are successive because the person is in time. When person is in time, the past moment can never be recaptured in the same way. Thus we can never be completely victims of the past. The person, in failing to give victory to the reality principle, can still reflect on the present moment, which may seem like a return to the past, and yet see it as distinct from the past. In making the distinction a telos emerges.

NOTES

[1] E. Pumpian-Mindlin (ed.), *Psychoanalysis as Science* (New York: Basic Books, 1952), p. 126.

[2] Bartlett H. Stoodley, *The Concepts of Sigmund Freud* (Glencoe, Ill.: The Free Press, 1959), p. vii.

[3] Rapaport, "The Structure of Psychoanalytic Theory: A Systematic Attempt," p. 20. Ernest Jones, *The Life and Work of Sigmund Freud* (3 vols.; New York: Basic Books, 1961-65), III, 310.

[4] Rapaport, "The Structure of Psychoanalytic Theory: A Systematic Attempt," p. 20.

[5] Sigmund Freud (1924), *An Autobiographical Study*, in *The Complete Psychological Works of Sigmund Freud*, ed. and trans. by James Strachey, XX (London: Hogarth Press, 1966), p. 8. Hereafter, unless otherwise specified, all references to Freud's works will be taken from this collection with the specific

date and title mentioned. David Rapaport, "The Structure of Psychoanalytic Theory: A Systematic Attempt," *Psychological Issues Monograph*, No. 6, III (1960), II. Fritz Wittels, *Freud and His Time* (New York: Liverright, 1931), Chapter I, *passim.*

[6]Rapaport, p. 22.

[7]*Ibid.*

[8]Morton Beckner, *The Biological Way of Thought* (New York: Columbia University Press, 1959), p. 97.

[9]Rapaport, "The Structure of Psychoanalytic Theory: A Systematic Attempt," p. 22.

[10]Sigmund Freud, "Letter to Karl Abraham," (11 Nov. 1917), in Jones, *The Life and Work of Sigmund Freud*, III, 312.

[11]Rapaport, "The Structure of Psychoanalytic Theory: A Systematic Attempt," p. 23.

[12]Walther Riese, "The Pre-Freudian Origins of Psychoanalysis," *Science and Psychoanalysis*, Jules H. Masserman (ed.). (New York: Grune & Stratton, 1958), p. 62.

[13]Jacob Arlow, "The Concepts of Regression and the Structural Theory," *Psychoanalytic Concepts and the Structural Theory*, Jacob Arlow and Charles Brennen (New York: International Universities Press, Inc., 1964), p. 57.

[14]Riese, "The Pre-Freudian Origins of Psychoanalysis," p. 63.

[15]Riese, "The Pre-Freudian Origins of Psychoanalysis," p. 60.

Arlow, "The Concepts of Regression and the Structural Theory," p. 56.

[16]Riese, "The Pre-Freudian Origins of Psychoanalysis," p. 60.

[17]Riese, "The Pre-Freudian Origins of Psychoanalysis," p. 62.

[18]*Ibid.*, p. 63.

[19]"Impressive analogies from biology have prepared us to find that the individual's mental development repeats the course of human development in an abbreviated form." Freud (1910), "Leonardo Da Vinci and a Memory of His Childhood," XI, 97.

"In his mental development, the child would be repeating the history of the race in an abbreviated form, just as embryology long since recognized was the case with somatic development." Freud (1926), "The Question of Lay Analysis," XX, 212.

"In the last few years, psycho-analytic writers have become aware that the principle that 'ontogeny is a repetition of phylogeny' must be applicable to mental life; and this has led to a fresh extension of psychoanalytic interest." Freud (1913), "The Claims of Psycho-analysis to Scientific Interest," XIII, 184.

"Ontogenesis may be regarded as a recapitulation of phylogenesis in so far as the latter has not been modified by more recent experience. The phylogenetic disposition can be seen at work behind the ontogenetic process. But disposition is ultimately the precipitate of earlier experience of the species to which the more recent experience of the individual, as the sum of the accidental factors, is super-added." Freud (1914), "Preface to the Third Edition of *Three Essays on the Theory of Sexuality,*" VII, 131.

[20]Freud (1905), *Three Essays on the Theory of Sexuality*, VII, 241.

[21]Freud (1905), *Three Essays on the Theory of Sexuality*, VII, p. 162, n. 2, 1915. (This note was added in 1915).

[22]Freud (1912), *Totem and Taboo*, XIII, 90.

"It seems as if each one of us has been through a phase of individual development corresponding to this animistic stage in primitive man, that none of us has passed through it without preserving certain residues and traces of it which are still capable of manifesting themselves, and that everything which now strikes us as 'uncanny' fulfills the condition of touching those residues of animistic mental activity within us and bringing them to expression." *Ibid.*, p. 241.

[23]Freud (1916), "Introductory Lectures on Psychoanalysis," XVI, 370.

[24]Freud (1916), "Introductory Lectures on Psychoanalysis," XVI, 371.

Freud (1938), *An Outline of Psychoanalysis*, XXIII, 188-89.

[25]"The overcoming of the Oedipus complex coincides with the most efficient way of mastering the archaic, animal heritage of humanity. It is true that that heritage comprises all the forces that are required for the subsequent cultural development of the individual, but they must be sorted out and worked over. This archaic heirloom is not fit to be used for the purposes of civilized social life in the form in which it is inherited by the individual." Freud (1919), "Preface to Reik's *Ritual: Psycho-analytic Studies,*" XVII, 262.

"Although the majority of human beings go through the Oedipus complex as an individual experience, it is nevertheless a phenomenon which is determined and laid down by heredity and which is bound to pass away according to programme when the next pre-ordained phase of development sets in. This being so, it is of no great importance what the occasions are which allow this to happen, or, indeed whether any such occasions can be discovered at all." Freud (1924), "Dissolution of the Oedipus Complex," XIX, 174.

[26]*Ibid.*

"Every individual has in fact gone through this phase (Oedipal) but has afterwards energetically repressed its purport and succeeded in forgetting it. A horror of incest and an enormous sense of guilt are left over from this prehistoric epoch of the individual's existence. It may be that something quite similar occurred in the prehistoric epoch of the human species as a whole and that the beginning of morality, religion and social order were intimately connected with the surmounting of the primaeval era." *Ibid.*, p. 221.

[27]Freud (1938), *Moses and Monotheism*, XXIII, 99.

"Behind this childhood of the individual, we are promised a picture of phylogenetic childhood—a picture of the development of the human race, of which the individual's development is in fact an abbreviated recapitulation influenced by the chance circumstances of life." Freud (1919), *Interpretation of Dreams*, V, 548.

[28]Freud (1926), "Question of Lay Analysis," XX, 212.

[29]Freud (1900), *The Interpretation of Dreams*, IV, 60.

[30]*Ibid.* (1914), V, 591.

[31]*Ibid.* (1919), p. 548.

[32]*Ibid.*, p. 549.

"Furthermore, dreams bring to light material which cannot have originated either from the dreamer's adult life or from his forgotten childhood. We are obliged to regard it as part of the *archaic heritage* which a child brings with him into the world, before any experience of his own, influenced by the experience of his ancestors. We find the counterpart of this phylogenetic material in the earliest human legends and in surviving customs. Thus dreams constitute a source of human pre-history which is not to be despised." Freud (1938), *An Outline of Psychoanalysis*, XXIII, 167.

[33]Freud (1915), *Introductory Lectures on Psychoanalysis,* XV, 199.

[34]"Shall we succeed in distinguishing which portion of the latent mental processes is derived from the individual prehistoric period and which portion from the phylogenetic one? It is not, I believe, impossible that we shall. It seems to me, for instance, that symbolic connections, which the individual has never acquired by learning, may justly claim to be regarded as a phylogenetic heritage." Freud (1915), *Introductory Lectures*, XV, 199.

[35]Freud (1905), *Three Essays on the Theory of Sexuality*, VII, 173, 173 n. 1.

[36]Freud (1938), *Origins of Psychoanalysis*, XXIII, 206.

". . . I regard it as a methodological error to seize on a phylogenic explanation before the ontogenetic possibilities have been exhausted. I cannot see any reason for obstinately disputing the importance of infantile prehistory while at the same time freely acknowledging the importance of ancestral prehistory. Nor can I overlook the fact that phylogenetic motives and productions themselves stand in need of elucidation, and that in quite a number of instances this is afforded by factors in the childhood of the individual. And finally, I cannot feel surprised that what was originally produced by certain circumstances in prehistoric times and was then transmitted in the shape of a predisposition to its re-acquirement should, since the same circumstances persist, emerge once more as a concrete event in the experience of the individual." Freud (1914), "From the History of an Infantile Neurosis," XVII, 97, 121.

[37]Freud (1914), "From the History of an Infantile Neurosis," XVII, 103, n. 1.

[38]". . . development . . . involves two dangers—first, of *inhibition*, and secondly, of regression . . . in view of the general tendency of biological

processes to variation, it is bound to be the case that not every preparatory phase will be passed through with equal success and completely superseded: portions of the function will be permanently held back at these early stages, and the total picture of development will be qualified by some amount of developmental inhibition." Freud (1915), "Introductory Lectures on Psychoanalysis," XVI, 339.

[39] *Ibid.*, p. 340.

[40] Freud (1911), "Psycho-analytic Notes on An Autobiographical Account of a Case of Paranoia," XII, 78.

[41] Freud (1915), "Introductory Lectures," XVI, 340.

"The normal sexuality of adults emerges from infantile sexuality by a series of developments, combinations, divisions and suppressions, which are scarcely ever achieved with ideal perfection and consequently leave behind predispositions to a retrogression of the function in the form of illness." Freud (1913), "Claims of psychoanalysis," XIII, 180.

[42] Freud (1915), "Thoughts on War and Death," XIV, 285-86.

[43] Freud (1901), "Fragment of an Analysis of a Case of Hysteria," VII, 50.

[44] Freud (1905), "Three Essays on the Theory of Sexuality," VII, 170.

[45] Freud (1909), "Five Lectures on Psycho-Analysis," XI, 46.

[46] Freud (1911), "Formulations on the Two Principles of Mental Functioning," XII, 224.

[47] Freud (1912), "Types of Onset of Neurosis," XII, 232, 236. Freud (1911), "Psycho-analytic Notes on an Autobiographical Account of a Case of Paranoia," XII, 62, 77. Freud (1915), "Mourning and Melancholia," XIV, 249.

[48] Freud (1913), "The Disposition to Obsessional Neurosis," XII, 318. Freud (1915), "Introductory Lectures on Psychoanalysis," XVI, 421.

[49] Freud (1909), "Five Lectures on Psychoanalysis," XI, 45.

[50] Freud (1914), "From the History of an Infantile Neurosis," XVII, 86.

"If he is left to himself, a neurotic is obliged to replace by his own symptom formations the great group formations from which he is excluded. He creates his own world of imagination for himself, his own religion, his own system of delusions, and thus recapitulates the institutions of humanity in a distorted way which is clear evidence of the dominating part played by the directly sexual impulsions." Freud (1921), "Group Psychology and the Analysis of the Ego," XVIII, 142. Freud (1923), "A Short Account of Psycho-Analysis," XIX, 206.

[51] Freud (1912), *Totem and Taboo*, XIII, 66. Freud (1915), "Instincts and Their Vicissitudes," XIV, 131.

[52] Freud (1916), *Introductory Lectures*, XVI, 362.

[53] Freud (1916), *Introductory Lectures*, XVI, 366.

"The aetiology common to the onset of a psychoneurosis and of a psychosis always remains the same. It consists of a frustration, a non-fulfillment, of one of those childhood wishes which are forever undefeated and which are so deeply rooted in our phylogenetically determined organization." Freud (1923), "Neurosis and Psychosis," XIX, 151.

[54]Freud (1925), "Inhibitions, Symptoms and Anxiety," XX, 154.

[55]*Ibid.*, p. 155.

[56]Freud (1914), "Preface to the Third Edition of *Three Essays on Sexuality*," VII, 131.

[57]Freud (1914), "From the History of an Infantile Neurosis," XVII, 97.

[58]Freud (1905), *Three Essays on the Theory of Sexuality*, VII, 198.

[59]Freud (1915), *Introductory Lectures on Psychoanalysis*, XVI, 314.

[60]Freud (1923), *The Ego and the Id*, XIX, 29.

[61]Freud (1905), *Three Essays on the Theory of Sexuality*, VII, 198.

[62]*Ibid.*, p. 181.

[63]*Ibid.*, p. 182.

[64]Freud (1913), "The Disposition to Obsessional Neurosis," XII, 321.

[65]Freud (1911), "Formulations on the Two Principles of Mental Functioning," XII, 222.

"The employment of a fiction like this (that only the pleasure principle is operative) is, however, justified when one considers that the infant—provided one includes with it the care it receives from its mother—does almost realize a psychical system of this kind. It probably hallucinates the fulfillment of its internal needs; it betrays its unpleasure, when there is an increase of stimulus and an absence of satisfaction, by the motor discharge of screaming and beating about with its arms and legs, and it then experiences the satisfaction it has hallucinated." *Ibid.*, p. 220.

"We have put forward the fiction that we did always possess this ability to hallucinate and that at the beginning of our mental life we did in fact hallucinate the satisfying object when we felt the need for it. But in such a situation satisfaction did not occur, and this failure must very soon have moved us to create some contrivance with the help of which it was possible to distinguish such wishful perception from a real fulfillment and to avoid them for the future. In other words, we gave up hallucinatory satisfaction of our wishes at a very early period and set up a kind of 'reality testing.' " Freud (1915), "A Metapsychological Supplement to the Theory of Dreams," XIV, 231.

[66]Freud (1905), *Three Essays on the Theory of Sexuality*, VII, 218.

[67]Freud (1938), *An Outline of Psychoanalysis*, XXIII, 150.

[68]Freud (1914), "On Narcissism: An Introduction," XIV, 76.

"Recent investigations have directed our attention to a stage in the development of the libido which it passes through on the way from auto-erotism to object love. This stage has been given the name of narcissism. What happens is this. There comes a time in the development of the individual at which he unifies his sexual instincts (which have hitherto been engaged in auto-erotic activities) in order to obtain a love-object; and he begins by taking himself, his own body, as his love-object . . .'' Freud (1911), ''Psycho-analytic Notes on an Autobiographical Account of a Case of Paranoia,'' XII, 60.

[69]Freud (1938), *An Outline of Psychoanalysis*, XXIII, 150.

[70]Freud (1911), ''Notes on a Case of Paranoia,'' XII, 60.

[71]Freud (1932), *New Introductory Lectures on Psychoanalysis,* XXII, 99.

[72]Freud (1905), *Three Essays on the Theory of Sexuality*, VII, 198.

[73]Freud (1914), ''On Narcissism: An Introduction,'' XIV, 90.

[74]Freud (1905), *Three Essays on the Theory of Sexuality*, VII, 198.

[75]*Ibid.*, p. 199.

[76]Freud (1913), ''The Disposition to Obsessional Neurosis,'' XII, 321.

[77]Freud (1938), *Outline of Psycho-analysis*, XIII, 154.

[78]Freud (1915), ''Instincts and Their Vicissitudes,'' XIV, 139.

[79]Freud (1905), *Three Essays on the Theory of Sexuality*, VII, 186.

[80]Freud (1917), ''Transformations of Instinct,'' XVII, 130.

[81]Freud (1932), *New Introductory Lectures on Psychoanalysis*, XXII, 99.

[82]Freud (1938), *Outline of Psycho-analysis*, XXIII, 154.

[83]*Ibid.*, p. 155.

[84]Freud (1905), *Three Essays on the Theory of Sexuality*, VII, 199, n. 2 (1924).

[85]*Ibid.*, XXIII, 189.

[86]*Ibid.*, p. 191.

[87]Freud (1923), *Ego and the Id*, XIX, 32.

[88]Freud (1905), *Three Essays on the Theory of Sexuality*, VII, 197.

[89]Freud (1905), *Three Essays on the Theory of Sexuality*, VII, 207. Freud (1909), *Five Lectures on Psychoanalysis*, XI, 44-45. Freud (1915), *Introductory Lectures on Psychoanalysis*, XVI, 308, 329. Freud (1923), ''Infantile Genital Organization: An Interpolation into the Theory of Sexuality,'' XIX, 142.

[90]Freud (1905), *Three Essays on the Theory of Sexuality*, VII, 217.

[91]Freud (1938), *Outline of Psychoanalysis*, XXIII, 155.

[92]Freud (1905), *Three Essays on the Theory of Sexuality*, VII, 207.

[93]Freud, ''Extracts from the Fliess Papers—Draft H. Paranoia (Jan. 24, 1895),'' I, 211.

[94]Freud, (1911), ''Psychoanalytic Notes on an Autobiographical Account of a Case of Paranoia,'' XII, 71.

[95]Freud (1914), ''On Narcissism,'' XIV, 74. Freud (1915), ''The Unconscious,'' XIV, 203.

[96]Richard S. Rudner, *Philosophy of Social Science* (Englewood Cliffs: Prentice-Hall, Inc., 1966), p. 24. Peter Achinstein, ''Models, Analogies, and Theories,'' *Philosophy of Science* (1964), pp. 329-330.

[97]Rudner, *Philosophy of Social Science*, p. 25. Else Frenkel-Brunswik,

"Psychoanalysis and the Unity of Science," *Proceedings of the American Academy of Arts and Sciences*, LXXX, 291-92. P. Henry Van Laer, *The Philosophy of Science*, I (Pittsburgh: Duquesne University Press, 1963), 119.

[98]Heinz Hartmann, "Psychoanalysis as a Scientific Theory," *Psychoanalysis, Scientific Method, and Philosophy*, ed. by Sidney Hook (New York: New York University Press, 1959), p. 17.

[99]Rudner, *Philosophy of Social Science*, p. 26.

[100]*Ibid.*, p. 27.

[101]*Ibid.*

[102]Freud (1938), *Moses and Monotheism*, XXIII, 100.

[103]Herbert Weiner, "Psychoanalysis as a Biological Science," in *Psychoanalysis and Current Biological Thought*, Norman S. Greenfield and William C. Lewis (eds.). (Milwaukee: University of Wisconsin Press, 1965), p. 15.

[104]David Rapaport and Merton M. Gill, "The Points of View and Assumptions of Metapsychology," *The International Journal of Psychoanalysis*, XL (1959), 158.

Morton Beckner, *The Biological Way of Thought* (New York: Columbia University Press, 1959), p. 95.

[105]Ernest Nagel, *The Structure of Science* (New York: Harcourt, Brace and World, Inc., 1961), p. 25.

[106]*Ibid.*, p. 26. Rudolf Allers, *New Psychologies* (London: Sheed & Ward, 1932), p. 11.

[107]Nagel, *The Structure of Science*, p. 568.

[108]Weiner, "Psychoanalysis as a Biological Science," p. 15.

[109]Freud, "Abstracts of the Scientific Writings of Dr. Sigmund Freud 1877-1897," III, 228-29.

[110]Freud (1915), "Thoughts on War and Death," XIV, 285-86.

[111]Freud (1915), *Introductory Lectures*, XVI, 341.

[112]Weiner, "Psychoanalysis as a Biological Science," p. 15.

[113]Beckner, *The Biological Way of Thought*, p. 107.

[114]Alfred S. Romer, *The Vertebrate Body* (Philadelphia: W. B. Saunders Co., 1949), p. 112.

[115]*Ibid.*, p. 113.

[116]B. I. Balensky, *An Introduction to Embryology* (Philadelphia: W. B. Saunders Co., 1961), p. 9.

[117]Weiner, "Psychoanalysis as a Biological Science," p. 15.

[118]*Ibid.*

[119]*Ibid.*, p. 104.

[120]Beckner, *The Biological Way of Thought*, p. 105.

[121]*Ibid.*, p. 106.

[122] *Ibid.*

[123] Philip Rieff, *Freud: The Mind of the Moralist* (New York: Viking Press, 1959), p. 292.

[124] We will deal with this problem at length in Chapter V.

[125] Gustav Bergmann, "Psychoanalysis and Experimental Psychology: a review from the standpoint of scientific empiricism," *Psychological Theory,* Melvin H. Marx (ed.) (New York: Macmillan Co., 1951), p. 355.

[126] In the course of our work, we propose to show that there is a full dialectic indicating a clear telos and a synthesis.

Chapter II

Psychoanalytic Concepts Descriptive of Person: Genesis and Telos

We examined in broad outline the ontogeny of person and have shown that a deeper view of the Freudian analysis of person is seen when we allow for a dialectic of genesis and emerging teleology.[1] We will attempt to make a further analysis of the human psyche by way of the psychoanalytic concepts.[2] However, we will treat only those concepts which will have some bearing on our study of man as religious.[3]

As we cannot understand Freud's view of man as religious without first understanding Freud's view of man, so too we cannot understand the psychoanalytic concepts describing the religious man without a prior examination of these psychoanalytic concepts. We believe that it would be fruitless to discuss concepts which are supposed to be telling us about the human psyche unless we first establish that they do say something. Freud proposed psychoanalysis as a science which by definition means it is supposed to be describing the empirical world. Therefore, through the use of philosophy of science, we must examine the concepts in order to find out whether they take their meaning because of a relation to reality or whether they are merely of the conceptual order without referent. To determine their meaningfulness we will examine their relationship to observables which they are supposed to describe; we will see whether they may be verified and falsified; and we will mention the need for proper linguistic usage in order that the concepts maintain their meaningfulness.

Having been satisfied with their meaningfulness, we will go on to consider the way the concepts give an accounting of the human psyche. We shall find that while the concepts have their genetic side, they also have an implicit teleological aspect. When both poles (genetic and teleological) are seen to be operative, a richer meaning of the Freudian analysis of psyche is seen to emerge. We examine this polarity with reference to the unconscious-conscious, ego-id-superego, identification and sublimation. With regard to sublimation we will see clearly the necessity of making a reductionism in order to understand its genetic side; but at the same time we are still faced with explaining the sublimation that has been achieved. We are thus forced to see a dynamism operative in the human psyche which is responsible for the forward movement. Understanding the genesis makes us all the more aware of an implicit *telos*.

A. *Philosophical Analysis of Psychoanalytic Concepts*
1. *Concepts borrowed from other sciences to describe the human psyche*

Freud's concepts have been subject to a great deal of criticism. We find, for example, such statements about psychoanalysis as:

> The psychoanalytic explanation either of behavior or of consciousness by impulses, repressions, traumas, complexes, compulsions, ids, libidos, and ''the play of mental forces,'' rather than by imaginable neural or spiritual realities, is like the apocryphal Scholastic's explanation of a clock's behavior by an essence of horadicity rather than by wheels and springs.[4]

> . . . I felt that these other three theories [including psychoanalysis] posed as sciences while in fact they were of the character of primitive myths rather than of science; that they resembled astrology rather than astronomy.[5]

> The false reasoning consequent on this use of an important term in two different significances is the well-known logical *fallacy of ambiguous middle:* one of the devices most favoured by all the great company of slipshod thinkers. By emphasizing now one meaning, now another meaning, of the term, dubious transitions may be made with ease and a principle may be applied over a much wider range than exact knowledge would permit.[6]

At first blush it seems as if his thoughts [Freud's] are expressed with crystal clarity. However, as soon as one begins to analyze some of his fundamental concepts such as libido, instincts, affect, psychic energy, one becomes bogged down in a maze of elusive or analogical notions, few of which are defined with any clarity.[7]

When we examine the criticism brought against Freud's concepts, we find that one objection is that he takes his concepts from the physical sciences and applies them to psychology without indicating any change of sense, e.g. he speaks of certain ideas as cathected with energy and certain impulses having a greater or lesser energy. The question arises as to how an idea, a dream, or an image can be said to carry a quantum of energy.[8] The authors point to certain elaborations of the concept of libido which Freud first introduced as an abbreviation for a set of sexual needs but then proceeded to describe as "flowing," as being "damned up," as "tending to regress to early channels," as "being converted" into anxiety, and as "making its energy available" to the ego.[9]

The critics want to know the justification for describing libido in this fashion. In addition, the analogy to a hydraulic press is no longer valid in physiology. Further, there is no correspondence of this description to the structure of the nervous system.[10] Issue is taken with the term "energy" because the concept has essential application to physical reality. Thus when the term "energy" is applied to the psychical order, does this mean that the psychical is the same as the physical? Energy in the physical sciences means something which can be measured, changes form, and varies quantitatively and a literal application to the psychic realm causes problems. No quantifying solution has been worked out for the energy problem in psychoanalysis.[11] If energy is used metaphorically of the psychic, then this should be clarified.[12]

In response, it should be pointed out that Freud did not intend the concepts to be taken in a strictly physical sense: he relied, especially in the early writings, upon physiology, as a guide but he also saw that it was different from psychology. Besides the difficulties that arise from borrowing non-psychological concepts, we wish to indicate that the Freudian concepts and their use in theory will not have the same exactness and precision as in mathematical and physical theories. This is so because the concepts are used in an attempt to understand the human phenomenon.[13] ". . . these peculiarities of psychoanalytic concepts are such as to ensure that their central and basic place in psychoanalysis must give this discipline logical status different from, though not of course for that reason either inferior or superior to, that of sciences concerned with things other than human beings . . ."[14]

2. *Relation of concepts and structures to observables*

Another question which arises is whether the psychoanalytic concepts have a relationship to observable phenomena. Much of what psychoanalysis speaks about is in the realm of the unconscious and therefore the phenomena which the concepts and theories describe are not observable. This criticism is related to the objection that Freud's concepts are vague. For a theory to be empirically validated, we must be able to derive logically (*a priori*) certain outcomes from the assumptions of that theory. Thus before an examination of the empirical data, we must have a clear idea of the consequences of the theory.[15] For example, the question may be raised as to whether it can be shown *a priori* what the specific conditions are in which the sexual drive will discharge its energy rather than join with the aggressive drive. If the Freudian concepts are so vague that any consequences are compatible with them, then they are unscientific. In the use of metaphor or analogy, Freud employs them without giving specific rules as to how to expand them. In the case of "energy" and "level of excitation" these lack a "specific content" and therefore meaning can be given to them arbitrarily.[16] Thus it is possible that when an attempt is made to explain the behavior of a person in terms of a metapsychology whose rules of correspondence are vague, we might find that the explanation is arbitrary.[17] Therefore, for empirical validation *some* of the theoretical notions must be connected with definite and unambiguous observable phenomena.

These connections are established by "correspondence rules," "coordinating definitions," "operational definitions," "rules of coordination," and "semantical rules." Unless these conditions are met, the theory has no "determinate consequences" about empirical phenomena[18] e.g. "semantic rules" are regulations whereby the terms in the theory are related to terms in sentences which are directly testable.[19] Thus a system of axioms and a system of observed facts are joined by operational definitions. Where points of agreement are found between the theory and the data we have confirmation of the theory,[20] i.e. the abstract concepts must be considered along with their content.[21] In Freud's system we find propositions which are on different levels depending upon their distance from empirical data, e.g., level of observation (phenomena of conscious life and unconscious and preconscious as seen in psychoanalytic session), level of clinical interpretation (interconnections and their bearing on other behavior), level of clinical generalizations (character type, family constellation, neurosis), level of clinical theory (interpretations leading to formation of theoretical concepts: regression, defense, repression), level of metapsychology (abstract concepts: cathexis, eros, death instinct), and level of philosophy (positivism).[22] The lower level hypothesis may be deduced from the metapsychological hypotheses.

It would be unfair to impose upon psychoanalysis a strict operationism or empiricism which would demand that *all* concepts be founded on concrete observations.[23] For both psychoanalysis and modern physics make use of "fictitious" language in place of the "natural" language. In the long run, they are thus able to achieve a simple relationship with observable phenomena.[24] For concepts to be operationally meaningful they must be confirmable in principle at least. There must be some contact with observable phenomenon: A concept may be part of a system but somewhere there must be a relation to the observable. Further the concept or theory involving the concept must be grounded in operations which are definite, empirical, able to be carried out, and repeatable. In operationism full verifiability or full falsifiability will not be required but confirmability will suffice.[25]

> This, then, is modern operationism or empiricism. As applied to psycho-analysis, it means that psycho-analytic principles should be stated in terms so that they are, in some final analysis, in principle confirmable in terms of some ultimate observables.[26]

Some feel that there is ambiguity in the rules of correspondence which are supposed to hold between the concept of sexual drive and observable behavior as the concept is linked with myriad forms of sensuality. There is also a failing in precision in the correspondence

59

rules with reference to the concepts of id, ego and superego.[27] It is charged that concepts like "libido," "id," "mental life," "energy cathexis," are vague;[28] they may be used as hypothetical constructs but are difficult to validate or invalidate experimentally. Therefore, hypothetical constructs should be transposed into lower-order terms so that there will be less difficulty in experimentally validating them.[29]

3. *Concepts reformulated as observables*

Philosophers of science have made attempts to reformulate the concepts of Freudian theory in operational terminology thus indicating that the terms had the potentiality to be empirically confirmed. Freud set down his definitions of psychic structure after he had studied and repeated his clinical evidence. In cases of conflict, where certain functions were frequently grouped together in one formation as distinct from another formation, he was able to give names to these groupings. Thus the functions that were carried on in a mental process became the criteria for defining a psychic system.[30]

We will examine the attempt to connect Freud's concepts with observables. However, we will not show that the concepts are empirically verified because this is beyond the role of the philosopher of psychoanalysis. Rather, we will show that they can be reformulated in terms of observables,[31] e.g. the "id" can be grounded in experience as it can be seen operative in the life of a person because he has needs or drives such as hunger, sex, and thirst. These needs ("id") express themselves and can in turn be changed in view of social forces.[32] The "ego" can be observed in the following phenomena: the person has the ability to think, to perceive, to remember and to evaluate self and others and the core of these activities is called the "ego" by Freud. We might reformulate the "superego" operationally: the person is influenced in his behavior by what the parents have called "good" or "bad." Where the person sees a great many of his actions as bad, we have a guilty person or one who has a strong "superego," to use Freud's term.[33] Thus there are observational data proposed which would aid us in distinguishing the components of the psychic structure.

> In the structural hypothesis, . . . , id, ego, and superego are defined in terms of their roles in the pursuit of instinctual gratification. The distinction between ego and id was required by

the clinical facts of neurotic conflict in which one unconscious agency concerned with ultimate consequences attempts to impede the strivings of another. The distinction between superego and ego was required by the clinical facts of psychosis in which one agency of the ego seems to watch, criticize and attack the rest of the ego. Because their definitions are functional, it is possible to look for correlates about the ultimate structure of each of the three institutions, its function and its mode of operation.[34]

We attempt now an operational reformulation of "*repression,*" e.g. when the person realizes that he has done something "bad," he tries to avoid thinking of it again; he may succeed in forgetting it and thus save his ego pain. These processes take place unconsciously and yet we can obtain some indication that these things are going on from the fact that in a relaxed mood, some of the situations come back to consciousness. The person may act in such a way as to show he does not wish to remember.[35] The *Oedipus complex* can be reformulated operationally as follows: in the small family group as found in our culture, the little boy is aware that his father has a very important place with reference to his mother and he wishes that he could take the father's place.[36] Since the boy's sexual desires are denied an outlet they turn to his own mother. Because of his jealousy for his father and incestuous feelings, the boy may develop great hostility to the father and fear that the father will castrate him.[37] Thus meaning is given to the term, Oedipus complex, which is not far removed from terms employed in ordinary usage.[38]

In *sublimation* the person gives up a particular sexual *aim* but still retains interest in that object. The ordinary goal for libido is some form of sexual activity but it can be directed instead to some higher cultural activity. The mechanism of sublimation may be reformulated by considering a person who has no sexual outlet but expends his energy in artistic creations. With regard to *transference*, a patient may react to the analyst with the same feelings and complexes he felt toward his own parent(s). A reformulation of transference is seen with the employee who without sufficient reason reacts with hostility to his employer who is an older man. Thus he transfers to authority figures the same feelings he has had toward his own father (his first authority). In *identification* the child gives up the object-cathexis surrounding the

61

father and instead incorporates into his superego the father's image. We may reformulate this operationally by considering a person identifying with a well known celebrity although there may be no interest in or hope of knowing that individual personally.

Some authors use the terms "intervening variables" as the factors which form a link between hypothetical constructs (theoretical terms, e.g., "id") and the data of observation (manifest behavior).[39] The dispositional concepts of "reaction-formation," "displacement," and "projection" are examples of "intervening variables."[40] Intervening variables are concepts which are "directly abstracted" from observable phenomena by means of psychoanalytic techniques.[41] Here too there would be expected to be some empirical grounding which would give meaning to the intervening variables. A repetition of manifest behavior and other things known from the analytic setting would point to their existence. Therefore it appears that the psychoanalytic concepts discussed lend themselves to reformulation in terms of observables thus assuring us of their meaningfulness. We may be assured that we will be speaking meaningfully when we employ them in our discussion in this chapter and in our discussion of man as religious.

4. *Confirmability: verification and falsification*

Another important factor in the matter of theories (each concept may be considered a theory) is that a good theory cannot have implications for two incompatible outcomes. A theory must not only be able to be confirmed by observations but it, at least in principle, must be able to be falsified by observable data. Therefore, the theory must be such that it cannot be used so that it can explain any body of observations regardless of whether the set of data is in contradiction to another set of data.[42] Some philosophers claim that the lowest level generalizations of psychoanalysis cannot be refuted; also the empirical consequences derived from generalizations cannot be tested so as to provide an opportunity to refute the generalization. The question, therefore, arises as to whether psychoanalysis is irrefutable and therefore unscientific.[43] At this point the philosopher must reformulate the different parts of the theory in order to see whether they can be refuted.[44]

a. *Oedipus Complex.* Special attention is given to the Oedipus complex as it is the key to much of what we will say later about religion. "A subject is usually regarded as unscientific if in principle no observable state of affairs could falsify its claims so that by ad hoc modifications its assertions can be made compatible with any state of affairs whatsoever."[45] In regard to the Oedipus complex, one could ask for evidence to count *against* its presence;[46] some authors have asked for *one* specific trait (agreed upon by all), rather than a constellation, to indicate that there is no Oedipal conflict present.[47] Attempts[48] have been made to describe things which would indicate the absence of an Oedipal conflict. However, to ask for a specific description of evidence which will *always* show that a boy lacks an Oedipus complex is difficult to come by. Data is hard to find which under all kinds of circumstances will verify or falsify something;[49] this type of criteria requested for falsification seems to be too rigorous.[50] Some argue that one must show that the phenomena under investigation can be explained *only* by the one theory under investigation. For it is conceivable that the murderous and incestuous feelings of all children could be explained in another way. For the Oedipal theory holds that these feelings are a very part of growth.[51] "It [psychoanalysis] must find ways of eliminating other hypotheses compatible with the same results."[52] Again this seems to be a very rigorous demand made upon psychoanalysis. "In sum, even the most careful and extensive test can neither disprove one of two hypotheses nor prove the other, thus strictly construed, a crucial experiment is impossible in science."[53] Rather what psychoanalysis should do here would be to gather more and more evidence which would point to its hypothesis and less for opposing hypotheses.

That a child is going through an Oedipal phase might be verified by a presence of possessiveness for the mother and resentment for the father. Indications that would falsify the presence of the Oedipal phase would be the little boy without romantic feelings or phantasies regarding his mother and he would express no desires for the ousting of the father. That a person has an Oedipus complex might be indicated by their unfounded hostility toward father figures. Factors pointing to falsification would be that the person, for the most part, is well adjusted to interpersonal relationships and that his feelings and reactions to persons are proportionate responses to the way others have extended or not extended themselves to him.

b. *Topological and structural concepts.* In regard to the theory of *instincts* (drives) which Freud divides into the ego (self preservative) and the sexual, we find that this classification can be refuted *in principle*. For it is conceivable that new clinical data may be forthcoming which would not fit into the present two-fold division and which would necessitate a change in the classification of the instincts. In Freud's own writings, he later had to take into account the death instinct.[54]

Some consider the "*ego*," "*id*," and "superego" merely as fictional constructs because they claim the concepts cannot be clearly identified with specific physiological or psychological structure. Therefore they would seem to be unverifiable or unfalsifiable.[55] When we come to the concepts of the psychic structures ("id," "ego," and "superego") the notions of refutability and irrefutability are not *directly* applicable.[56] But we believe, as has been pointed out, that these concepts would have to be first reformulated as operational definitions and then they could be subject to refutability. In the discussion of the "superego" we can think of it as loving, hating, being severe, and forbidding toward the person. These terms, it is true, are taken from ordinary language used with reference to a parent-child relationship. But the person will experience these same feelings in and outside of analysis.[57] If we make use of transferential feelings, the analyst becomes a parental figure or living representative of the person's own superego. It is possible to conceive that the person will not see the analyst as loving, hating, being severe and forbidding. In such event we will have evidence against the superego's presence, e.g., psychopathic personality. Thus there is room for refutability. In regard to the concepts of *regression* and *fixation*, they seem to be refutable. For it is conceivable that obstacles could be set up to interfere with ordinary growth, e.g., frustration; and we could observe whether or not regressive behavior resulted or not.[58] Fixation (habit) as a prerequisite to regression has been experimentally verified and it is refutable in theory.[59]

An objection could be brought against the above discussion. For the problem is whether psychoanalysis as given to us by Freud is refutable i.e. the question is whether it was refutable without a great deal of reformulation.[60] We believe that the reformulations do not radically alter Freud's theory. There is a problem in calling upon clinical observations to support the theory. For observations are interpretations made through the eyes of the theory. Thus one needs to set up criteria of refutation before one turns to the observations. Thus there could be factors which if observed would refute the theory.[61]

c. *Unconscious.* It is extremely important that the concept of the unconscious be examined philosophically to see whether it has meaning; this examination is important for our discussion because Freud points to religious activity as a manifestation of unconscious conflicts. If we cannot speak meaningfully of the unconscious, or if we cannot show its necessity in explaining the psyche, our religious discussion will be fruitless. The "unconscious" as given by Freud is a hypothetical construct which is made specific by its relation to the concepts of consciousness and preconsciousness.[62] The "unconscious" was part of a "conceptual framework" which he found to account for phenomena he discovered.[63] There is no objection to the "unconscious" as a hypothetical element because the physical sciences make use of the same type of constructs.[64] We will discuss the proper use of the concept and the evidence for its existence.

Proper Use of Concept. Confusion has been caused over the concept of *"unconscious" mind*[65] which is taken to be a contradiction because the mind is considered to be in its very nature "aware." To say one had knowledge of the "unconscious" mind is a contradiction for how can one have knowledge of the unknown?[66] Further, *"unconscious" feelings* must not be taken to mean feelings which no one knows about but rather they are feelings belonging to a person who is unaware of them. "Unconscious" feelings are not those of a person who cannot know of them but the way he does not know them is the way we do not see what is in the future.[67] We can speak of hidden objects and we can also set up criteria for identifying the objects which will then be no longer hidden.[68] As we become aware of the objects once hidden we also become aware of "unconscious" feelings once hidden. "But these processes or elements can be made actual even as regards awareness. This may therefore be considered as potential processes or elements of awareness."[69] It is conceivable also that another person may be aware of our "unconscious" feelings because he observes our behavior in various situations and scrutinizes our thoughts and feelings.[70] If we could see the person when given the interpretations by the analyst before the appearance of "unconscious" feelings and then following the appearance of unconscious feelings, we would appreciate the unity in a "feeling" which seemed to be so distant when referred to as "unconscious."[71]

It is important to speak of *"unconscious" wishes* rather than "unconscious" reasons for the latter concept sounds contradictory. The concept of "wish" is like the concept of "motive"; they both show some directedness. But a "wish" is not like "reasons" for "wish" does not show a comprehension of means to take in order to achieve an end.[72]

Since scientists are accustomed to use the term "cause" with reference to the observable order, difficulties are presented in speaking of an *unconscious "cause."* No one has ever seen the unconscious because it is not an entity which can be independently discovered. Thus when the unconscious is called upon to aid in an explanation, it does not explain as a puppet-operator explains the motion of the puppets.[73] Some authors are very much opposed to the use of the "unconscious" in causal explanations.

> . . . the word "unconscious" cannot appear in any genuine causal explanations, whether rigorously deterministic or probabilistic, whether in terms of the postulates of a rigorous theory of human behavior or, more modestly, in terms of pragmatically reliable generalizations, because its function is only to mark, not to *solve*, a problem of explanation.[74]

> Freud, when dealing in practice with particular cases, was concerned primarily with the *motives* for neurotic behavior, whereas, when theorizing and generalizing about his works, he often thought he had been dealing with something quite different, namely the alleged *efficient causes* of such behaviour.[75]

The concepts involved with the "unconscious" are dispositional concepts which might provide for *testability* but still leave more to be said in the way they give an *explanation*.[76] A person is said to have a peculiar disposition (K), if when he is subject to a particular stimulus (S), he responds in a certain way (R). Because of the unknown variable of the disposition (K), the relation between S and R is "probabilistic" rather than causal.[77] In a dispositional statement we are in expectation of the discovery of a causal relation. If we knew what K was, then along with S we might call them the cause of R.[78] When we try to explain a particular manifest behavior and say that it is due to an ''unconscious'' wish, we are not giving a causal explanation. Rather it is a dispositional state, not yet clarified, which is responsible for the manifest behavior.[79] When one person is said to have an ''unconscious'' dislike for another, it means that like any person with that property he will react in the same way given the same circumstances. When the property is discovered we then have a causal explanation and also the disappearance of the word ''unconscious.'' When nothing specific can be pointed to so as to describe the property, we may resort to the person's past experience and thus have some degree of probability.[80]

''Unconscious'' mental processes, since they have no location, cannot be spoken of as efficient causes which can lead to, for example, obsessive actions. It is better to explain a pattern of behavior in terms of motives[81] and thus psychoanalytic explanations are more like motive explanations than causal ones.[82]

> To study a person's unconscious motives is to study what he seemingly ''tries'' to do or bring about in situations where he is unaware of his objective and where he would not admit to any such trying in the ordinary sense of ''try.''[83]

When we say that a dream is wish fulfillment, we really mean that the dreams are motivated; the explanation of dreams is in terms of motives. Thus Freud, in the discovery of the unconscious, has not come upon a specific entity but rather has discovered that human behavior, especially neurotic, is explained in terms of motives previously not seen.[84] The ''unconscious'' is seen to provide an ''explanatory connecting link'' between manifest behavior which is separated both by space and time from its relation, e.g., previous childhood episodes.[85]

Some authors admit that people have thoughts and feelings which are unconscious but they maintain that these processes should not be under the *noun* ''unconscious'' which implies that there is such a specific entity.[86] It is inadequate to say merely that the ''unconscious'' exists. An explanatory theory always does much more; it tells us something about "properties," "powers" and "effects" of the entity in question. The theory of the "unconscious" is not made valid by only saying that an "unconscious" exists hidden in such a way that we cannot describe it. What we would have to look for are the ways in which the "unconscious" displays itself and how it then explains ideas and behavior. "The scientific point concerns not a concept but rather what consequences follow from a theory."[87]

Some consider Freud's "unconscious" as continuous with the way ordinary language is used i.e. it is a technical term which comes out of ordinary usage with the aid of a convention. To use the concept "unconscious" meaningfully several things must be kept in mind: it must be realized that under certain circumstances a specific phenomenon could appear in consciousness; the "conditions" under which the phenomenon would manifest itself would have to be spelled out in some detail; there would have to be distinguished "complications" which could stand in the way of the phenomenon manifesting itself even though in the technical sense the phenomenon is really present, i.e., unconsciously. Thus we are setting up predictions which could be subject to verification or falsification; with the above specification we would then be speaking meaningfully of unconscious phenomena.[88]

Evidence for Unconscious. We postulate the existence of the "unconscious" because there may be a portion of observed behavior the dynamic reasons for which the person is unaware.[89] Behavior which would display itself as "undiscriminating," "subliminal," "unremembered," "insightless," "uncommunicable," or "repressed" would point to the operation of the "unconscious." "If these conditions are fulfilled, then a logical operational inference of an unconscious can be made . . ."[90] That there are "unconscious" factors operative can be confirmed by post-hypnotic carrying out of commands which were given during hypnosis, predicting and observing latent processes becoming manifest,[91] and through slips of the tongue and errors.[92] The "unconscious" provides for an empirical interpretation by the fact of its reference to free associations and dreams[93] as in the latter the associations coming from the dream material presuppose that there must be some underlying stability which perdures throughout the process. The order that emerges where before there seemed to be disorder of intentions points to the "unconscious" link.[94]

The question also arises as to whether a phenomenon can equally well be explained without involving the concept of the "unconscious." What should be attempted first is a program of seeing whether all the areas of consciousness have been explored as possibilities of explanation. And if the program proves unsuccessful, then the believer in the "unconscious" has greater assurance.[95] Freud considered that under normal conditions behavior was to be considered purposive and that only when behavior departed from the ordinary fashion should we then look to the unconscious.[96] "But it is only when the stated reasons are unconvincing as explanations that we look around for unconscious wishes as *sufficient* explanations.[97] It was found that to provide a more comprehensive view of conscious behavior, it was necessary to look beyond to the "unconscious"; the conscious phenomenon then became intelligible. With the positing of the "unconscious" there opened the possibility of predicting future behavior which is the desire of all science.[98]

From our discussion of the "unconscious" it becomes apparent that the concept is meaningful when careful linguistic usage is observed. We have tried to show that causality in the unconscious is not the same as causality in the empirical world and to speak of an unconscious cause is not linguistically correct. However, we have tried to show that the empirical evidence does point to the existence of the unconscious. It may be concluded that, for the most part, the terms are meaningful as they are not so vague as to be irrefutable and they seem to give an accounting of the human psyche. Where there are weaknesses in the concepts, they are open to correction without destroying the essential meaning Freud intended them to have. Thus while we believe that the Freudian concepts are useful in explaining human behavior in such a way that his statements are said to have meaning, if taken in isolation the concepts may appear to be onesided in their genetic orientation.

B. *Dialectic of Genesis and Telos in the Psychoanalytic Concepts*

Having been assured that the Freudian concepts descriptive of person take on meaning because of a relationship to observables, we now proceed to analyze how well they explain the human psyche. We proceed in this study with the promise that we are speaking of the real world and not merely the conceptual order. What we propose to show in our analysis of the Freudian concepts is that there is an inner tension within them. On a first reading, they may appear to be susceptible of only a genetic interpretation, i.e., they chain the activities of the psyche to past episodes; they make the past genesis and the infantile totally explanatory of the present. We do not deny that the reductionist direction is present in the concepts for the field is called psycho-*analysis* and not psycho-*synthesis*. However, we propose to show that there is discovered an emerging teleology in Freud for to understand totally the human psyche it is necessary to have the two moments of regression and progression.

We will consider the confrontation between *conscious* and *unconscious* life and will see that a deeper psychic life emerges from their dialectic. The tension between the *ego, id* and *superego* will allow us to better appreciate the intersubjective features which allow for the person "becoming conscious." Further, the process of *identification* makes us aware of the forces of genesis and teleology in that it is only through the abandonment of an object-cathexis and a being reduced to narcissism that the ego incorporates into itself the object it has been in confrontation with and emerges enriched. Finally, *sublimation* points to a reductive movement; i.e., a regression of libido to a narcissistic level, a desexualization through the mediation of the ego and the emergence of creativity. However, Freud does not fully explain this creative moment but we feel the direction of his work points to it as the self seems to possess a driving force which moves forward even in the wake of opposition. Through confrontation the self becomes conscious. When we examine the process of "becoming conscious," we are made aware of Freud's dependency upon fate: id, superego, narcissism and death instinct all stand as a contrast to the emerging teleology.[99]

1. *Conscious and Unconscious*

It is the *unconscious* which is considered the primordial for not only does it have all the incidents of our own past but it contains the memories, at least implicitly, of the race. The unconscious holds everything that we are unaware of; even the actions which we consider most free may be unconsciously motivated. The unconscious may contain the desires which most truly tell us about our real feelings and yet we may not be aware (conscious) of this sphere of truth. The unconscious represents that moment which links us most to the past. It has our entire genesis. The unconscious is a chaos; there is no order. The unconscious only affirms and exempts itself from all negations and time. All our cravings, desires and wishes push for satisfaction. Yet there is no moment of awareness or reflection in the unconscious. There are desires of all types and they do have direction: they push for satisfaction. But they are never aware of their direction, still less their meaning.

The unconscious is involved in a continuous dialectic with the conscious. The conscious gives meaning to the unconscious. But the unconscious contains the origins of meaning. Only when the unconscious can be made to reveal itself to the conscious can we really know fully. Before the revelation of the unconscious, we do know the present moment in our conscious awareness but not fully because the unconscious holds those things which affect in part the way we know the present moment. The unconscious contains the desires concerning the way we would like reality to appear. Only when the conscious gives meaning to these desires does the self realize how much unconscious desires affect the present moment; in the present moment the self endeavors to see reality the way it is.

When conscious life is examined and our feelings are reduced to their genesis hidden in the unconscious, we see the two aspects of the psyche. Conscious life is not fully understood except in terms of the unconscious. Genesis tells us about the past incidents which have brought about the present feeling. Consciousness can reflect upon what it has been offered and can know the meaning of its past. However, the present moment is richer with the knowledge of its genesis. The present moment brings the psyche to a higher degree of consciousness than it was at the previous moment. The past which has been unknown, or rather forgotten, is brought to the attention of the conscious. In the forward movement, toward self-awareness, the conscious is seen to be less subject to the past as before.

The moment of becoming aware of what the unconscious contains is a moment of negation for the conscious. For some the moment may be too overwhelming and not all that the unconscious contains will be seen. But whatever has been seen will become part of the next forward moment. It is true that the analytic session brings out best the dialectic between the conscious and unconscious. The moment forward may not be apparent outside of the session and the concept of unconscious divorced from the session takes on a forbidding look. It seems so much our adversary rather than our aid or like the force of the past holding unknown threats to the future moment.

2. *Ego, Id, Superego*

The dialectical relationship between the conscious and unconscious does not allow us to see totally the intersubjective relationships involved in ''becoming conscious.'' Rather it is the topography of ego, id, and superego which allows the intersubjective to emerge i.e. we are able to see the impersonal, personal and superpersonal all in confrontation (ego-id, ego-superego, ego-world).[100] The ego is alienated from itself when it fails to achieve its desire and thus meets opposition; it sees itself in confrontation and thus discovers the other. From the confrontation it emerges with greater self-consciousness.[101] The ego must confront the forces of the past and those presently seeking satisfaction (id). At the same time the ego is forced into confrontation with the superego which represents authority with its cultural traditions and ideals from the past. The ego in the present moment must mediate between all these forces. The superego is derived from the parents and thus it is not a totally impersonal force. The ego carries with it the influences of the past and its present desires. In the present moment the ego confronts the world which is its moment of alienation only to give rise to the next moment of more heightened consciousness.

The moment of confrontation with the outside world is really a struggle for recognition. In the analytic situation involving transference, we have a view of the process of ''becoming conscious'' because the struggle of the patient with the analyst is one for recognition. When the alienation is over, then the analysis is terminated for the person has become a self.[102]

3. *Identification*

The process of *identification* does not seem to have the same reductionist tendency as the other concepts do or, at least, it opens itself more easily to teleology. For the child, the father represents what he would like to be and to have. The desire ''to be like'' is not reducible to the desire ''to have'' as they are two distinct things. We believe that where one cannot have the other, there is the moment of denial for one has come into confrontation with another. The denial makes one aware of himself and the other. The moment of recovery does not derive merely from the loss but rather from the self taking cognizance of what has been lost. This is a forward movement. For the self has lost but it has known the other. Thus the self, incorporating the other, moves to a state of more heightened consciousness.

For Freud there is an intersubjective process supposed here between the consciousness of one and the consciousness of the other. However, the Freudian interpretation sees only the regressive aspects of identification because psychoanalysis only realizes vaguely the process of consciousness to consciousness.[103] Freud sees that if one has lost any object or has been forced to give it up, one compensates by identifying with the lost object which is set up in the ego. For Freud, object-choice *regresses* to identification[104] i.e. the only way that an erotic object-choice can make an alteration on the ego is to replace the object-choice by an identification.

The question may arise as to whether the loss of an object is truly a regressive process—a return to narcissism. It might, on the other hand, seem like a time for growth for in the Oedipus complex, where the child abandons and renounces the strong object-cathexis surrounding his parents, we have a creative process. There is a process of identification and a setting up of the structure of personality. For in my relationships with the other I am in a way negated because other stands against me by his own consciousness; but at the same time I grow in virtue of the fact of our encounter. It is only through negation that desire is educated.[105] Thus we see in the Freudian concept of identification there is opened the possibility of a process of growth in the face of negation. However, Freud does not have the full appreciation of the inter-subjective encounter; he is ambivalent in considering the movement from "to have" to the next stage "to be like" as regressive. His ambivalence, we feel, is an opening for the implicit teleology.

4. *Sublimation*

In his early writings, Freud speaks of *sublimation* as a deviation of the aim of the libido but there is no substitution of a new object. The deviation is connected with activities prior to coitus; these acts (perversions: seeing, concealing, revealing) can become separate aims taking the place of genital intercourse. Thus sexual curiosity may be sublimated in art where interest is shifted away from the genitals to the appearance of the body as a whole.[106] Sublimation may take place when there is a deviation from the usual aim because of the forces of "disgust, shame and morality."[107] Sublimation is considered as a discharge and use of strong excitations in an area other than sexuality e.g. artistic creativity is one of the manifestations of the sublimation.[108]

In the introjection of the parents in the formation of the superego the abandonment of the sexual aim takes place and there is an exchange between the object and the ego. (The object-libido is transformed into narcissistic libido and also becomes desexualized.) Freud calls this desexualization a type of sublimation. Freud wonders whether all sublimation takes place through the action of the ego; the ego changes sexual object-libido into narcissistic libido and then gives it another aim.[109] Accordingly, in Freud's later writings there have been two changes: (1) Desexualization becomes a central issue where before we had deviation. We thus have a neutral and displaceable energy which can be given over to the erotic or destructive instincts. (2) The ego becomes the necessary agent in the transformation. Therefore, it is apparent that sublimation is related to the alteration of the ego which we also saw in identification. In identification we saw that the model-image of the father was involved and thus the superego is implied in both desexualization and sublimation. From this discussion we see that sublimation is no longer considered a perverse infantile component which has turned toward the non-sexual. Rather sublimation is an object-cathexis of the Oedipal stage which has been taken into the psyche by means of desexualization and the forces at play at the time of the breakup of the Oedipus complex.[110]

In Freudian terms sublimation can be looked at as a regression to narcissism but we feel that the regression does not seem to give a full accounting of the process. There seems to be need for the concept of "progression." For the question arises as to how narcissism differentiates itself in all the varied sublimations. Also the identifications that are taken in by the ego (modifying it, confronting it) imply that there is a progressive movement.

Thus psychoanalysis reveals the archaic and infantile in our sublimations and thus makes us, by contrast, focus more intensely on the fact of emergence of the sublimation. There seems to be the forward moving dynamism of the self left unaccounted for. Freudian theory seems to play down the aptitude for progression which, however, is found in the analytic session.[111] The fact that we have a reductionism of sublimation to its genesis in the infantile makes us look for the factor which allows for the emergence of the sublimation. Thus we consider that sublimation points to an implicit teleology which has not been fully articulated in Freud for reductionism alone does not fully explain the sublimation. Thus in this Chapter we have seen that the psychoanalytic concepts are meaningful. The concepts have a reductionist tendency in that they reduce psychological phenomena to their genesis but the revelation of the genesis points to the fact that there must be a teleology operative to have brought us to the present psychological moment which transcends the genesis.

NOTES

[1]Chapter I.

[2]Chapter II.

[3]Chapter III.

[4]Donald C. Williams, "Philosophy and Psychoanalysis," *Psychoanalysis, Scientific Method and Philosophy*, ed. by Sidney Hook (New York: New York University Press, 1959), p. 173.

[5]K. R. Popper, "Philosophy of Science: A Personal Report," *British Philosophy in the Mid-Century*, ed. by C. A. Mace (London: Allen & Unwin, 1957), p. 157.

[6]Knight Dunlap, *Mysticism, Freudianism and Scientific Psychology* (St. Louis: Mosby, 1920), p. 97.

[7]Patrick Mullahy, *Oedipus—Myth and Complex* (New York: Hermitage Press, Inc., 1952), p. 317.

[8]Rudolf Allers, *The Successful Error* (New York: Sheed & Ward, 1940), p. 59.

[9]Else Frenkel-Brunswik, "Psychoanalysis and the Unity of Science," *Proceedings of the American Academy of Arts and Sciences*, LXXX, 308. Eugene Pumpien-Mindlin, "Propositions Concerning Energetic-Economic Aspects of Libido Theory: Conceptual Models of Psychic Energy and Structures in Psychoanalysis," *Conceptual and Methodological Problems in Psychoanalysis*, L. Bellak (ed.), *Annals of the New York Academy of Sciences*, LXXVI, Art. 4 (Jan., 1959), 1038. Mullahy, *Oedipus—Myth and Complex*, p. 319.

[10]Frenkel-Brunswik, "Psychoanalysis and the Unity of Science," p. 309.

[11]Heinz Hartmann, "Psychoanalysis as a Scientific Theory," *Psychoanalysis,*

Scientific Method, and Philosophy, ed. by Sidney Hook (New York: New York University Press, 1959), p. 12.

[12]H. Wildon Carr, "Philosophical Aspect of Freud's Theory of Dream Interpretation," *Mind*, New Series, XXIII, (1914), 326.

[13]Ernest Nagel, "Methodological Issues in Psychoanalytic Theory," *Psychoanalysis, Scientific Method, and Philosophy*, Ed. by Sidney Hook (New York: New York University Press, 1959), p. 39. Philipp Frank, "Psychoanalysis and Logical Positivism," *Psychoanalysis, Scientific Method and Philosophy*, ed. by Sidney Hook (New York: New York University Press, 1959), p. 310. Sidney Hook, "Marx and Freud: Oil and Water," *The Open Court*, XLII (1928), 20.

[14]Antony Flew, "Motives and the Unconscious," *Minnesota Studies in the Philosophy of Science*, ed. by H. Feigl & M. Scriven, I, (Minneapolis: University of Minnesota Press, 1956), 156.

[15]Nagel, "Methodological Issues in Psychoanalytic Theory," p. 39.

[16]*Ibid.*, p. 41.

[17]*Ibid.*, p. 43.

[18]*Ibid.*, p. 40. B. A. Farrell, "The Status of Psychoanalytic Theory," *Inquiry* (1964), p. 109.

[19]Frank, "Psychoanalysis and Logical Positivism," p. 309. Arthur C. Danto, "Meaning and Theoretical Terms in Psychoanalysis," *Psychoanalysis, Scientific Method and Philosophy*, ed. by Sidney Hook (New York: New York University Press, 1959), p. 317.

[20]Frank, "Psychoanalysis and Logical Positivism," p. 312. John E. Gedo *et. al.*, "Studies in Hysteria: A Methodological Evaluation," *Journal of American Psychoanalytic Association* (Oct. 1964) XII, 750.

[21]Elizabeth Zetzel, "An Approach to the Relation Between Concept and Content in Psychoanalytic Theory," *The Psychoanalytic Study of the Child*, XI (1956) (New York: International Universities Press), 119.

[22]Robert Waelder, *Psychoanalysis, Scientific Method and Philosophy* (Review), ed. by Sidney Hook, *Journal of the American Psychoanalytic Association*, X (1962), 620. Benjamin B. Rubinstein, "On the Inference and Confirmation of Clinical Interpretations," Presented in abbreviated form to the New York Psychoanalytic Society, 28 May 1968. Francis W. Gramlich, "On the Structure of Psychoanalysis," *Psychoanalysis, Scientific Method and Philosophy*, p. 300.

[23]Frenkel-Brunswik, "Psychoanalysis and the Unity of Science," p. 275.

[24]*Ibid.*, p. 276.

[25]Albert Ellis, "An Operational Reformulation of Some of the Basic Principles of Psychoanalysis," *Minnesota Studies*, I, 132.

[26]*Ibid.*, p. 135.

[27]Nagel, "Methodological Issues in Psychoanalytic and Scientific Method," p. 305.

[28]Dunlap, *Mysticism, Freudianism and Scientific Psychology*, p. 97. T. R. Miles, *Eliminating the Unconscious* (New York: Pergamon Press, 1966), p. 110.

[29]Ellis, "An Operational Reformulation," p. 136.

[30]H. Hartmann, A. Kris, R. Loewenstein, "Comments on the Formation of Psychic Structure," *Psychoanalytic Study of the Child*, II (New York: International Universities Press, 1946), 15.

[31]Ellis, "An Operational Reformulation," p. 150.

[32]*Ibid.*, p. 140.

[33]*Ibid.*, p. 141.

[34]Mortimer Ostow, "The Structure Model: Ego, Id and Superego," *Conceptual and Methodological Problems in Psychoanalysis,* ed. by L. Bellak, *Annals of the New York Academy of Sciences*, LXXVI, Art. 4 (Jan., 1959), 1123.

[35]Ellis, "An Operational Reformulation," p. 144. Else Frenkel-Brunswik, "Meaning of Psychoanalytic Concepts and Confirmation of Psychoanalytic Theories," *Scientific Monthly*, LXXIX (1954), 297. Zetzel, "An Approach to the Relation Between Concept and Content in Psychoanalytic Theory," XI, 101. Miles, *Eliminating the Unconscious,* p. 115.

[36]Ellis, "An Operational Reformulation," p. 147.

[37]*Ibid.*, p. 148.

[38]Charles Frankel, "The Status of Freud's Ideas," *Psychoanalysis, Scientific Method, and Philosophy*, ed. by Sidney Hook (New York: New York University Press, 1959), p. 325.

[39]Hartmann, "Psycho-analysis as a Scientific Theory," p. 29.

[40]*Ibid.*, p. 30.

[41]Ellis, "An Operational Reformulation," p. 132. Frenkel-Brunswik, "Meaning of Psychoanalytic Concepts," p. 297.

[42]Nagel, "Methodological Issues," p. 40.

[43]Gail Kennedy, "Psychoanalysis: Protoscience and Metapsychology," *Psychoanalysis, Scientific Method, and Philosophy*, ed., by Sidney Hook (New York: New York University Press, 1959), p. 269.

[44]B. A. Farrell, "Can Psychoanalysis Be Refuted?," *Inquiry*, IV, (Spring, 1964), 17.

[45]Hook, "Science and Mythology in Psychoanalysis," p. 214.

[46]*Ibid.*, p. 215.

[47]*Ibid.*, p. 217. Danto, "Meaning and Theoretical Terms in Psychoanalysis," p. 317.

[48]Jacob A. Arlow, "Psychoanalysis as a Scientific Method," *Psychoanalysis, Scientific Method, and Philosophy* ed. by Sidney Hook (New York: New York University Press, 1959), *passim.*

[49]C. S. Schoenfeld, "Three Fallacious Attacks on Psychoanalysis as Science," *Psychoanalytic Review*, XLIX (Winter, 1962), 38.

[50]William P. Alston, *Philosophy of Language* (Englewood Cliffs: Prentice-Hall, Inc., 1964), p. 71.

[51]Frankel, "The Status of Freud's Ideas," p. 326.

[52]Hook, "Science and Mythology," p. 219.

[53]Carl G. Hempel, *Philosophy of Natural Science* (Englewood Cliffs: Prentice-Hall, Inc., 1966), p. 28.

[54]Farrell, "The Status of Psychoanalytic Theory," p. 18.

[55]Ellis, "An Introduction to the Principles of Scientific Psychoanalysis," p. 169.

[56]Farrell, "The Status of Psychoanalytic Theory," p. 23.

[57]Leo A. Spiegel, "Superego and the Function of Anticipation with Comments on 'Anticipatory Anxiety,' " *Psychoanalysis—A General Psychology* (New York: International Universities Press, Inc., 1966), p. 316.

[58]Robert R. Sears, *Survey of Objective Studies of Psychoanalytic Concepts* (Social Science Research Council, 1943), p. 96.

[59]*Ibid.*, p. 138.

[60]Michael Martin, "Mr. Farrell and the Refutability of Psychoanalysis," *Inquiry*, VII (Spring, 1964), 87.

[61]Popper, "Philosophy of Science: A Personal Report," p. 161, n. 2.

[62]Frenkel-Brunswik, "Psychoanalysis and the Unity of Science," p. 282.

[63]Hartmann, "Psychoanalysis as a Scientific Theory," p. 7.

[64]F. Aveling, "Is the Conception of the Unconscious of Value in Psycholo-gy?," *Mind* (1922), p. 426.

[65]Ilham Dilman, "The Unconscious," *Mind* (1959), p. 463. John Laird, "Is the Conception of the Unconscious of Value in Psychology?," *Mind* (1922), p. 442.

[66]Dilman, "The Unconscious," p. 463.

[67]*Ibid.*, p. 461.

[68]*Ibid.*, p. 463.

[69]Aveling, "Is the Conception of the Unconscious of Value in Psychology?," p. 431.

[70]Dilman, "The Unconscious," p. 461.

[71]*Ibid.*, p. 462.

[72]R. S. Peters, *The Concept of Motivation* (New York: Humanities Press, 1958), p. 63.

[73]Miles, *Eliminating the Unconscious*, p. 81. Nagel, "Methodological Issues in Psychoanalytic Theory," p. 47.

[74]Arthur Pap, "On the Empirical Interpretation of Psychoanalytic Concepts," *Psychoanalysis, Scientific Method, and Philosophy*, ed. by Sidney Hook (New York: New York University Press, 1959), p. 288.

[75]Antony Flew, "Psychoanalytic Explanation," (revised) *Philosophy and*

Analysis, ed. by Margaret Macdonald (Oxford: Blackwell, 1954), p. 140.

[76]Pap, "On the Empirical Interpretation," p. 284. Frenkel-Brunswik, "Psychoanalysis and the Unity of Science," p. 294.

[77]Pap, "On the Empirical Interpretation," p. 284.

[78]*Ibid.*, p. 285.

[79]*Ibid.*, p. 286.

[80]*Ibid.*, p. 287.

[81]Antony Flew, "Psychoanalytic Explanation," *Analysis*, I (Oct., 1949), p. 11. Stephen Toulmin, "The Logical Status of Psychoanalysis," *Analysis*, IX, No. 2 (Dec., 1948), 28.

[82]Flew, "Psychoanalytic Explanation," p. 12.

[83]Miles, *Eliminating the Unconscious*, p. 93.

[84]Flew, "Psychoanalytic Explanation," p. 12.

[85]Michael Martin, "The Explanatory Value of the Unconscious," *Philosophy of Science* (1964), p. 124.

[86]Frenkel-Brunswik, "Psychoanalysis and the Unity of Science," p. 283.

[87]J. O. Wisdom, "Psychoanalytic Technology," *British Journal for the Philosophy of Science*, VII, No. 25 (May 1956), 16.

[88]Abraham Edel, "The Concept of the Unconscious: Some Analytic Preliminaries," *Philosophy of Science* (1964), p. 21.

[89]William Herron, "The Evidence for the Unconscious," *Psychoanalytic Review*, Part I (1962), p. 86. Hartmann, "Psychoanalysis as a Scientific Theory," p. 6.

[90]Herron, "The Evidence for the Unconscious," p. 86.

[91]Frenkel-Brunswik, "Psychoanalysis and the Unity of Science," p. 280.

[92]Herron, "The Evidence for the Unconscious," p. 87.

[93]Frenkel-Brunswik, "Psychoanalysis and the Unity of Science," p. 282.

[94]Paul Ricoeur, *Freedom and Nature: The Voluntary and the Involuntary*, trans. by E. V. Kohik (Evanston: Northwestern University Press, 1966), p. 282.

[95]Edel, "The Concept of the Unconscious," pp. 23-24. G. C. Field, "Is the Conception of the Unconscious of Value in Psychology?," *Mind* (1922), p. 423.

[96]Peters, *The Concept of Motivation*, p. 55.

[97]*Ibid.*, p. 61.

[98]O. Fenichel, *The Psychoanalytic Theory of Neurosis* (New York: W. W. Norton & Co., Inc., 1945), p. 7.

[99]Paul Ricoeur, *Freud and Philosophy*, trans. by David Savage (New Haven: Yale University Press, 1970), p. 468.

[100]*Ibid.*, p. 477.

[101]*Ibid.*, p. 474.

[102]*Ibid.*, p. 474.

[103]*Ibid.*, p. 480.

[104] *Ibid.*, p. 479.

[105] *Ibid.*, p. 482.

[106] Freud, *Three Essays on Sexuality*, VII, 156-57.

[107] *Ibid.*, pp. 178-79.

[108] *Ibid.*, p. 238.

[109] Freud, *The Ego and the Id*, XIX, 30.

[110] Ricoeur, *Freud and Philosophy*, p. 488.

[111] *Ibid.*, p. 492.

Chapter III

The Religious Neurosis: Genesis and Telos

We have seen the validity of Freud's ontogeny of person[1] and of the psychoanalytic concepts descriptive of person;[2] we have tried to illustrate the deeper meaning of the Freudian analysis by showing the dialectic of *genesis* and *telos* operative in our study. In Chapter III, we are now ready to understand Freud's analysis of the person as *religious* which he considered to be a manifestation of neurotic conflict or wish fulfillment. Thus religious experience is usually reduced to one of these categories. The case studies which we will examine, while they deal with the religious behavior of neurotics, are not "qualitatively"[3] different from the religious experience of all men, according to Freud. The way we have set forth the religious neuroses in this Chapter is in hierarchical order i.e., from the most regressive to the least regressive. In this manner we try to highlight the evolution of man's growing awareness of the way reality is. The neurotic religious symptom stands for a compromise between the impulse of the repressed and the repressive activity of the ego. As we trace the neuroses we will see the gradual "return of the repressed" with less and less distortion. The "return of the repressed" is basically the infantile Oedipal conflict. (We will see in Chapter IV that the race has experienced the gradual "return of the repressed" from the primal crime to the crucifixion of Christ.) When the person has come to terms with the "repressed," he is freed from religion.

The hypothesis propounded by Freud, on the basis of the cases treated, is that religious activity is a manifestation of unconscious conflicts. But before we can look to a deeper significance of the religious neuroses, we have to be assured that Freud's hypothesis had some foundation. Since he proposes the cases as scientific, we have to make an examination of the methodology involved from the perspective of philosophy of science which interestingly shows the probability of the hypothesis.

We will then go on to investigate and develop the further significance of the religious symptom for a philosophy of religion. We believe our treatment of the cases can be made to reveal an evolution in awareness of the "Wholly Other" or, at least in a negative way, an evolution in less distorted views of the "Wholly Other." A reductive interpretation of religious neurosis in itself does not give a full accounting of the phenomenon. However, we will see that a reductive interpretation of the religious neurosis is a necessity for revealing its teleological horizon. From the analysis of our cases we will see the frequent repetition of the mechanism of sublimation which in itself reveals the locus of the union of genesis and telos. We will examine the religious neurosis showing that it is a symbol because it arises at the intersection of the dialectic of genesis and telos. A symbol points in two directions: to the past and to the future; the past is genesis—the future is telos. True, the reduction of the religious neurosis reveals the infantile but at the same time at the horizon of its telos the sacred symbol appears which bears witness to the approach of the "Wholly Other." An act of faith in the "Wholly Other" transcends knowledge and is a precarious experience for faith very easily becomes objectified into an idol; religion is faith reified. These notions will be developed in the course of our discussion.

In the analysis of the cases, Freud engages in a *reductive* interpretation i.e. the religious manifestation is interpreted on the model of the neurosis. Basically, the neurosis is an escape from a portion of reality and there is regression to the point of weakness in the ontogeny of the person. By means of regression, the ego repressed the unwanted impulse. From the incompleteness of the repression the religio-neurotic symptom is born. In the unconscious there is an Oedipal conflict which manifests itself through the religious symptom. In this first analysis, we will give all our attention to the reductive moment even though there might appear at times an implicit teleology. We give emphasis here to the genesis in order to all the more fully appreciate our discussion of *telos* later in the Chapter.

In the cases involved, we move through the neuroses[4] of dementia praecox, paranoia, obsession, phobia and hysteria. We have given a brief statement about each type of neurosis in order to show an evolution in the distortion of reality or, positively speaking, an evolution in awareness of the way reality is. In each neurosis we may note a predisposition which comes from a weakness at the time of the *early* ontogeny (oral, anal, phallic) of the person; the weakness is brought on by traumatic experience(s) which the person has never resolved and which remains in the unconscious. In later life, there arises some precipitating incident which activates again the conflict; the ego reacts to the danger with anxiety and begins the task of repressing the impulse. Where the impulse cannot fully express itself and where repression is not entirely successful, we have the formation of a neurotic symptom. The symptom, as a result of regression, will take a form dependent upon the predisposition of the person i.e., oral, anal, phallic. Thus the neurotic seems to be a victim of his past.

A. *Exposition of Cases Dealing with Religious Phenomena: Genesis*

In each of the cases dealing with religious neurosis we will see Freud's *reductive* analysis to the unconscious Oedipal conflict. This procedure should be kept in mind, so that the order of the cases may be readily understood. It may seem that the enumeration of the cases indicating a reduction to the Oedipus complex is repetitious but, when we deal with their teleological aspect the need for repetition will become apparent.

1. *Paraphrenias*
   a. *Dementia praecox*
   1. Mechanism in dementia praecox, the most regressive of the neuroses, there is a complete abandonment of object-love and a return to infantile auto-erotism[5] which is the lowest level of sexuality with no psychosexual aim and which is satisfied by local feelings of gratification.[6] A turning away of the libido from the external world is a very clear feature in dementia praecox. The hallucinations show the struggle between repression, and at the same time an attempt at recovery which is an endeavor to bring libido back to objects through the use of an hallucinatory mechanism. Any attempt at reconstruction is unsuccessful and victory lies with the repression.[7] In hallucinatory

psychoses, the hallucination gives all the appearance of reality even in the use of the perceptual system except that the images seen in consciousness have escaped reality-testing.[8]

Finally, let us once more glance at the significant light which the *topography* of the process of repression throws for us on the mechanism of mental disturbances. In dreams the withdrawal of cathexis (libido or interest) affects all systems equally; in the transference neuroses, the *Pcs.* cathexis is withdrawn; in schizophrenia, the cathexis of the *Ucs.*; in amentia, that of the *Cs.*[9]

Hallucination consists in a cathexis of the system *Cs (Pcpt.)*, which, however, is not effected—as normally—from without, but from within, and that a necessary condition for the occurrence of hallucination is that regression shall be carried far enough to reach this system itself and in so doing be able to pass over reality-testing.[10]

2. *The American Physician.* As an example of dementia praecox with religious symptomatology, we find in Freud's writings the case of the American Physician.[11] Freud received a two-page letter from the physician in answer to the former's own personal unbelief. The physician recalled a scene of a "sweet-faced dear old woman" being brought into a dissecting room. His response was that there could not be a God because He would not have allowed such a woman to be brought to the dissecting room; so the doctor discontinued going to church and had many doubts about Christianity. Then the physician claimed a voice spoke to him advocating caution in the step he was taking; he replied that if he were convinced of the veracity of Christianity and the Bible, he would accept them.[12] In a few days it was revealed to him that the Bible was the word of God, the teachings of Jesus were true and Christ was his hope. Following this revelation, he accepted the things in question and took Christ as a personal Saviour. Further God continued to manifest Himself by "many infallible proofs."[13]

Freud opened his analysis of this experience with the question as to why hostility against God was precipitated at the time of the dissecting room incident;[14] he felt that the sentiments which the woman evoked in the physician were due to the memory of his own mother.[15] A longing for the mother was stirred up because of his own Oedipus complex along with hostility toward his father. "His ideas of 'father' and 'God' had not yet become widely separated"; and the death wishes towards the father came to consciousness as a disbelief in the existence of God. Further, a justification for his unbelief came about because of the terrible treatment directed to the mother-object as children typically regard what the father does to the mother in intercourse as ill-treatment.[16]

Thus the impulses that were coming to the fore were being displaced into the religious realm. However, these impulses were repeating the Oedipus complex and, even though displaced into the religious realm, had their fate already *determined*. While the conflict was in process, the displacement level was not quite parallel: we hear of no arguments in justification of God and are not told what the signs were that God gave to prove His existence to the doubter. "The conflict seems to have been unfolded in the form of an hallucinatory psychosis: inner voices were heard which uttered warnings against resistance to God." Thus the Oedipal conflict expressed itself again in the religious realm with an already determined outcome: "complete submission to the will of God the Father." The physician became a believer accepting all that had been told him about God and Christ or in Freud's words "He had had a religious experience and had undergone a conversion."[17]

Freud admits that all situations of conversion are not this easily understood. However, the point to be remembered is the predetermined nature of the conversion: skepticism and finally the act of belief.[18] Thus we see an apparent religious experience reduced to the Oedipal conflict with the "return of the repressed" so distorted as to be infantile or hallucinatory.

b. *Paranoia*

1. Mechanism. After dementia praecox, paranoia[19] shows regression to the earliest stage of development. Paranoids seem to be fixated at the narcissistic stage as libido is not sent out to other objects but rather centers on the self. In this neurosis we find the tendency to reconstruct the world in the person's own image; moreover this world is set up after a model based upon the figures of the paranoid's early

past. The paranoid symptom will occur when some later incident (intolerable to the ego) activates the early trauma which will bring on defense and repression;[20] there are three phases of repression: (1) fixation which is a precursor and necessary condition of every repression. (2) repression proper which is an active process on the part of the ego. (3) "the return of the repressed" or the failure of repression. Symptom-formation begins at the point of fixation i.e. there is a regression of libidinal development back to that point.[21] Those who have not moved successfully through their narcissistic stage or are fixated at that stage may thus have a disposition to later illness.[22]

When the ego cannot tolerate a certain portion of reality because it appears to be too threatening, it engages in a process of repression by means of which it withdraws libido from the objects it once cathected. This object-libido, now withdrawn, becomes ego-libido. If a large degree of libido cannot find release, it may sexualize social instincts and upset sublimations; paranoids continually try to protect themselves against this sexualization of their "social instinctual cathexes."[23] In the normal person, when libido is withdrawn from an object, he looks toward someone else to receive the libido. In the paranoid, there is a return to the stage of narcissism for the sexual object *is* his own ego.[24]

> The highest phase of development of which object-libido is capable is seen in the state of being in love, when the subject seems to give up his own personality in favour of an object-cathexis; while we have the opposite condition in the paranoic's phantasy (or self-perception) of the "end of the world."[25]

In paranoia, libido has been withdrawn from all objects, and the patient takes back from persons and the external world the libidinal cathexis which before he attached to them. The new world has to be built up all over again and this he does by delusion. "The delusional formation, which we take to be the pathological product, is in reality an attempt at recovery, a process of reconstruction."[26] At the same time with the "return of the repressed" in distorted form, the defense has failed.[27] ". . . mnemic hallucinations in paranoia undergo a distortion . . ."[28]

In repression proper there is a detachment of libido from objects previously loved. In the process of recovery the person undoes the work of repression and restores the libido to the people it had abandoned through the mechanism of projection. For the paranoid, what was removed from within returns from outside.[29] He dissolves the person (whom he loves and identifies with) into many different persons each having one or more of the traits of the original person loved and sets up again all the figures he loved as a child and had abandoned. The ego itself becomes split up into extraneous figures;[30] and the paranoid is seen to be a victim of the past. His own reconstruction of the world shows the distortion that the "return of the repressed" has undergone.

2. Schreber case. We will consider a case dealing with a paranoid who manifested his disorder by means of a form of religious manifestation. Freud worked on an autobiographical report of Daniel Paul Schreber—a paranoid[31] who believed the study of his case could be of value for "religious truths." The development of the case was in two phases: (1) feelings of persecution and homosexuality; (2) feelings of being a redeemer, megalomania and religious ideas. In a dream-like state Schreber thought it would be nice to be a woman submitting to copulation.[32] At the same time that these homosexual thoughts were breaking forth, he felt persecuted by Dr. Flechsig, the director of the hospital in which he was detained.[33] Schreber felt that Dr. Flechsig attempted to commit "soul-murder" upon him i.e., an effort made to get control or possession of his soul like a demon would do.[34] Schreber thought of Flechsig as an enemy and God as an ally. In addition, he divided Flechsig's soul into an "upper Flechsig" and a "middle Flechsig."[35]

Schreber also felt that he had a special mission to accomplish for God and that he was called to suffer for a holy purpose like the Prophets. However, to accomplish this purpose, it was necessary to be transformed from a man into a woman.[36] His femaleness would become prominent and he would thus be impregnated by God in order to give birth to a new race of men;[37] he had delusions of being in mystical communion with God, and a plaything of devils. While at times his relationship with God was good, there were ambivalent feelings witnessed in his belief that God was Flechsig's accomplice in abusing him. Even though God was involved, Schreber believed that they would not succeed because the "Order of Things" were on his side.[38] Even the emasculation was in keeping with the "Order of Things."[39]

Schreber believed that after creation, God left the world to fend for itself, only giving attention to taking back the purified souls of the dead, performing a rare miracle or attending to some gifted people.[40] In his delusional system God was made up of the "anterior realms" and the "posterior realms." God is a unity but the upper and lower realms are still separate beings and each vies with the other for first place.[41] In accordance with the "Order of Things" God became endangered because the nerves of living men were exercising power over Him; Schreber was able to do this also and, as a consequence, suffered.[42] Thus God's own self-preservative reaction made His nature evidently different from the perfections ascribed to Him by religions, e.g. God really knew nothing about living men. Thus God instigated a plot against Schreber taking him for an idiot and subjecting him to ordeals and because of this persecution, Schreber was forced to become a scoffer of God.[43] Accordingly, Schreber displayed ambivalent feelings toward God: on the one hand he was critical and rebellious (which Schreber is privileged to be over other humans): on the other hand, he made repeated attempts to justify God's behavior. His attempt is ". . . similar in ingenuity to any theodicy . . ." For God needs to preserve Himself. Yet in the end the "Order of Things" will provide the victory for man. Only in the last stage does Schreber take on the classical redeemer phantasy. No human being who dies can enter the stage of bliss as long as the greater part of the rays of God are tied up, by attraction, to Schreber's person. Finally, his identification with Jesus Christ appears clearly.[44]

Bliss, to Schreber, was the intensive continuation of sensual pleasure of earth.[45] The rays of God are no longer hostile when they go into his body and there they experience spiritual voluptuousness (sexual satisfaction);[46] and further he believed that the cultivation of "voluptuousness" was a duty.[47] Before the time of the delusional system, Schreber engaged in sexual asceticism and was a doubter in God but in the delusional system he was a devotee of "voluptuousness" and a believer in God. He felt that he was God's wife; the nerves of God impregnated him and he felt the stirrings of a child.[48]

Freud gives a psychoanalytic explanation of the case.

In Schreber's system the two principal elements of his delusions (his transformation into a woman and his favoured relation to God) are linked in his assumption of a feminine attitude towards God. It will be an unavoidable part of our task to show that there is an essential *genetic* relation between these two elements.[49]

In the beginning, the relationship between Schreber and his doctor, Flechsig, was good.[50] However, there was a return of the phantasy that it would be nice to be copulated with as a woman. The disease began at this time and it seemed to be due to an outburst of homosexual libido.[51] In addition Schreber believed there was a conspiracy to have his body delivered up; this was changed to having his body sexually abused.[52] It might have been that his friendly feelings toward the doctor were transferential, thus reminding him of his brother or father. However, there was a defensive struggle against passive homosexuality which by means of projection took on the form of persecution.[53] To avoid the passive homosexuality toward Flechsig, Schreber replaced him by God. To provide God with the voluptuous sensations was not repulsive to his ego and the emasculation was consonant with the "Order of Things";[54] further his megalomania enabled him to become reconciled to the persecution. Yet his relationship with God was *ambivalent* showing a mixture of rebelliousness and reverence.

In Schreber's mind Flechsig and God belonged to the same class as the persecutor was divided into upper and middle Flechsig and lower and upper God; these two in turn were further divided into two personalities. "A process of decomposition of this kind is very characteristic of paranoia." Paranoia decomposes just as hysteria condenses or rather, paranoia resolves once more into their elements the products of condensations and identifications which are effected in the unconscious.[55]

All of this dividing up of Flechsig and God into a number of persons thus had the same meaning as the splitting of the persecutor into Flechsig and God. They were all duplications of one and the same important relationship. But in order to interpret all these details, we must further draw attention to our view of

89

this decomposition of the persecutor into Flechsig and God as a paranoid reaction to a previously established identification of the two figures or their belonging to the same class. If the persecutor Flechsig was originally a person whom Schreber loved, then God must also simply be the reappearance of some one else whom he loved, and probably some one of greater importance.[56]

Since Schreber's father was a very important physician it is not impossible that he be transfigured into a God in the memory of his son,[57] for the infantile attitude of boys to their fathers is a prototype of their relation to God. When Schreber rebukes God for understanding corpses better than the living, he is really rebuking his father the physician.[58] The Sun, to which Schreber was related in an especially favored way, is also a sublimated symbol of the father.[59] Consequently the patient's struggle with Flechsig was revealed as a conflict with God which in turn sheds light on his conflict with his beloved father.[60]

The withdrawal of libido from Flechsig was a primary factor in Schreber's case; its removal was followed by delusion because of the return of libido to his own ego. The libido was directed again to Flechsig but negatively as he was seen as a persecutor. The great problem of repression began to ensue i.e. there was the struggle, by means of repression, to keep the libido from going to the external object—Flechsig. Finally, repression won with the expressed conviction that the world was at an end and all that remained was the self. "If we review the ingenious constructions which were raised by Schreber's delusion in the domain of religion—the hierarchy of God, the proved souls, the fore-courts of Heaven, the lower and the upper God—we can gauge in retrospect the wealth of previous sublimations which were brought down in ruin by the catastrophes of the general detachment of his libido."[61] The phase of the intense hallucinations represents the combat between the forces of repression and the attempt at recovery. The struggle was to direct the libido towards objects again and the hallucinations were a compromise.[62] Thus the Schreber case illustrates unconscious father conflicts being played out by means of religious symbols on the conscious level. All manner of disguise seems to have been employed to ward off his true wishes for his father. The "return of the repressed" comes about through great distortion.

90

And finally, Schreber's religious experience is reduced to his unresolved Oedipus complex.

2. *Obsessions*

a. *Mechanism.* In obsessional neurosis, the person is still fixated at the anal-sadistic level of development. Therefore, the neurotic symptom arising will resemble the psychic behavior of the anal stage as the person tries to handle anxiety-provoking situations or represses the original trauma; the neurosis indicates an escape from a portion of reality and a return to an infantile mode of behavior. Further, the obsessional symptom blocks the person from seeing reality the way it is. However, reality does not suffer from as severe a distortion as in the more regressive neuroses already examined. Prerequisites for obsessional neurosis are that the genital organization of the libido be very weak and that the person still be somewhat organized at the anal-sadistic level.[63] In defending itself the ego "throws back" (regression) the genital organization to an earlier anal-sadistic level.[64]

> In obsessional neurosis, . . . it is the regression of the libido to the preliminary stage of the sadistic-anal organization that is the most striking fact and the one which is decisive for what is manifested in symptoms. The love-impulse is obliged, when this has happened, to disguise itself as a sadistic impulse. The obsessional idea "I should like to kill you," when it has been freed from certain additions which are not a matter of chance but are indispensable, means at bottom nothing other than "I should like to enjoy you in love." If you consider further that there has been a simultaneous regression in regard to the object, so that these impulses apply only to those who are nearest and dearest to the patient, you can form some idea of the horror which these obsessions arouse in him and at the same time of the alien appearance which they present to his conscious perception.[65]

The motive for the defense is the castration complex; the ego tries to fend off the threats of the Oedipus complex.[66] However, within the obsessional neurotic there is a regressive degradation of libido and severe superego activity leading the ego to strong reaction-formation

91

such as conscientiousness, pity, cleanliness along with a cessation of all masculine activity.[67] The father is depersonalized in the guise of the superego; the fear of castration may be transformed into a vague feeling of social or moral anxiety.

> But this anxiety is concealed. The ego escapes it by obediently carrying out the commands, precautions and penances that have been enjoined on it. If it is impeded in doing so, it is at once overtaken by an extremely distressing feeling of discomfort which may be regarded as an equivalent of anxiety and which the patients themselves liken to anxiety.[68]

The superego acts as if there were no repression, for it understands the real meaning of the aggressive impulse and accordingly punishes the ego[69] which believes it has done nothing but still feels guilty. The true disposition is intelligible to the superego because of its connection with the id. On the other hand, the ego is unaware because it is cut off from the *id* by repression. In some obsessional neurotics, no guilt is experienced because a set of symptoms (penances, restrictions) have been set up.[70] These symptoms display masochism and are reinforced by the regression.[71]

Freud also saw the origins of obsessional neurosis in a sexual trauma followed by self-reproach and repression. When the repression was unsuccessful, because the ego could not control the instinctive impulses, one had the formation of symptoms.[72] The ego defends itself from a portion of reality, which it cannot tolerate, by the formation of compromise symptoms. If the defense begins to fail against the derivatives of the repressed memory, then the obsessional neurotic may create further symptoms which are called the "secondary defense." If these additional protective measures succeed in repressing the symptoms of the trauma which are coming to consciousness, then the obsession is transferred to the protective measures which are called obsessional actions.[73]

> Secondary defense against obsessional *affects* leads to a still wider set of protective measures which are capable of being transformed into obsessional acts. These may be grouped according to their purpose: *penetential* measures (burdensome

ceremonials, the observation of numbers), *precautionary* measures (all sorts of phobias, superstition . . .)[74]

The obsessional action is really a compromise: it shows an effort at expiation and at the same time it is a substitute act for compensating the prohibited instinct.[75] In order to prevent the occurrence or recurrence of some particular event, precaution is the first underlying motive of obsessional ceremonials.[76] The obsessional neurotic may give the appearance that a ceremonial is attached to his ordinary activities. But there is repetition of the same thing over and over again. These defense symptoms indicate the sublimation of the anal-erotic components.[77]

b. *Obsessions and Religious Practices.* Freud believed that the resemblances between the "observances" of the pious and the ceremonials of the neurotic are not superficial; he thought that if he were able to find the origins of neurotic ceremonial then by "analogy" he could come to know about the underlying processes of religious life.[78] Of what do the neurotic ceremonials consist? To his ordinary life activities the person makes little additions or restrictions which must be executed in the same manner or, if varied, they must follow a set form. These ceremonials may appear meaningless to both the observer and even to the neurotic himself. ". . . the special conscientiousness with which it is carried out and the anxiety which follows upon its neglect stamp the ceremonial as a 'sacred act.' "[79] Neurotic ceremonials share the following resemblances with religious rituals: (1) an uneasy conscience in the face of their neglect; (2) the activities in question are isolated from other activities and are not to be interrupted; (3) there is conscientiousness even to minute detail. However, there are differences: (1) there is more variability in neurotic ceremonial while religious ritual is more stereotyped; (2) the neurotic ceremonial tends to be private while the religious is communal; (3) neurotic ceremonials do not seem to have an *apparent* meaning while the religious rituals have much symbolism.[80] "In this respect an obsessional neurosis presents a travesty, half comic and half tragic, of a private religion."[81] This last difference (no apparent meaning) disappears when psychoanalysis reveals the hidden meaning of the obsessive actions: ". . . they are consequently to be interpreted either historically or symbolically."[82] The obsessive action expresses *un-*

93

conscious motives and ideas while the usual pious believer performs a ceremonial without knowing its true significance. (The priests and scholars may understand the symbolic meaning of the ritual.)[83]

Ceremonials and obsessive actions serve as a defense against temptation and as protection against expected danger. When the protective measures are "insufficient then prohibitions which ward off a dangerous situation come into play."[84] Some of these neurotic manifestations may also be seen in religious life. "The formation of a religion, too, seems to be based on the suppression, the renunciation, of certain instinctual impulses." In religion, these impulses are not all sexual (as in neurotics) but are also of an anti-social nature. In religion where there is constant temptation, a sense of guilt follows along with an expectant anxiety of punishment from God. As in neurosis, so too in religion, suppression of instinct is an interminable process perhaps because of the sexual admixture. Even more than neurotics, pious people relapse into sin which in turn leads them to acts of penance which are also found in the obsessional neurosis.[85] Displacement is a mechanism employed in obsessional neurosis by which trivial things take on great significance because they are now acting as substitutes for the original thing. Displacement is found in religion too: trite ceremonials become the essential thing with the "underlying thoughts" or values being neglected. "That is why religions are subject to reforms which work retroactively and aim at a reestablishment of the original balance of values."[86] "Compromise," which is the resultant of an impulse and a prohibition, is seen also in religion; what religion apparently wishes to prevent sometimes breaks forth and is justified in the name of religion.[87]

> In view of these similarities and analogies one might venture to regard obsessional neurosis as a pathological counterpart of the formation of a religion, and to describe that neurosis as an individual religiosity and religion as a universal obsessional neurosis. The most essential similarity would reside in the underlying renunciation of the activation of instincts that are constitutionally present; and the chief difference would lie in the nature of those instincts, which in the neurosis are exclusively sexual in their origin, while in religion they spring from egoistic sources.[88]

94

c. "*Rat Man.*" We turn now to some of the classical case studies; Freud tells us that "Rat Man" was "devoutly religious" up to his fourteenth or fifteenth year, but then became a free-thinker. He points out that the religion which "Rat Man" had outgrown still seemed to maintain a hold on him.[89] When "Rat Man" felt attracted to women, the immediate accompanying response was fear of the death of his father. The unconscious process revealed that his father's command prevented him from associating with women and there was the resultant hostile reaction towards his father. However, the fear of his father's death gave rise to impulses to do something to prevent this coming evil; these impulses eventually developed into "protective measures."[90] In obsessional neurosis it is sometimes necessary to fill out the ellipsis as in the example of "ascetic prohibition": "If I marry the lady, some misfortune will befall my father (in the next world)." From the analysis Freud shows:

If my father were alive, he would be as furious over my design of marrying the lady as he was in the scene in my childhood; so that I should fly into a rage with him once more and wish him every possible evil; and thanks to the omnipotence of my wishes these evils would be bound to come upon him.[91] In the Spring (1903) he felt violent self-reproaches (why?). A detail brought the answer. He suddenly fell on his knees, conjured up pious feelings and determined to believe in the next world and immortality. This involved Christianity and going to Church in Unterach after he had called his cousin a whore. His father had never consented to be baptized, but much regretted that his forefathers had not relieved him of this unpleasant business. He had often told the patient that he would make no objections if he wanted to become a Christian. Might it be, perhaps, I asked, that a Christian girl had appeared just then as a rival to his cousin? "No." "The Rubenskys are Jews, are they not?" "Yes, and professing ones." Indeed, if he had become a Christian it would have meant the end of the whole R. scheme [a Jewish marriage]. So, I replied, his kneeling must have been directed against the R. scheme and he must have known of this plan before the scene of the kneeling. He thought not but admitted that there was something he was not clear about.[92]

Thus embracing the Christian religion would have excluded the possibility of a Jewish marriage which would have been forbidding due to his fear of his father. And for the father who stood in his way, there was the corresponding hostility which undoubtedly evoked in "Rat Man" correspondingly intense self-reproaches. Religion was the means of keeping away his dreadful thoughts about his father. His extension of obsessional fears to the "next world" were a reaction to the death-wishes against his father; for the "next world" could be understood to mean "if my father were still alive."[93] Thus part of his obsession was a fear of extending punishment to his loved ones both to this world and for all eternity.

As a reaction to his unconscious hostility, "protections" were set up.[94] There was a return to piety with the offering of many prayers which became longer and longer lasting for an hour and a half. The reason for their length was due to the fact that as he prayed a negative term would interject itself into the prayer. Thus the prayer was turned into the opposite of its first intention: "E.g., if he said, 'May God protect him,' an evil spirit would hurriedly insinuate a 'not.' " The thought even occurred to him to curse with the expectation that the opposite would result. In this last thought Freud feels that the true intention, masked by the praying, was coming to consciousness. Finally, he gave up the prayers and made use of a short formula derived from the beginning letters of several prayers which was repeated rapidly thus preventing other words from intervening.[95]

The uncertainty or anxiety of neurotics at prayer is due to unconscious thoughts coming to consciousness, mixing with the prayers and thereby disturbing the person. In the case of the "Rat Man," when he prayed for his lover: "May God protect her," a hostile "*not*" came through from the unconscious and inserted itself; this seemed like an attempt to curse. If the "not" had not intervened, he would have still remained uncertain and continued to pray indefinitely. Once the "not" came forward he ceased to pray.[96] But before this cessation, he did everything possible to prevent the opposite feeling from coming through; e.g., shortening the prayers or saying them more quickly.[97]

In the case of "Rat Man" he suffers a great deal of anxiety with reference to women because of fear of his father towards whom a great deal of unconscious hostility is directed. At the same time, "Rat Man" engages in a devout religious life especially with regard to prayer. Freud points out the relationship between his religious life and his conflicts, namely that prayer is used as a defense against the appearance of unacceptable impulses. Freud saw the "Rat Man" as three personalities: one unconscious and two preconscious between which consciousness could fluctuate. In the unconscious were his evil impulses. In his normal state he was "enlightened" i.e., free of religion, but in his third state "he paid homage to superstition and asceticism."[98] Thus with the "Rat Man" we have the case of a person whose apparently religious behavior (prayer-life), was really a manifestation of unconscious conflicts. As the unconscious conflicts began to appear or as the defenses began to fail, the repressed material became more and more intermingled with the religious. Finally, the religious behavior was abandoned because it was seen as ineffective in helping to resolve the unconscious conflicts now become conscious. Thus Freud reduces "Rat Man's" religion to the Oedipal conflict.

d. "Wolf Man"

In the case of the "Wolf Man," Freud saw his childhood made up of four phases: (1) the earliest period from the time he witnessed the primal scene of his mother and father having relations *a tergo* to the seduction by his sister and threat of castration by Nanya at age three; (2) the alteration in his character up till the anxiety dream (the fear of wolves eating him) at four years old; (3) the period of animal phobia till his initiation into religion at age four and a half; (4) the time of the obsessional neurosis till ten years.[99]

At age four and a half "Wolf Man" displayed a great deal of irritability and so his mother read to him stories from the Bible. With this initiation into religion the anxiety symptoms (phobia) of the previous stage were replaced by obsessional symptoms.[100]

> Up to then he had not been able to get to sleep easily because he had been afraid of having bad dreams like the one he had that night before Christmas;[101] before he went to sleep he was obliged to pray for a long time and to make an endless series of signs of the cross. In the evening, too, he used to make the round of all the holy pictures that hung in the room, taking a chair with him, upon which he climbed, and used to kiss each one of them devoutly . . . perhaps it was quite consistent with it—that he should recollect some blasphemous thoughts which used to come

into his head like an inspiration from the devil. He was obliged to think ''God-swine'' . . .[102]

Freud was very impressed with the maturity of the child's critique of religion which insight few adults achieve:[103] ''Wolf Man'' did not like the idea of the sufferings of Christ; he was dissatisfied with God the Father; he further maintained that if God is Almighty, then He is responsible for wickedness and Hell and should have made all men good; he found the doctrine of ''turn the other cheek'' as objectionable; he felt that Christ did not want to suffer on the cross and that there was no miracle to prove He was the Son of God. The child was severe in his criticism of the Scriptures.[104] Along with these criticisms of the Bible, there arose other *doubts* which incline one to look for the operation of ''hidden impulses.'' He wondered whether Christ had a ''behind''; he did not wish to subject Him to this type of scrutiny but the further *doubt* as to whether Christ defecated came to consciousness.

Freud now makes an attempt to understand the ''hidden impulses.'' The rejection of his genital overtures by Nanya led him to sadism and masochism[105] and in his sadistic attitude (beating animals) he maintained his identification with his father. But in his masochistic attitude (being beaten) he chose his father as a sexual object. He was, therefore, in the stage of pregenital organization which is often a predisposition to obsessional neurosis.[106] Freud considers that the dream about the wolves in an upright position recalls in some way the primal scene—the wolves being father-surrogates. This dream would have provided a transition from his masochistic attitude toward his father to a feminine attitude to him—homosexuality. However, the dream ended in anxiety. Because of his narcissistic masculinity he was prevented from acting like a woman toward his father and the sexual relation was thrown further back to a ''more primitive stage,'' i.e., the fear of being eaten by the wolf.[107]

From the time of the dream onwards, in his unconscious he was homosexual, and in his neurosis he was at the level of cannibalism; while the earlier masochistic attitude remained the dominant one. All three currents had passive sexual impulse, but that impulse had become split up along three different levels.[108]

"Wolf Man" made use of the sacred story as a means of sublimating his masochistic attitude toward his father. He identified with Christ and thus became important as a person and as a *man*. The repressed homosexuality was seen in his doubts about whether Christ had a "behind" which meant that he questioned whether he himself could be used like a woman by his father. The fact that he did not want to think of the sacred figure in this way indicated the repression of his passive homosexuality. He was making great efforts to keep his sublimation free from the derivatives of the repressed. In this he did not succeed.[109] He began to rebel against the passive character of Christ and also the ill-treatment that He was subjected to by his Father. Thus he seemed to be renouncing his masochistic ideal even in the sublimation.[110] In the situation of God the Father and God the Son, he felt that the intimate relationship was far from what it ought to be.[111] "The boy had some kind of inkling of the ambivalent feelings towards the father which are an underlying factor in all religions, and attacked his religion on account of the slackening which it implied in this relation between son and father." His opposition turned against the figure of God for He had treated His Son terribly and acted the same way toward men. He sacrificed His own Son and Abraham was ordered to do the same thing. "Wolf Man" began to be afraid of God.[112]

If he thought of himself as Christ, then God was his father. But the God that religion gave him was no replacement for the father he had loved and did not want taken from him. His love for his own father gave him this ability to discriminate and thus he rebelled against God so as to be able to hold on to his own father. He was keeping the old father in preference to the new one and was experiencing the difficulty of breaking away from his own father.[113] In his earliest childhood, the love for his own father provided the strength and insight to criticize the new God and religion. However, his hostility to the new God had its sources, too; its prototype was his hostility to his own father which was precipitated by the anxiety-dream. Thus, his relation to God was a revival of a relation to his own father:[114] his father was turning into a forbidding figure who could threaten with castration; and at the same time, he felt that God was cruel because he made men sinful and then punished them; He sacrificed His own Son and the sons of men. This God was like his father. Yet at the same time he did not wish his father

to be like God.[115] Thus the two opposing feelings—love and hatred, which remained with him during his life, expressed themselves in the ambivalent struggle with religion. The struggle thus led to symptoms of blasphemous ideas and the compulsion to think ''God-swine'' which were products of compromise connected with his anal-eroticism.[116]

To atone for his blasphemies he engaged in pious ritual which consisted in breathing in a ceremonious manner. Every time he made the sign of the cross, he had to breathe in and exhale with great energy. Breath and Spirit are the same word in his language and thus he had to breathe in the Holy Spirit and breathe out the evil spirits. The evil spirits were responsible for his blasphemous thoughts. He had to exhale when he saw beggars or cripples fearing that he might become as them.[117] In association with the beggars and cripples, there was his sick father at the sanitorium for whom he felt very sorry. Thus the father could be considered a prototype of the cripples and beggars. Freud sees here both a negative and positive identification with the father. ''Wolf-Man'' did not want to become like the cripples or become like his father; but nevertheless he was imitating the father of the primal scene by breathing like him. Thus the Holy Spirit was derived from the male sensual excitement but repression had turned this breathing into evil spirits.[18]

His condemnation of the evil spirits indicated his own asceticism. The story of Christ casting out evil spirits into the swine which rushed into the sea reminded him of his sister rolling down to the beach from the cliff-path. He considered her an evil spirit and a swine. And it was not difficult to understand the obsessive thought ''God-swine'' for his father, too, was a slave to sexuality.[119] He likened himself to Adam who was seduced by a woman (his sister); but even after confession, his sister still remained a source of occasion to anger. However, his strict piety was seen to fade away through the influence of his tutor who was like a father-surrogate[120] who paid no attention to piety or the supposed truths of religion. At the same time, ''Wolf Man's'' dependence on his father diminished as the more social father-surrogate took his place.

''Wolf Man'' had a predisposition to obsessional neurosis since he had an anal-sadistic personality organization[121] along with a masochistic and repressed homosexual current. His ego repudiated all of these. The effect of his conflict was seen in a movement from wolf phobia to a phase of religious piety. In "Wolf Man" a transformation took place because his mother brought him the doctrines of religion and the Bible which helped to achieve a restraint on sexual impulses through sublimation; religion also decreased the importance of family relations and increased the importance of the world community. [122] "As Christ, he could love his father, who was now called God with a fervour which had sought in vain to discharge itself so long as his father had been a mortal." He was thus able to discharge his unconscious homosexuality without guilt; and his masochistic impulses found a sublimation, without too much renunciation, in the sufferings of Christ. [123] "So it was that religion did its work for the hard-pressed child—by the combination which it afforded the believer of satisfaction, of sublimation, of diversion from sensual processes to purely spiritual ones, and of access to social relationships."

In the case of "Wolf Man," we see again a manifest religious behavior which masks unconscious conflicts. His attitude toward Christ was colored by his attitude toward his own father; and his ambivalent attitudes (love and hate) towards his father were found reflected in his relation to God. To ward off the hostile impulses, he engaged in pious ritual. The opposition which "Wolf Man" offered to religion had a three-fold origin: (1) He did not have the ability to make changes readily, was fearful of the new, and was afraid of a change in libido which became apparent in his reluctance to substitute loving God for loving his own father. [124] (2) In religious doctrine itself there is an ambiguous relation towards God the Father i.e., both love and fear. (This ambivalent attitude can be traced back to the very origins of religion.) "Wolf Man's" own high degree of ambivalency towards his own father made him more aware of this ambivalency in religion [125] (3) His homosexual desires were not entirely sublimated by religion but were rather repressed and thus were active unconsciously; his questionings, which implied he was wondering about whether Christ could serve a sexual function for God the Father, indicated his own unconscious conflicts. His denial of these impulses came forth in obsessive blasphemous thoughts; and thus his affection for God took the form of debasement. At the same time, in order to overcome these

101

emerging bad thoughts, he struggled vehemently. Thus there could be seen gross and obsessive exaggeration of all his activities which dealt with the piety and love of God.[126]

"Religion won in the end, but its instinctual foundations proved themselves to be incomparably stronger than the durability of the products of their sublimation." The new father-surrogate (his tutor) was against religion and so "Wolf Man" dropped religion and replaced it with something else. Thus his piety which originated under the influence of women was ended by men.[127] The fear of assuming a feminine attitude toward men was taken care of by the religious sublimations; however, his new interest in the military provided a more effective sublimation.[128]

After the removal of the obsessional symptoms, there were still some effects that remained behind. For the previous success of the "faith of piety" had impaired his faculty for critical investigation and brought about repression of his homosexual attitude rather than entirely sublimating it.[129] The latter drive remained in the unconscious directed to its original aim.[130] "He developed no zeal for learning, he showed no more of the acuteness with which at the tender age of five he had criticized and dissected the doctrines of religion."[131] The case of "Wolf Man" shows that his religious activities and his personal relationship with God were but the manifest behavior of his unconscious conflicts. The father-complex, of which he was in turmoil, expressed itself in his varying attitudes toward the God-head.

3. *Hysteria*

   a. *Anxiety Phobia*

   1. Mechanism. Phobias seem to be experienced by those whose libidinal development is more or less centered around phallic pleasure and the time of the Oedipal phase. Therefore, object relations will center around both parents. Phobic symptoms do not ordinarily show regression as in obsessional neurosis, paranoia, and dementia praecox. Freud claimed that in phobia there was an earlier phantasy which became intensified and forced its way into consciousness. At the same time, the ego tries to defend itself by the repression of the phantasy. With regard to the phobic idea, it is a substitute for the unconscious feared idea; the original idea loses its phobic *affect* when its memory comes to consciousness; the substitute idea must be of such nature as to be united with the quality of the liberated affect or

have some relationship to the incompatible idea. Thus anxiety, arising from a sexual origin incompatible to the person, will attach itself to the common fears or phobias of man e.g., animals, darkness, thunder storms, etc.[132] In the beginning of *anxiety hysteria* (phobia), anxiety may appear without the person knowing why he is fearful.

Clinical data show that a child with an animal phobia experiences anxiety under two conditions: when the repressed love-impulse becomes intensified and when he sees the feared animal. Substitution of a phobic idea more and more comes into operation and therefore there is less and less chance of the child being affected by his own father to whom the real fear is directed. Excitation coming from the outside environment, because of its connection with the substitute idea, will give rise to some anxiety and this is a signal to repress.[133]

All three, phobias, conversion hysteria, and obsessional neurosis, have as their outcome the destruction of the Oedipus complex; and in all three the motive force of the ego's opposition is, we believe, the fear of castration. Yet it is only in the phobias that this fear comes to the surface and is acknowledged.[134]

The child's hatred for his father (because of competition for the mother) is in conflict with admiration for the father. Relief is given by displacing the hostility and fear onto a substitute. The ambivalence is displaced onto the animal.[135]

In the case of phobia, the neurotic symptom represents a distortion of reality i.e. the person is not able to see the true meaning of his actions. For the threatening idea there has been substituted another idea. Thus reality has been disguised or masked; the person does not see the world as it is. Psychosexual development centers around phallic pleasure, and thus phobic symptoms do not distort reality as much as dementia praecox, paranoia and obsessional neurosis. We see for the first time the unconscious fear appearing in conscious life and receiving acknowledgement by the person. The phenomenon of phobia is significant for our study because frequently the fear is of an animal which from psychoanalytic investigation, is really a substitute for the father. Further, phobias bear a relationship to totemism which is a significant stage in the evolution of religion (Chapter IV). The cases of phobia, which Freud deals with, do not make direct mention of religion but we treat them because of their importance in understanding totemism and as they are a stage in the evolution of a greater awareness of reality.

2. "Little Hans." In the case of "Little Hans," at age three, he was threatened with castration by his mother for touching his penis;[136] at the same time he was frightened of horses fearing that they would bite him.[137] Here we have the beginning of Hans' anxiety and his phobia[138] which was attached to horses who might bite his finger (penis).[139] Freud pointed out that for Hans there were many similarities between his father and the horse.[140] Little Hans was afraid that horses would be injured if they fell down (which he wanted to happen). This indicated ambivalent feelings toward his father[141] because the horse was a substitute for the father whom he really feared. When the boy's fear of his father was lessened, it became clear that he wished his father to go away (die) as his father was regarded as a competitor for the attentions of the mother.[142]

The hostile wishes directed toward the father were subject to repression which had taken place by transforming the impulse into its opposite i.e., by means of projection, it appeared as if the father were aggressive to the son. This aggressiveness is centered in the sadistic phase of the libido with only slight degradation needed to bring it to the oral phase—the fear of being bitten or devoured. There was repression of passive "tender" impulses directed toward his father which were on the phallic level and which were more important because they went through a deeper regression thus influencing the make-up of the phobia.[143] In the case of "Little Hans" there seems to be merely a replacement of the psychical representative (castration by his father) with a regressive form of *expression*—the fear of the horse biting him.[144] Thus sadistic aggressiveness and passivity to the father are seen as a pair of opposites. In the case of "Little Hans" the repression affected all parts of the Oedipus complex: hostility and tenderness to the father and tenderness to the mother. The formation of the phobia did away with the tender impulses toward the mother but the make-up of the phobia did not display this sign.[145] "Little Hans" repressed out of fear of castration; he feared the horse would bite him—castrate him. Being bitten by a horse was a distorted substitute for the idea of being castrated by the father; this idea had undergone repression.[146] The anxiety arose not from repression but rather the repression took place as a means of defense against the anxiety experienced in the ego.[147]

3. "Wolf Man." We treat here *another* aspect of "Wolf Man" namely, his phobia. He displayed fear, hostility and kindness to various animals.[148] He feared that the wolves he had dreamt about would eat him[149] and had a terrible fear of all father substitutes.[150] "His last sexual aim, the passive attitude toward his father, succumbed to repression, and fear of his father appeared in its place in the shape of the wolf phobia."[151] "Wolf Man's ego reacted to the deep homosexual aims with the formation of a phobia which was organized around the genital level and displayed the mechanism of anxiety-hysteria. His ego reacted with anxiety as a protection against homosexual enjoyment. In the process of repression the object to which the libido was directed was replaced by a different one in consciousness. "What became conscious was fear not of the *father* but of the wolf."[152] The anxiety, which led to the phobic symptom, was due to castration fear.[153] The instinct repressed is the libidinal attitude directed to his father along with fear of him. With repression, this impulse is gone. Substituted for the father is an animal which became the transferred source of anxiety. The ideational portion has changed but the quantitative portion is still there transformed into anxiety. "The result is fear of a wolf, instead of a demand for love from the father." The person has not been saved from unpleasure and thus the neurosis goes into a second phase—the *phobia proper*: the person sets up avoidances (phobia), so as to prevent the outbreak of anxiety.[154]

The idea of being devoured by the father shows in a regressive degraded way the passive tender impulse to be loved by him in a genital-erotic sense. The genital impulse does not seem to be apparently tender here but rather to be in a phase between the oral and sadistic organization of libido. In the case of "Wolf Man" it was a genuine regressive degradation of his genitally directed impulse.

In the case of "Little Hans" we find a child struggling with the Oedipal conflict. The hostile wishes for his father were repressed and it seemed as if the father was threatening. However, a further displacement took place—he feared a horse instead of his father. With "Wolf Man" there was an unresolved Oedipal conflict; it centered around his fear of being sexually used by his father and the fear was displaced onto wolves. The case of "Little Hans" and "Wolf Man" are so different yet the result for both was a similar phobia.[155] They both repressed out of fear of castration. "Little Hans" feared the horse would bite him—castrate him and "Wolf Man" feared that to be loved by his father meant becoming a woman, i.e., castration. "The ideas contained in their anxiety—being bitten by a horse and being devoured by a wolf—were substitutes, by distortion, for the idea of being castrated by their father. This was the idea which had undergone repression."[156] In the cases of animal phobias, we engage in a reductionism and find that the animals are substitutes for the father and this substitution will have an important link with totemism.

b. *Conversion Hysteria*

1. Mechanism. Freud claimed that in some forms of hysteria there was not one great traumatic experience but many smaller ones. ". . . There was usually a sexual factor found to be at the core of the aetiology of the neurosis."[157] Repression and the outbreak of defensive symptoms came later when the *memory* of the unpleasure connected with the trauma arose.[158] There are both somatic and psychical signs indicated in an hysterical attack. Freud adopted Charcot's mechanism to explain hysteria which represents the return of a memory of a psychical trauma.[159] The hysterical attack may appear as an hallucination reproducing the traumatic experience and its memory is from the unconscious.[160] If the person wishes forcibly to repudiate, forget, inhibit or suppress an experience, intention or idea, then these psychical acts enter the unconscious to return as memories evocative of an hysterical attack. The nervous system disposes excitation through association or discharge by motor activity; in hysteria these psychical events have not been properly discharged.[161] Hysterical symptoms are mnemic symbols of certain operative (traumatic) impressions and experiences."[162] The mnemic residues are not translated into verbal images.[163]

> The return of the repressed in visual images approaches the character of hysteria rather than obsessional neurosis; but hysteria is in the habit of repeating its mnemic symbols without modification, whereas mnemic hallucinations in paranoia undergo a distortion . . .[164]

106

". . . there is an uninterrupted series, extending from the unmodified *mnemic residues* of affective experiences and acts of thought to the hysterical symptoms, which are the *mnemic symbols* of those experiences and thoughts."[165] Hysteria repeats the classical cycle of infantile sexual activity with repression, failure of the repression and finally the return of the repressed.[166] In each hysterical attack the person is hallucinating the very event which produced the first hysterical attack; hysterical symptoms were made to disappear when the precipitating event was recalled and the effect brought forth.[167] The following words of Freud should be given very careful attention and recalled later in the discussion of religion on the cultural level.

Anxiety is not newly created in repression; it is reproduced as an affective state in accordance with an already existing mnemic image. Affective states have become incorporated in the mind as precipitates of primaeval traumatic experiences, and when a similar situation occurs, they are revived like mnemic symbols. I do not think I have been wrong in likening them to the more recent and individually acquired hysterical attack and in regarding them as its normal prototype.[168]

We seem to see deeper in the case of some affects and to recognize that the case which holds the combination we have described together is the repetition of some particular significant experience. This experience could only be a very early impression of a very general nature, placed in the pre-history not of the individual but of the species. To make myself more intelligible—an affective state would be constructed in the same way as a hysterical attack and, like it, would be the precipitate of a reminiscence. A hysterical attack may thus be likened to a freshly constructed individual affect, and a normal affect to the expression of a general hysteria which has become a heritage.[169]

This does not imply that anxiety occupies an exceptional position among the affective states. In my opinion the other affects are also reproductions of very early, perhaps even pre-individual, experiences of vital importance; and I should be inclined to regard them as universal, typical and innate hysterical

107

attacks, as compared to the recently and individually acquired attacks which occur in hysterical neuroses and whose origin and significance as mnemic symbols have been revealed by analysis.[170]

It may happen in hysteria that the person does not remember anything of that which has been forgotten and repressed but rather "acts it out."[171] The event is reproduced not as a memory but as an act for the patient is not aware that he is repeating. This is his way of remembering.[172] Repeating may replace remembering in the way he handles other relationships that he is not engaged in.[173]

There is no libidinal regression, properly speaking, in hysteria. The mode of thought expression which the hysteric uses may, however, be regressive.[174] The hysteric is considered to be allo-erotic i.e., his identification is with the person loved, not himself.[175] Freud infers, but with some uncertainty, that when a person of the erotic type falls ill he will develop hysteria just as the obsessional type will develop obsessional neurosis.[176] Hysteria thus bears a close relationship to the phase of genital primacy and the reproductive function. In hysterical neurosis, genital acquisition is subjected to repression; however, there is no regression to a pre-genital phase.[177] Whatever regression there might be it would be to the primary incestuous sexual objects. Yet, this is not really a regression to an earlier stage of sexual organization.[178] In hysteria as in all neuroses there is a confrontation with the Oedipal complex. The symptoms expressed are the ego's reaction to the anxiety arising from castration fear or loss which is experienced unconsciously.[179]

Hysteria, compared with the other neuroses, shows the least distortion of reality. There is no regression in hysteria as the person is functioning at the genital level. As in all the neuroses the symptom indicates the person's reaction to trauma which is bound up with the Oedipal conflict. The hysterical symptom is really the reoccurrence of some past memory attached to an unpleasant experience. Therefore, the symptom and the real event are not that different. As the hysteric suffers from reminiscences, so too the race on a cultural level, through the acting out of events, recalls its early traumas.

2. Haizmann. Freud worked on a seventeenth century manuscript[180] which came from the shrine of Mariazell at which place there

was reported a miracle in which a painter, Christoph Haizmann, was freed from a pact with the Devil through the intercession of the Virgin Mary. The painter had been subject to "convulsive seizures and visions."[181] Accordingly, Haizmann was examined by the Church in order to find out whether he had entered into any pact with the Devil. Because of worries about his work, he had agreed nine years earlier that after a lapse of nine years he would give Satan his body and soul. The time was about to expire.[182] He was convinced that the Mother of God at Mariazell could save him from the bond with the Devil.[183] After a period of prolonged penance and prayer at Mariazell, the Devil appeared to him on the eve of the Nativity of the Virgin and returned to him the pact written in blood.[184] He had other visions besides.

> In the grandest of these ecstasies the figure surrounded by light took him first into a town in whose streets people were perpetrating all the acts of darkness; and then, in contrast, took him to a lonely meadow in which anchorites were leading a godly life and were receiving tangible evidence of God's grace and care. There then appeared, instead of Christ, the Holy Mother herself, who, reminding him of what she had already done on his behalf, called on him to obey the command of her dear Son. "Since he could not truly resolve so to do," Christ appeared to him again the next day and upbraided him soundly with threats and promises.[185]

The painter stated that he had made up his mind to leave the world and from that time on he had no more visions or temptations.[186] However, returning phantasies went from temptations to ascetic thoughts and finally punishing ideas. The exorcism was a great miracle but as the Fathers honestly tell, it was not very long lasting. ". . . Fresh attacks began . . . paralysis of the legs, and so on." But it was not only the Devil who vexed him but also Christ and Mary; all these experiences he called the manifestations of the Devil.[187] He was tempted in a vision by a finely dressed cavalier to throw away his document of entrance into the Brotherhood of the Holy Rosary and enjoy the world instead. After these phantasies, a period of asceticism set in. ". . . a voice [of Christ] . . . commanded him to forswear this wicked world and serve God in the wilderness for six years." In the next attack, Christ made threats for his not obeying and also led him to

Hell to see the damned. And so he again entered Mariazell in order to obtain back from the Devil an earlier bond written in ink. The Blessed Virgin and the Fathers were again successful in obtaining this end for him. Haizmann later joined the Brothers Hospitallers but was continuously tempted by the Evil Spirit to make a pact.[188]

Like Charcot, Freud believed that the possessions and ecstasies of the past were really manifestations of hysteria e.g. demons were really bad wishes which had been repressed. The Middle Ages, by projection, made these wishes entities of the external world; we rather see them today as part of the patient's internal life.[189] Thus, Freud treated Haizmann's case as one of hysteria and proceeded to investigate the *motive* for the pact with the Devil. We are led to the problem of motivation, if we view the case history like that of a neurotic. For Haizmann's immortal soul, the Devil has much to offer: wealth, security, power, magic and women. All of these he refuses.[190] It is to be remembered that he was despondent over the death of his father and thus may have made the pact to be freed from depression. It is also to be noted that in the pacts nothing is mentioned as to what the Devil will give in return for his immortal soul.[191] The thought might arise that Haizmann was looking for a new father to make up for his dead father.[192] Thus he became a slave of the Devil and "had undertaken to lead a sinful life and to deny God and the Holy Trinity."[193]

Freud considered the hypothesis of the *Devil as a Father-Substitute*. If the pact with the Devil was a neurotic phantasy, then the matter could be treated psychoanalytically.[194] The Devil, in his first encounter with the painter, appeared as an honest man. However, the appearance changed becoming more terrifying—more mythological. It might appear strange as to why the Devil was selected as a Father-substitute. Freud next considers this matter.

> To begin with, we know that God is a father-substitute; or, more correctly, that he is an exalted father; or, yet again, that he is a copy of a father as he is seen and experienced in childhood—by individuals in their own childhood and by mankind in its prehistory as the father of the primitive and primal hordes. Later on in life the individual sees his father as something different and lesser. But the ideational image belonging to his childhood is preserved and becomes merged with the inherited memory-

traces of the primal father to form the individual's idea of God. We also know, from the secret life of the individual which analysis uncovers, that his relation to his father was perhaps ambivalent from the outset, or, at any rate, soon became so. . . . It is our view that the same ambivalence governs the relations of mankind to its Deity. The unresolved conflict between, on the one hand, a longing for the father and, on the other hand, a fear of him and a son's defiance of him, has furnished us with an important characteristic of religion and decisive vicissitudes of it.[195]

The anti-thesis to the concept of God would be the Devil. Freud believed that God and the Devil were originally identical but then the one figure broke up into two—with each representing two opposite attributes. In early religion God possessed those traits which were later attributed to the Devil.[196] Here we see a process in which an idea with a contradictory or ambivalent content becomes sharply divided into its opposites.[197] "The contradictions in the original nature of God are, however, a reflection of the ambivalence which governs the relation of the individual to his personal father." If a good God is the substitute for a loving father, it should not be surprising that there be a Devil representing the hate and fear for the same father; for the father is the individual prototype of God and Satan. The mark of the primal father, more like the Devil than God, should be expected in religions.[198]

Freud began to look for causes in the life of Christoph Haizmann that would bring about a negative attitude toward his father. Freud hit upon the number nine which is frequently mentioned in the report (a bond for nine years, tempted nine years).[199] The number nine is frequent in neurotic phantasies and bears a relationship to pregnancy. In addition the Devil appeared to him in traditional guise (large penis ending in a snake) but also with two pairs of female breasts. Freud speculated on the negative attitude: the painter was rebelling against his feminine attitude toward the father culminating in a phantasy of giving him a child i.e. the nine years. Haizmann's mourning for his father and his longing for him reactivated the repressed phantasy of pregnancy which he warded off by neurosis and by "debasing his father."[200] Two explanations (not mutually exclusive) are offered on

111

the phantasy of the Devil *with breasts*: (1) the son's rejection of the feminine attitude toward the father is his revolt against castration. This repudiation often finds expression in the phantasy of castrating the father i.e., making him a woman.[201] (2) The son's feelings toward the mother may have been displaced on to the father. This might mean that there was a strong attachment to the mother with the accompanying increase of hostility to the father.[202]

It was clear from the *pious* visions that what was being offered was a way of life in which he would no longer have to worry about his sustenance as the old man in the cave who was fed each day by God's angels.[203] Haizmann found it difficult to give up the world; nevertheless, he finally succeeded (Holy Orders). At the same time, the internal struggles and material needs ended. In regard to the neurosis, the seizures and visions were finished at the exorcism from the first bond written in ink.[204] He wanted to make his life secure: first he tried the help of the Devil, at the price of salvation; then with the help of the clergy at the price of freedom of enjoyment.

Freud felt that the painter's economic situation intensified a longing for the father which in turn led to a demonological neurosis. With the removal of the melancholia and the Devil, there still remained a conflict between the libidinal enjoyment of life and the interests of self-preservation which demanded renunciation and asceticism. "On the other hand, he made no sharp distinction between the operations of the Evil Spirit and those of the Divine Powers. He had only one description for both: they were manifestations of the Devil."[205] Thus it might seem to be really one being in question, the Devil (his father), with two manifestations of his personality: Good and Evil. Thus Freud reduces the religious experience with God and the Devil to unconscious conflicts centering on the Oedipus complex.

3. Dostoevksy. Another case of hysteria, which is relevant for our purposes, is that of Dostoevsky. Freud believed that his epileptic seizures were really hysterical symptoms which were an expression of guilt and self-punishment for the death wishes he harbored for his father. He pointed out that Dostoevsky struggled with the problem of the individual (with all his instinctual cravings) in conflict with the demands of the community. His Oedipal conflict predetermined the course of action he took; " . . . he landed in the retrograde position of submission both to temporal and spiritual authority, of veneration

112

both for the Tsar and the God of the Christians . . ." This behavior Freud considered the weak point of his personality. Dostoevsky referred to himself as epileptic and was considered so by other people. Freud claimed that it was "highly probable" that the epilepsy was symptomatic of neurosis and thus was "hystero-epilepsy"—"severe hysteria." However, Freud admitted that he could not be sure.[206]

He felt that it was a "probable assumption" that Dostoevsky's hysterical attacks went back to early childhood; he showed biographical evidence[207] which indicates that this is possible. These milder forms of attack became epileptic after the experience in his eighteenth year—someone murdered his father.[208] At this point Freud indicated that it would be good[209] [for Freud's theory] if the evidence showed that the hysterical attacks disappeared during Dostoevsky's Siberian exile following the murder. The Siberian exile would then be acting as punishment enough for Dostoevsky's unconscious desire for his father's death. There would be no need, therefore, for *somatic* signs [hystero-epilepsy] of self-punishment. Freud, however, mentioned that most accounts and even that of Dostoevsky indicated that the "illness only assumed its final epileptic character during the Siberian exile."[210] Immediately Freud adds:

Unfortunately there is reason to distrust the autobiographical statements of neurotics. Experience shows that their memories introduce falsifications which are designed to interrupt disagreeable connections. Nevertheless, it appears certain that Dostoevsky's detention in the Siberian prison markedly altered his pathological condition.[211]

Freud believed that Dostoevsky's early childhood epileptic attacks stood for death because they began with a fear of death, lethargy and somnolescence. Further, he used to leave notes indicating that if these states occurred, he should not be buried for five days.[212] These "death" attacks might be either an identification with a dead person or the wish for someone's death. "At this point psycho-analytical theory brings in the assertion that for a boy this other person is usually his father and that the attack (which is termed hysterical) is thus a self-punishment for a death-wish against a hated father."[213] Freud goes on to point out that every punishment is in the last analysis a castration—or taking the passive (feminine) attitude toward the father. "Even Fate is, in the last report, only a later projection of the father."[214]

> You wanted to kill your father in order to be your father yourself. Now you *are* your father, but a dead father!—the regular mechanism of hysterical symptoms. And further— "Now your father is killing *you*."[215]

Dostoevsky was never free of guilt feelings which were due to his intention of patricide. These guilt feelings affected his behavior in two other areas where the "father-relation" comes into play: the State and belief in God. He submitted to his "Little Father," the Tzar but was a little more free in the religious areas; he wavered between faith and atheism all the way to his death bed. Because of his genius he was very much aware of the "intellectual difficulties" which arise when one takes the path of faith. He found a liberation from his guilt by identifying with Christ and used his own suffering as analogous to the sufferings of Christ. The fact that he did not arrive at freedom from religion was due to his filial guilt (found generally in mankind) which arrived at a "super-individual intensity" not to be overcome even by his great intellect. And religious feeling is built upon this filial guilt.[216] ". . . Dostoevsky's decision has every appearance of having been determined by an intellectual inhibition due to his neurosis.[217] Thus the religious experience of Dostoevsky is *reduced* to the Oedipal conflict.

4. "*Un-neurotic*" - Leonardo.

Finally we come to Freud's analysis of Leonardo da Vinci. Here we have an example of a person whose psychic life resembled somewhat that of an obsessional neurotic[218] and whose sexual orientation was not fully heterosexual but had ("ideal sublimated") homosexual overtones.[219] However, his total personality did not betray the usual symptoms of neuroses because of the perfect sublimation he was able to achieve.[220] Leonardo is of interest to us because he did not become engaged in religious activity of the traditional sort. Because of the vicissitudes of Leonardo's life, he did not know his father who was missing during the first four years of his childhood. Through an examination of his phantasies, Freud analyzed Leonardo as identifying with the Christ child and as seeing his mother as the Blessed Virgin.[221] For like Christ, he was without a father. Freud felt that in the case of Leonardo, libido had escaped repression by being sublimated from the beginning into curiosity and the thirst for research. But through the well-ordered sublimation, he escaped the turbulent eruptions from the unconscious which mark the neurotic.[222]

Leonardo is seen as the first modern natural scientist for he looked down upon authority and those who imitated the Ancients; he believed the study of nature was the source of all truth. The Ancients and authority could be seen as corresponding to the father while nature represented the mother. Leonardo was so different from ordinary persons who find support for authority so compelling that the world for them collapses without it[223]; he could not have abandoned authority so easily were it not that he had already learned from the first years of his life to do without a father. His scientific work is marked by a certain liberty and independence which point to the existence of a previous infantile sexual research freed from the scrutiny of a father and now minus the sexual element.[224] Freud believed that when one escaped being "intimidated" by the father in earliest childhood and thus had no authority interfering with his investigations, then it was expected that the person would not remain a believer in "dogmatic religion."[225]

Leonardo had been accused by his contemporaries of being irreligious.[226] He did not allow the Bible to mislead him in his research; he doubted a world-wide Flood and his calculations in geology were far beyond the time scale in the Scriptures. He also attacked the practice of praying to images of saints.[227] Yet he insisted that the Creator was best known and loved by an examination of creation.[228] In his discoveries he was filled with ecstasy and realized the splendor of creation revealed in the portion he had studied. He was filled with religious emotion when he looked at natural science.[229] However, there is nothing in Leonardo's writings to indicate that he was looking for a "personal" relationship with God. The writings of his last years show a spirit of resignation[230] to the law of nature or *Ananke* (Necessity). He looked for no special gifts from God. "There is scarcely any doubt that Leonardo had prevailed over both dogmatic and personal religion, and had by his work of research removed himself far from the

115

position from which the Christian believer surveys the world."[231] A reduction of Leonardo's views on God and religion revealed an absense of any unresolved Oedipal conflicts.

Thus we have examined all the major cases of religious neuroses which Freud dealt with and have seen that he applied the methodology of psychoanalysis to these studies. Analysis is essentially reductionistic; it explains a present phenomenon in terms of its genesis. We have seen that the genesis of the religious experience reveals the Oedipus complex, the religious experience thus was found to be a manifestation of latent conflicts.

We may now sum up briefly our findings having traced the various neuroses with religious content to the unneurotic with no religious content. Central to all of the cases we examined was the father-conflict. In all the cases there was an attempt at a "return of the repressed." It is the opposing forces of instinct and repression which lead to the neurotic symptom. With the more regressive neuroses the attempt at the repressed returning shows itself with greater distortion i.e., we cannot readily see what the repressed impulse is because the symptom is too disguised. However, as we moved from case to case the "repressed impulse" revealed itself ever more clearly. The person is playing out, on an individual level, the drama of the primal crime with all its accompanying ramifications. After this extended treatment of the neuroses and religion, it would be interesting to consider whether there has been an ever more clear "return of the repressed" as we moved from the most regressive to the least regressive neuroses. The repressed comprised murderous wishes for the father accompanied by guilt for having the wish, fear of retaliation for the offense and longing for the father.

In *dementia praecox* there is a "return of the repressed" in terms of an hallucinatory symptom. There were voices telling the American physician to return to the God he had denied; finally, he submitted to the Father.

In *paranoia* there is a "return of the repressed" in terms of a projection symptom. Schreber had hostile wishes toward God; he feared God and he submitted to Him by way of a special cosmogeny with a redeemer phantasy. He sacrificed himself to the Father like Christ but there was great distortion of the classical myth.

In *obsessional neurosis* there is a "return of the repressed" in terms of the symptoms of protective measures. "Rat Man" placated the wrath of the father by prayer, which also acted to protect against the emergence of death wishes. So too in the obsessional neurosis there was a return of the repressed in terms of the symptoms of compulsive religiosity. "Wolf Man" identified with Christ and the sacred drama so as to alleviate his guilt and satisfy his intense longing for the father.

In *phobia* there is a "return of the repressed" in terms of the symptoms of animal fear. "Wolf Man" feared the animals which were father substitutes. In this episode, he feared retaliation from the father for his murderous wishes. He also feared being eaten which fact draws us closer to the primal episode.

In hysteria there is a "return of the repressed" in terms of some somatic sign. Dostoevsky identified with Christ; his hysterical symptoms were like Christ's sufferings and his own sufferings relieved him of his guilt which arose from his patricidal intentions. In hysteria there is a "return of the repressed" in a way unique to this neurosis: the frightful return of *the* very memory of the trauma or an acting out of the trauma. After the death of his father, Haizmann longs for him. His hysterical symptom is seen in the fantasy of entering into a covenant with the Devil to whom he united himself as a son and promised to serve. The Devil is closer to the image of the primal father than to God. For the primal father castrated the sons who in turn murdered Him. Thus the *memory* of the repressed has finally returned in its full splendor!

We end with Leonardo, the *un-neurotic* and the man of science who has no father-complex because he knew no father and thus needed no personal Father or religion.

b. Philosophical Critique of the Methodology Employed in the Cases

We have examined in some detail the major neuroses involving religion as part of the symptomatology. What we will now attempt to do is examine the methodology employed in these cases which are supposed to support the *reductive* hypothesis that religious manifestation is an expression of an unconscious father-complex. The methodology will influence the credibility of the hypothesis. Our position is that since Freud was dealing with psychic phenomena, we cannot expect him to have had the same rigor in his methodology as we would expect of the physicist. However, we do believe that Freud, for the most part, conforms in his methodology to the norms set down by philosophy of science. It is immediately obvious that all the cases cannot be evaluated by the same criteria because the conclusions which Freud arrived at in these cases were based upon *different* quantitative and qualitative evidence.

With respect to "Rat Man" and "Wolf Man" we have extended studies. Freud analyzed these men over a long period and kept adequate notes on the analytical sessions. Thus on these two cases we can evaluate adequately the methodology employed. In regard to "Little Hans", Freud directed the investigation through the father of the child but only saw Hans himself one or two times. In the case of the "American Physician," Freud only had a letter on which he based his conclusions. The work on Schreber was based on an autobiographical report. And in regard to Haizmann, he based his analysis on a seventeenth century monastic manuscript. For Leonardo and Dostoevsky, Freud was able to use their works and available biographical material. Thus he never once interviewed any of these last five men.

1. *Experimental Setting: Interview*

We will begin with an analysis of the psychoanalytic methodology with specific reference to "Rat Man" and "Wolf Man." We will also consider the criteria which philosophy of science sets down concerning good methodology, namely, the experimental setting, the scientific status of the hypotheses which will involve us in a discussion of clinical inference, the causal relationship, prediction, postdiction, overdetermination and refutability. "Every one of his comprehensive case histories is at the same time a study in psychoanalytic theory. I mention them at this point because they show the constant mutual promotion of observation and hypothesis formation, the formation of definite propositions which make our knowledge testable, and the attempts to validate or invalidate them."[232] It is the task of the philosopher to state the logical criteria which a scientific theory must have. Were the logical criteria to be missing in a scientific theory it would be poor.[233] The philosopher is also concerned with the methodology employed in the validation of psychoanalytic propositions.

". . . Sooner or later the ever more precise empirical test becomes an essential element of any system of scientific propositions."[234] The psychoanalytic interview is a setting of an experimental type with rules of procedure. Each analytic session provides a setting for testing long-range predictions. Each time the subject reacts to something which the observer does, we have a reaction to a calculated change brought into the experiment.[235]

> The psychoanalytic situation can be regarded as an experiment in which the attempt is made to study the patient's behavior in interaction with the analyst's behavior as the principle variables. The analyst behaves in accordance with certain analytic hypotheses and the patient reacts correspondingly. Then the analytic session itself permits one to investigate the power of the hypotheses in helping us to understand, to predict, and to control behavior.[236]

The aim in the analytic session is to keep certain variables constant and allow others to vary. Furthermore, "Every aspect of psycho-analytic technique is oriented towards preserving the objective, neutral, uncontaminated relationship of the field of observation."[237] "Objective," "neutral," and "uncontaminated" mean that in the analytic situation the analyst for the most part is a passive observer.[238] Distortions that might arise on the part of the observer have been removed by his having undergone personal analysis;[239] thereby the analyst remains a blank so that the patient can project onto him; the analyst expresses no emotional reactions, no thoughts about politics and religion and says nothing about his personal life.[240] Here it may be mentioned that although Freud kept the analytical sessions ideal according to the above criteria, there was one major inadequacy. Freud was never analyzed himself; he did a self-analysis and thus ran the risk of deceiving himself. The fact that we found in the cases, when juxtaposed, similar interpretations especially in regard to religion makes us wonder whether Freud fell victim to projection. Is it possible that there were so many Christ figures? Is it an accident that Freud selected to work with and write up these particular cases? Is it not interesting that Leonardo, "Wolf Man" "Rat Man," and Dostoevsky all were engaged in a battle to retain the freedom of the intellect against the inhibiting forces of religion? While it is possible

119

that some degree of projection on Freud's part could have taken place, we believe his conclusions are essentially correct. Subsequent analysts, who have undergone personal analysis, still maintain the same essential conclusions of Freud.

2. *Scientific Status of Interpretation (hypothesis)*

Clinical interpretations in psychoanalysis may be considered the same as *hypotheses* in the sciences.[241] "Now interpretation is tentative explanation, and therefore close to hypothesis."[242] "To say that a statement is an interpretation, is to say (i) that the analyst sees in the associations a relationship between networks of ideas, which (ii) is governed by one or other of the component theories."[243] One of the hypotheses that Freud made in the case of "Rat Man" and "Wolf Man" was that their apparent religious behavior was motivated by unconscious conflicts, specifically the father-complex. Thus the analyst is concerned with the observation of data and the "sequences" that may be found in the data. A tentative interpretation may be made if some particular theme seems to run through the sequences. Then the interpretation must be checked out by examination of past and future data.[244]

a. *Clinical Inference.* In forming a hypothesis, the analyst must follow a certain set of rules; namely, rules of clinical inference[245] which would point to possible but not necessarily actual relationships.[246] In the case of "Rat Man" the neurotic symptoms began to show the "return of the repressed." Prayers for protection for the father were being colored by just the opposite invocation. Here we see the use of clinical inference by Freud: he infered from the conscious behavior the presence of unconscious hostility which was seeking fulfillment. So too with "Wolf Man", the pre-occupation with the sexual features of Christ (whose identity was at one time used as a means of sublimation) led Freud to infer the gradual emergence of the unconscious wishes that "Wolf Man" had for his own father.

It might be objected that Freud's inferences already presuppose Freudian theory. This objection can be met if we understand the relationship between higher and lower level hypotheses. The Freudian lower level hypotheses about "Wolf Man" and "Rat Man" must of course, as in the case of other scientific low level hypotheses, be formulated in terms of higher level hypotheses. As with all scientific procedure, one cannot question the higher level hypotheses at the same time as one questions the lower level hypotheses. In order to test the lower level hypotheses, one must accept the higher level hypotheses. In other words, before an interpretation can be made there must be agreement about the frame of reference e.g., unless we have accepted the theories of the Oedipus complex or infantile sexuality, any interpretation made within this frame of reference would be rejected.[247] It is obvious that we must accept Freudian theory before we can accept the hypotheses propounded in the cases of both "Rat Man" and "Wolf Man."

b. *"Causal" relationship.* Psychoanalysis presupposes that the psychic flux is not a matter of pure chance as psychic life has some degree of stableness and permanence which are a necessity for any scientific attempt; without some degree of stability and identity in psychic life it cannot be understood.[248] However, this does not mean that psychic life must be understood in terms of strict causal necessity but only that the statements of psychoanalysis express well confirmed probabilistic relations. Causality in psychoanalysis, as in other empirical sciences, is to be interpreted only as probability statements which would show certain actions as probably coming from other preceding actions. Analysis would show that slips of the tongue, dreams and neurotic symptoms are not haphazard i.e., they are probably connected with certain unconscious factors.[249] Thus in the case of "Rat Man" Freud was satisfied with setting up correlations between the unconscious conflicts and the protective measures (religion) taken. With "Wolf Man" the correspondence was even greater: the very unconscious impulses he felt toward his father were being expressed toward God.

Psychoanalysis has a problem peculiar to itself not found in other empirical sciences in that it seeks to establish a causal relationship between latent and manifest phenomena. (The latent phenomena are the desires and conflicts operative in the unconscious; the manifest phenomena are those actions which are apparent to conscious observation.) Psychoanalysis maintains that the latent and the manifest phenomena may be associated with each other by way of *similarity* and *contiguity.*[250]

Similarity, contiguity, frequency. We look to the similarity between the unconscious conflict and the manifest symptom in the case

121

of "Rat Man." Hostility toward his father, fear of carrying out the hostility along with the accompanying fear of retaliation by his father—all these things seem to bear similarity to prayers offered in his father's behalf which always ran the risk of becoming curses. There is quite a degree of similarity between the latent conflicts and manifest religious attitudes of "Wolf Man." The hostility toward his father and the compulsive blasphemies hurled at God; his own unconscious masochism toward his father, and his identifying with Christ as suffering at the hands of his Father; his desire to be loved by his father, and his wanting to be loved by God the Father; his desire to identify with the (sexual) Power of his father and his "breathings" in imitation of the Holy Spirit (Breath).

Because of past associations in a person's life history, Freud believed that events which are *contiguous* are causally related. In this sense we can say that one event evokes another event, e.g., with "Rat Man" the unconscious conflict when activated evoked the neurotic symptom (religion). This is established because of the association between the two forementioned phenomena. When "Rat Man" felt attraction to women, this attraction was associated in his unconscious mind with the fear of what his father might do, hostility toward the father, and repression of the hostility. Evocation of these intervening variables by the attraction to women resulted in an increase in prayer life (religion). For "Wolf Man" the unresolved father-complex when activated was capable of evoking the religious symptomatology. To satisfy the impulses to be loved as a woman by his father, he sought to be loved by God which was a sublimated form of the initial wish.

When two things are associated with a certain degree of *frequency* or repetition, we are in a better position to link them causally.[251] Throughout the cases of both "Rat Man" and "Wolf Man" we have the same repetition of the neurotic symptom (religion) pointing to the unconscious conflict.

c. *Prediction and Postdiction.* The scientific status of an hypothesis is bound up closely with prediction and postdiction. If the predicted event arrives, we regard the hypothesis as confirmed.[252] That there must be regularities in the events under consideration is only one condition for predicting. The analyst must understand the regularities and must have sufficient information relating to the system under question. In regard to the last factor, it may be that the means for knowing this information are not yet available.[253] When any of these factors under consideration is lacking or insufficient, then prediction is made difficult. In psychoanalysis there seems to be a limitation on the possiblity of precise predictions because the factors which bring this about seem to be ''inherent'' in the subject itself.[254] In empirical science, predictions are based on the ''relative frequency'' of the occurrence of an act in a certain class of events. However, Freud tended to see prediction only in terms of the individual case he was working on.[255]

The analyst predicts that observable events in some way related to the hypothetical unconscious motive will occur sometime in the course of the analysis; in his prediction he may indicate events which may be used as means for the fulfillment of the hypothetical unconscious motive or things which may be avoided on the way to fulfillment of the motive.[256] If ''Rat Man's'' religious behavior was contingent upon the unresolved father-complex, then Freud should have been able to *predict* that with the resolution of the conflict or the ineffectiveness of the defense, the corresponding religious behavior would disappear. Freud did point out situations in which ''Rat Man'' was relatively free of unconscious conflicts and at these times he was ''enlightened'', i.e., free of superstition and asceticism. Further, when ''Rat Man'' himself saw the ineffectiveness of prayer as a defense against unwanted impulses, he abandoned the devotion. The fact that there were unconscious hostile motives directed toward his father became evident in the course of the analysis as the form of prayer for the father became curses for him.

It is already clear that ''Wolf Man's'' unconscious ambivalent feelings toward his father manifested themselves in extreme ambivalence in his relationship with God. An analytic prediction regarding ''Wolf Man's'' behavior might be that if the conflict with the father-figure were resolved, then his religious behavior would change. It is therefore interesting to note that when a new father substitute (tutor) was found, he did not need the sublimation which religion had afforded him; and at this time his religious activity diminished along with dependence upon his father.

The analyst, on the basis of the known situation, may *predict* the stirrings of a particular disposition. Given an aroused disposition, he may *postdict* the situation that stirred up the disposition;[257] he can make predictions about the past in virtue of the genetic viewpoint of psychoanalysis.[258] Freud was able to *postdict.* Knowing that "Rat Man" became both enraged and frightened toward his father when he met women, it seemed reasonable to postdict that something similar had occurred in his childhood; Freud did, in fact, find this to be so. Also, since "Rat Man's" behavior seemed to fluctuate, in the analysis, between periods of religiosity and freedom from compulsion, perhaps his *previous* behavior displayed the same pattern. This seemed to be true in that he was deeply religious up till age fifteen, then became a free thinker and again he had periods of religious compulsion. Having analyzed "Wolf Man's" psychic make-up in relationship to his father, Freud theorized that there must have been a witnessing of the primal scene in his childhood. He then found, through an analysis of "Wolf Man's" dreams, that this had occurred. The primal scene that had been witnessed had evoked the ambivalent disposition of taking the role of both father and mother. The religiosity at a very early age pointed to the manifestation of these premature fears and desires.

d. *Overdetermination.* There are limitations on predictions in psychoanalysis because of so many factors determining activity and analysts realize the over-determination of action.[259] "A phenomenon is said to be over-determined if there exists more than one set of antecedent conditions or causes, and if each set *alone* is capable of explaining how it occurs."[260] In explaining a neurotic disturbance, for example, there may be a plurality of causes: hereditary traits, predisposing conditions and precipitating conditions. There is the problem of distinguishing which are the relevant causes.[261] *Ideally* the relationship between the two phenomena should be one in which the supposed cause is necessary, unique, and sufficient to explain the effect. With "Rat Man" we find various factors (the unconscious conflict, environmental influences) which could be responsible for his religious neurosis. It might be argued that Freud is not justified in claiming that it is the unconscious conflict that caused the religious neurosis but rather the environmental factors i.e., he may have been religious because of his family upbringing. In the case of "Wolf Man," it is very clearly indicated that he was presented with religious material at a very early age with which he might play out the drama of his unconscious conflicts. Thus one could argue that environmental

124

factors were as important as unconscious conflicts. It is evident that in some of Freud's studies over-determination is found.

However, Freudian theory can meet the charge of over-determination, if it adopts the following criteria for testing an interpretation. An interpretation which is made up of a clinical hypothesis is established if the response to the interpretation can be interpreted in terms of the *same* clinical hypothesis. The point is that if one were allowed to interpret a response by using *any* theory then we would find that every response would be confirming the theory being tested.[262] "Hence our criterion for testing would be *that a response corroborates an interpretation embodying a hypothesis about clinical content provided it can be interpreted by means of the same hypothesis about clinical content even though with a different hypothesis of defense.*"[263] With regard to the analyst, he should be able to predict what kind of defense will be made in the response. Will the response now give the preceding associations greater clarity after the interpretation is made or will there be a strong defense? The analyst should also specify what probable defense, if any, would have occurred had he not intervened with the interpretation. One could determine the probability of the influence of an interpretation by counting the proportion of predictions that are correct when interpretations are not given and the proportion when they are given.[264]

With "Rat Man" there was one incident when Freud did propose to him his interpretation of the religious phenomenon. "Rat Man's" response was to disagree with Freud but with some degree of uncertainty. The response seems to be so limited that it would seem very tenuous to use it to support or not support the interpretation. If he looked at the non-committal response as a defense, then we can neither say that it clarified the interpretation nor that it was a strong defense. Freud does not show us in the case whether he made any prediction as to the kind of response or defense that would be made. Therefore, for Freud the case was over-determined.

e. *Refutability.* We turn now to an examination of the possible refutability of a psychoanalytic interpretation. An interpretation could be considered false if the subsequent associations are not relative to the interpretation.[265] However, the desire of some to ask for one specific *crucial experiment* to validate or invalidate an interpretation is too strict a requirement which is not even required in physics.[266] We will examine the possibility of refutation of the hypothesis that "Rat Man's" and "Wolf Man's" religious activities were but a manifestation of unconscious conflicts. There are difficulties here because Freud had a tendency to see all religious manifestation as indicative of unresolved conflicts and needs. Thus it would seem that *a priori* Freud would search out unconscious conflicts wherever he encountered the religious phenomenon; it would seem that there were no criteria acceptable to him which would indicate that the religious manifestation was free of neurotic involvement;[267] it would seem that no evidence could count against the relationship between neuroses and religion. Therefore, one might conclude that the interpretation is unfalsifiable. However, even though Freud did not provide specific criteria which would falsify his hypothesis, he did admit that psychoanalysis did not totally exhaust the meaning of religious experience.[268] Thus, at least in theory, his hypothesis is falsifiable. "If the application of the psychoanalytic method makes it possible to find a new argument against the truths of religion, *tant pis* for religion; but defenders of religion will by the same right make use of psychoanalysis in order to give full value to the affective significance of religious doctrines."[269]

1. Control. There is need of control groups so that an interpretation may have validity. ". . . The fact that some event or attribute B occurs with a certain relative frequency p when some other event or attribute A occurs is not sufficient to show that A and B are significantly related—unless there is further evidence that the relative frequency of B in the absence of A, or the relative frequency of the non-occurrence of B in the presence of A, is markedly different from p."[270] Thus the fact that religious manifestation occurs with a certain frequency (p) when there is an unresolved father-complex is not sufficient to show that religious manifestation and father-complex are significantly related—unless there is further evidence that the relative frequency of religious manifestation in the absence of a father-complex is different markedly from p. And the relative frequency of the non-occurrence of religious manifestation in the presence of a father-complex is markedly different from p. In other words, to show a significant relationship between father-complex and religious manifestation, we would want to see a decrease in the frequency of religious manifestation where there is no father-complex or good

frequency of occurrence of the father-complex where religious manifestation is revealed. This information cannot be established on the basis of one or two cases.

Because someone shows *apparently* no personal relationship to God, it does not mean that he has resolved his father-complex. The absence of religion does not indicate the resolution of unconscious father conflicts, but rather may show that they are successfully repressed or sublimated at least for the time being. Also it may mean that the person does not choose to "play out" the conflicts by means of religious symbols; he may find another mode. The data must be so analyzed that comparisons with a control group can be made; then we could be assured of a causal inference.[271] Freud can be justifiably criticized on the grounds of insufficient controls.

2. Lack of data. Psychoanalysis has been criticized for using a small amount of data upon which it bases interpretations which it attempts to validate; and that psychoanalysis has dealt with a relatively small number of cases. In answer to this objection, it must be pointed out that in each individual case there is an enormous amount of data which has a bearing on the problem. In each case there are hundreds of facts which can be used to test an hypothesis and predict future outcomes. However, it is true that sometimes there is difficulty in validation because it is impossible to repeat the experimental procedures under the same conditions;[272] and therefore there is a lack of repeatable data.

3. Not Public. Another criticism that is brought against psychoanalysis is that its procedure in formulating and validating an interpretation is not open to public scrutiny.[273] In answer, it could be proposed that two psychoanalysts be asked to report on what happened in a recorded session and another two could be asked to predict the content of future sessions.[274] Statistical comparisons of how the analysts agreed or disagreed could be made. By recording this data a psychoanalytic session would be a "publicly demonstrable and repeatable experiment." The results would also be open to further scrutiny by other analysts.[275] In regard to the privacy of the sessions, there is data e.g., early traumas that could be verified by the family.[276]

Free association is one of the chief methods for both forming and verifying an hypothesis; through free association, the analyst is enabled to obtain an excellent sample of all that is going on in the mind.[277] Yet there is no way of proving that the associations are really

127

free[278] as the analyst may become somewhat "directive" in the session; it is said that patients dream according to the mode of the one analyzing them.[279] The question arises as to whether the analyst influences the reactions and responses of the client by means of suggestion.[280] The answer to this objection can be found in the following comment: "Every element in the formal analytic situation, i.e., the analytic incognito, the constancy of external variables, the non-interference by the analyst, the calculated interpretation, the watchful eye on counter-transference pressures and the tracing of transference attitudes to their sources, is essential to the facilitation of free associations."[281] Although there may be some influence of the analyst on the patient in spite of the above precautions, there is a reasonable probability that this influence would not be of major significance.

3. *Non-Experimental Setting of Cases*

a. *Absent Patient.* As we deal with the remaining studies, we will not do an exhaustive analysis of them for the reason that they are not scientific case studies according to the norms of psychoanalytic practice. ". . . In his case histories Freud never *reported* the facts but *interpreted* them; what passes for description in the Freudian method is already judgment."[282] This last statement we accept for the following discussion but not entirely for "Wolf Man" and "Rat Man."

Psychoanalytic theory becomes the less reliable the less it is applied to live patients. The less the object of study is able to respond—if we apply the theory to remote historical figures . . . —the less reliable the theory. As various symptoms appear, and as the patient reacts to therapeutic behavior, an analyst with a live patient before him will be guided in his theoretical formulation. Almost each segment of patient behavior permits a considerable range of interpretations from which the analyst chooses. His choice is shown to be appropriate or inappropriate by the patient's reaction. The trouble in interpreting the behavior of . . . absent persons is that they do not respond with reactions that can be utilized to narrow the interpretative range. As a result, that range remains insufficiently restricted to be meaningful; there are quite a number of interpretations compatible with general psychoanalytic principles that could "explain" the behavior of absent patients . . . . Hence, the explanation chosen

128

tends to reflect predilection which is not fully justified. I think that Freud here allowed himself to be seduced by his own speculations. But we need not follow him. Moreover, we seldom will even approximate knowledge of the relevant facts as well with . . . absent patients, as we do with live individual patients. This leads me to conclude that we should leave absent patients alone (or be aware that we are playing a parlor game) . . .[283]

It would seem that the lack of scientific value with regard to the cases dealing with non-live patients would militate against their being discussed here. However, because of their importance for Freud's philosophy of religion, it is essential that we give them some consideration. The significance of the case of "Little Hans" for religion is that an animal phobia was substituted for fear of the father; further, a stage of religion through which mankind evolved was *totemism* where we really have a disguised father figure. However, the validity for the substitution cannot be established from the case of "Little Hans" because Freud never analyzed the boy. "Wolf Man's" case seems to point to the possibility of a substitution but one or two cases are inadequate to establish this possibility with any degree of certitude.

b. *Overdetermination.* From a methodological viewpoint there could have been any number of factors which could have led to the fear of a particular animal. Freud himself admitted that there were no extensive studies available at the time; he did not believe that the scarcity of material was essential. Here he could be easily challenged. Because it would be in harmony with one's theory that an animal and father be interchangeable, does not excuse from further collection of adequate data. Why the case of "Little Hans" can be so misleading is due to the fact that Freud knew what he wanted to find *a priori* and thus risked selecting from the case the things he needed. Further, his instructions to Hans' father could be misleading i.e., they could lead to just the data Freud wanted. The father was not an analyst and certainly would not have been the right person for obtaining psychoanalytical material from his own son.

The *Schreber case* is inadequate methodologically because there were no interviews but only the person's autobiography. However, we might examine the case to see its inner consistency. Freud presumes that the hospital director was a substitute for Schreber's father. This presumption would allow Freud to say that the transferential feelings he showed for the director were the same as he held for his own father. There was a correspondence in his attitude toward God and the hospital director and by implication toward his own father. But Freud had no way of verifying the interpretations with the patient; there was no historical data available to shed any light on the relationship of Schreber and his own father.

   c. *Inaccurate Historical Data.* It would be beyond the scope of this work to show the other possibilities of interpretation that could be made of this autobiography. It will suffice to mention that other analysts have disagreed with Freud on this study.[284] ". . . the method of presenting and using findings collected from outside sources and not from the patient himself, differs from the accepted analytic method of gaining access to such data which in analysis, of course, originate from one source alone i.e., the adult patient."[285]

In regard to the interpretation of the diabolical possession case of the hysteric *Christoph Haizmann,* Freud makes use of the material to suit his convenience. The words "ex morte parentis" appear in the manuscript. From the word "parentis" we cannot tell whether this is the mother or father. Freud takes the liberty of saying it was the death of Haizmann's father.[286] If it is the time of Haizmann's father's death, then we could explain a longing for him and satisfaction with the Devil. If it were the death of the mother, then how explain the interest in the Devil? But the case can be played that way too because the Devil at times took on the attributes of a woman! Thus we reach the conclusion quickly that without the scientific methodology of a psychoanalytic session, we continuously run the risk of finding supporting evidence for whichever theory meets our fancy.

It is surprising that Freud felt the information yielded by the study was far superior to the orthodox procedure of psychoanalysis namely, associations and symptoms. At the same time he did admit that the present problem of gaining information on the negative attitude toward his father would be less difficult in an analytical setting.[287] But then he went on to say that he would look for things in the case indicative of a negative view to the father.[288] However, the manuscript does not have the ability to respond but rather remains passive to any interpretation Freud wishes to make. Studies have also pointed out that Freud's information on factors associated with mythology and demonology were incorrect. In spite of the incorrect data, he was able to make the material work for *his* theory.[289]

We have already seen the manipulation and selective choice of possible events which Freud made in his treatment of *Dostoevsky*. And so we will go on to the study of *Leonardo*. Freud mentioned in the context of this study that psychoanalytic inquiry works upon the life history of the person: chance events, background and the reactions of the person. With psychoanalytic theory ("knowledge of psychical mechanisms") as a tool the analyst looks to the type of reactions so as to understand the dynamic structure of the person's psyche.[290] There is obvious limitation in the quality and quantity of reactions because Leonardo is not present. Freud did admit that much of the material he used on Leonardo was uncertain and incomplete.[291] Nevertheless, in spite of this, he could not resist the temptation to analyze. His knowledge of mythological data, which he uses in the case of Leonardo, was called into quesiton but this factor alone would not have been the major criticism usually offered. Besides making complex interpretations on the basis of a single factor, Freud did not give due emphasis to history, the social situation and environment.[292] "Freud has misinterpreted Leonardo, and he admits more than once in his book how speculative his attempt is, it was in part because he ignored or misread certain facts."[293] The incorrect conclusions do not point to the invalidity of the psychoanalytic method but rather to an unjustified application.[294]

Freud also claimed that Leonardo was free from the father-complex because of the absence of his father. However, he is not consistent from case to case; he is prone to allow the phylogenetic influence to account for the presence of castration fears (coming from the father) when he cannot find the father making the threat in the case (e.g. "Wolf Man"); but in the case of Leonardo, he chooses not to consider the possibility of a phylogenetic influence or other father surrogate influences. Freud should be required to tell *why* the phylogenetic influence was *not* felt in the case of Leonardo. Also we might ask for the evidence that Freud has to show that where the father is absent the children do not believe in "dogmatic religion." He claimed that he had "evidence" to show that the young abandon religion when the father's authority wavers; yet we do not find this evidence ever given in Freud's writings.

Conclusion

We have been concerned with the hypothesis that religion is a manifestation of an unresolved father-complex. The data given were the clinical cases whose methodology we examined. We look now to a conclusion of this study. A challenge that might be brought against the hypothesis is that the cases all dealt with neurotics. It might be argued that neurotics are not like ordinary people; neurotics use religion as a way of manifesting their unconscious conflicts; ordinary ("normal") people do not use religion in this fashion. Freud would answer that there are not "qualitative" differences between the neurotic and the "normal"—only quantitative differences. There are no sharp distinctions between one person's personality and another unless we compare extremes: the bizarre behavior of a psychotic and the behavior of a so-called well adjusted individual. Everyone has gone through the Oedipal phase; and the only difference between the normal and the neurotic is the degree to which each person has outgrown it. Thus the possibility is open that the "normal" person, who is religious, may be "playing out" in a modified form his own unconscious conflicts in the same way as the neurotic. This is a possibility. With the idea of continuity of personality types it might be a likely possibility.

Our analysis of the methodology has indicated the various weaknesses and strengths in the hypothesis. From Freud's study, the most we can say is that some people who are religious may be merely displaying their own unconscious conflicts. The correlation of the two factors has not been conclusively shown in even some cases. However, the little evidence[295] seems to point to some correlation; to say more than this would be difficult for the philosopher of psychoanalysis as he would have to rely on further investigation in order to reevaluate the methodology. In summary, we have seen the reductive interpretation of the religious neurosis in terms of the Oedipus complex and the support given to this hypothesis by philosophy of science.

C. Reductive Analysis of Religious Phenomena in the Cases Allows for Possible Emergence of Sacred: Telos

1. Exploration of the Notions of Symbol, Sacred, "Wholly Other," Religion and Faith

Thus far we have given emphasis to the reductionistic tendency in Freud's treatment of religion which can be considered the first moment of our dialectic. We will explore whether the meaning of the religious neurosis has been exhausted in its genesis. It is our contention that genesis only constitutes one moment in the dialectic. We will first attempt to explore the notions of symbol, sacred, "Wholly Other", religion and faith in terms of the dialectic; we will be interested in the moment at which they occur in that dialectic. Having explored these notions we will employ them with reference to Freud's treatment of religious neurosis. It is our hope that a deeper meaning will be seen to emerge when we attempt to understand Freud's analysis as an important moment in the dialectic.

If we try to examine a moment of the dialectic, which is in continuous process, we may see the history of past experiences or genesis. The movement of the dialectic shows the previous past moment in confrontation with the present with all its novelty and newness. The present, while maintaining a link with the past, is also a shadow of the future or the moment of synthesis (telos).

We will try to locate symbol in this dialectic. When we consider something as symbolic we mean that it says something more than what an ordinary word conveys. The ordinary word gives us a meaning which is ordinarily immediately apparent to the one who speaks and the one who listens. However, with symbol the meaning may be immediately understood on one level, but there are other meanings not immediately understood. Symbol might be considered in a way analogous to a sound going through an echo chamber: it begins as one thing and through confrontation with different opposing and reinforcing forces takes on different sounds as it spreads out or goes beyond its point of origin. The full appreciation of the sound's richness is only understood when we experience not only where it has taken us but also where it is leading; it is this ability to lead and to take us beyond ourselves that is the unique quality of symbol.

Within the symbol there is an inner tension or dialectic in process.

The symbol has come to stand for many experiences of the past and at the present moment bears all the meanings of the past. Thus the symbol can give us a glimpse of its own history or origin. But as we trace its development back to its origin or engage in a reductionism we find ourselves involved in a dialectic in reverse: synthesis, anti-thesis, thesis. When we take the dialectic forward we then become aware that the history of the symbol is best seen in its forward movement where it takes us beyond ourselves. At the present moment the symbol is best appreciated for we can ourselves *experience* its inner dynamics as we are led forward. Symbol as it moves towards the future has taken into itself the present moment; by adding the present moment to its history it becomes all the more profound and richer. For as we now encounter the symbol it has more echoes of the past which can evoke responses from the depths of our own genesis; we are drawn to the symbol not fully understanding why. Having been attracted and taken by the symbol we are led beyond ourselves; for while the symbol bears the past it also gives the promise of revealing the future (telos). We and the symbol are both involved in the dialectic. Our dialectic of experience and the symbol's journey through time intermingle. Both move on together.

With reference to religious symbol and sacred symbol we have a dialectic of past and present. Religious symbol contains all the past experiences of man grasping for the "Wholly Other." A symbol from its very beginning has a capacity to take man beyond himself and is the best instrument available to show the striving of man for the "Wholly Other." Yet, if the world is taken to be in process and if we consider the "Wholly Other" to be revealed through the world, then the symbol which begins with the known and strives to grasp the unknown is also in process.

It becomes evident that to take the symbol at one particular time in history and to say that it is adequate enough to aid man in his striving for the "Wholly Other" is not to understand the "Wholly Other" as being in time. Religious symbol is inadequate because it represents a stabilization of that which by its very nature is in process. This stabilization places too much emphasis on a *past* encounter but religious symbol is viable when it is placed in the framework of a dialectic. When religious symbol is seen as in process, then we really have sacred symbol. Symbol has its past, its present moment of confrontation and its rising to a new moment. If the symbol cannot become enriched by the present moment, i.e., retain its meaningfulness and its ability to take us forward (telos), then it dies. Symbol grows in richness by confrontation with the present; symbol in order to remain viable must encounter fully the present moment. A symbol which is still able to take man beyond himself in his adventure or journey toward the "Wholly Other" we speak of as sacred.

Symbol never arrives at the thing symbolized for if it did, it would no longer be the symbol but the thing. In the dialectic of sacred symbol there is a pointing to the "Wholly Other." If we take Anselm's words that "God is that than which no greater can be conceived" then we have a viable sacred symbol. For the symbol continues to point beyond. True, men at different times thought they had captured in some way "that than which no greater can be conceived." Yet with time their ideas proved inadequate in the face of a reality which opens up newer and wider horizons. "That than which no greater can be conceived" opens up the mind to infinity. Man in growing in consciousness appreciates more and more the implications of infinity. The world that was revealed to man in the past enabled him to contrast the finite with the infinite. By way of contrast, he intuited in some way the infinite. "That than which no greater can be conceived" takes on deeper meaning for present-day man. For reality has since revealed much more and infinity must be all the greater. Thus the Anselmic phrase continues to be a sacred symbol and will continue to be so because it is involved in the dialectic of the past and the present: it best shows man straining to the utmost to transcend himself.

Since the "Wholly Other" is entirely other we never truly understand God; we see a manifestation of the "Wholly Other" in the world. Symbol, as we have seen, begins with the world and strives to transcend it. Our dialectic may show us the direction toward the "Wholly Other" but it will never give us the "Wholly Other." We can rise from an understanding of beings to that which has the fullness of being; but we only intuit in a clouded way, a Being which possesses all and upon which all are dependent. Our dialectic in a way is an odyssey of the mind searching to grasp reality—more specifically—searching to grasp that Being who is the fullness of reality. Our instruments, which ultimately are reduced to human reason, we saw to be helpful but incomplete. The dialectic as it raises us higher and higher in consciousness enables us to see more and more the world as it is; the world continues to reveal itself and we understand all the more clearly the beings of that world.

If we have been on a journey where we have tried to grasp in a better way the beings of the world then by implication it is a sacred journey. For the endeavor to understand being in greater depth implies that there is a striving to understand Being; for the beings we have employed in our quest are shadows of Being; they participate in Being; their contingency or finitude implies something beyond them; our use of symbol best illustrates a beginning in finitude and a launching out to infinity. We then see man in process—man striving to transcend himself—man grasping onto symbols to take him beyond—man's mind opening up to infinity. We reflect over these experiences. Man could view the cosmos as totally alien and meaningless; he could withdraw into himself rather than attempt to make sense out of what seems to be a chaos. On the other hand, man can also look out at the cosmos as revelatory and meaningful; here he makes an act of faith. This act of faith is not unlike the leap of faith which the existentialists make in the wake of a world which seems to be absurd.

When the act of faith is made, then some order or meaning seems to be further revealed. To launch out in an endeavor to understand being presupposes a faith which believes that there is such a thing as understanding and something to be understood. If we were in the area of theology we would take faith to be a belief in a God who has revealed himself through the Scriptures but whom we have never seen. The faith we have been speaking of, while it might not be the same as theological faith, does share some of its characteristics. Our faith in the ability of being to reveal meaning implies that there may be a source of being which is also the fountain of meaning. Our faith in the ability of being to unveil more and more the depths of reality implies that there is a source of the whole of reality which continues to reveal. In a way we are involved in an *Itinerarium Mentis ad Deum* with a pre-requisite of the journey being faith. For without faith we would never understand; and, having understood, we believe.

2. *Religious Neuroses: Sign of Sublimation, Identification and Archaic Symbol of the Sacred*

Having explored the ideas of symbol (both religious and sacred),

"Wholly Other" and faith we consider these notions with reference to Freud's analysis of religious neurosis. We would like to point out that Freud's analysis of the religious neurosis was not totally reductionistic but allowed for development of teleology specifically in the matter of sublimation and identification. Thus the *religious* neurosis marked or revealed the locus of confrontation between genesis and telos in sublimation and identification. We will endeavor to see now the deeper meaning of the religious manifestation in these cases: we will discuss sublimation, as it relates to the religious and sacred as seen in the cases specifically; then religious symbol and sacred symbol; and finally we will see the evolution in awareness of the "Wholly Other" as other.

In the case of the American physician his unresolved Oedipus complex ("return of the repressed") became activated on the occasion of a contemporary incident. There was the risk that the sublimations operative in his personal relationships, which were influenced by the Oedipal complex, could be broken down. However, the physician was able to sublimate the ambivalent feelings he had for his father through an identification with Christ and God. The physician exchanged the "to have" for a "to be like." He could not have his father but he could be like him. Thus we have an identification with Christ. Further, libido has been transformed (desexualized or sublimated) into a different aim. And all of these processes indicate a teleology which cannot be reduced. The fact that we are involved in a religious symbol must also be considered. Identification with Christ does not tell us anything new about the sacred and is thus relegated to the religious because it is the sacred become deified.[296] What makes the religious symbols archaic is the fact that they are products of hallucination and therefore do not witness a free encounter with the "Wholly Other."

However, a reduction of the religious symbol may enable us to see more. What did the religious symbol really mean when it was a sacred symbol or sign of the approach of the "Wholly Other"? In a way it may have been an act of faith in the face of confrontation, struggle, and alienation. The physician did not make an act of faith in his father but in the "Wholly Other." Whether a "Wholly Other" exists or not his faith is in something transcendent which is found not to be reducible to the father. An attempt at reduction to the genesis which shows the child's utter dependence upon the father does not explain away the present awareness of one's utter contingency, the contingency of all beings, and the present faith in a Being upon which all are dependent. All we can *understand* is religious symbol because it becomes part of the profane; sacred symbol goes beyond the grasp of knowledge. We can be aware of the latter but we cannot know it; the religious symbol points to the sacred but is not sacred or the "Wholly Other." Thus amidst the distortion and hallucination of the neurosis reductionism reveals that at one time the "Wholly Other" may have approached.

In the case of Schreber, Freud indicated that the patient felt the danger of his libido entering into his social relationships and sexualizing them along with the sublimations breaking down. Therefore, he made the attempt to withdraw libido from objects and return it to the ego. This redirection accomplished, Schreber was able to reconstruct reality; he also struggled to maintain his social relationships. The homosexual feelings ("to have") toward his own father, which he could not face, he transferred to God. Schreber was not able to move completely from the "to have" to the "to be like" with reference to God[297] and thus arrested psychosexual development interfered with his relating to God as the "Wholly Other." Schreber made an attempt to overcome the "return of the repressed" (Oedipal conflict) but only through a delusional system. He made use of religious symbol as a means of projecting his unconscious conflicts and the symbolism employed is very archaic and regressive. If we try to engage in a reduction of the religious symbol, we find we have a person not completely giving up the "to have" (he wants to be God's wife). Yet there is a movement toward the "to be like" (he carries out God's work as a redeemer). Thus some teleology is seen for his own consciousness must have been negated in some way (through not being satisfied completely with the "to have") in order to have moved on to the next moment—the "to be like" (identification); the process of identification shows a forward direction. Do these religious symbols in any way through their reductionism point to signs of the sacred? We may answer in the affirmative because they show man in that transitional stage with the "Wholly Other" where he begins to realize that he cannot possess the "Wholly Other" and accordingly begins to move on to an imitation (through identification) of the

138

"Wholly Other." These signs of the sacred are veiled in the form of religious symbols. Due to Schreber's paranoia, he makes use of archaic forms of religion by means of which he may project his conflicts. Schreber's religious symbols when reduced show us that the "Wholly Other" has approached—not in the present but in the archaic *past*. For the "Wholly Other" is not seen in religious symbol but in the sacred which comes in the *present* moment.

In the case of the "Rat Man" we see him struggling with the unconscious hostile feelings toward his father. These do not find expression in open hostility to other father surrogates or in a hostile relationship with God. Rather he goes beyond and engages in religious behavior which serves to prevent hostile and unsocial impulses from appearing. Thus he attempts to engage in a constructive transformation by the use of religion.

To see a deeper meaning in the religious manifestation we will engage in a reductionism. There is a struggle to overcome hostility and fear for the father by calling upon and placating a father surrogate (God). Here then is revealed the basic infantile attitude of the child to his father. However, from the point of view of telos, more is revealed besides the infantile. "Rat Man" is aware of his own limitation as witnessed by his calling upon God as an aid in keeping down his hostile impulses. He is also aware of the other (God) as *distinct* from himself for he has given up the "to have" and realizes that he cannot possess that which is "Wholly Other." He expresses his dependency upon the "Wholly Other" in his act of prayer which shows awareness of his own contingency and leads to an act of faith in the "Wholly Other." Nevertheless, there still predominate the infantile factors— looking for a God of consolation. As we shall show, this god of consolation is not "Wholly Other." It is only the act of faith in a being entirely different in His transcendence from the father, which allows us to be aware of a "Wholly Other."

With "Wolf Man" we see an obsessional neurotic who is able to sublimate the anal-erotic components of his personality through the use of religion. He had masochistic and homosexual tendencies which he was able to repress and through sublimation he put the libido at the service of the ego. Freud tells us that by sublimation of the libido into religion he was able to direct his attention to the service of the community rather than only the familial objects. Religion thus provided a new and more constructive avenue for the release of lower impulses. The religious manifestation as expressed in communal involvement can be taken as a symbol for it points in two directions— the past and the future: genesis with its unconscious infantile desires (anal-sadistic) and telos with its sublimation or overcoming of the infantile (communal involvement).

The process of identification was employed which, as in the case of sublimation, points to a teleology. "Wolf Man" had not successfully identified with his father; the identification would mean giving up the "to have" and replacing it with a "to be like." However, the religious drama enables him to remodel the father-son relationship: for the Son gives up the Father and identifies himself in doing the work of the father—namely, redemption. "Wolf Man" thus establishes the same type of relationship with his father. He gives up the "to have" and establishes a "to be like" by identifying with Christ as the latter relates to his Father. His libidinal desires for his father are sublimated through his love for God the Father and his identification with Christ. The building up of the sublimation thus enabled him more readily to engage in social activities. Unfortunately, the sexual impulses were not fully sublimated but rather were only repressed to remain in the unconscious with the concurrent problem of their coming to consciousness from time to time.

We see the person struggling to move again from the "to have" (possession) toward a "to be like" (identification). With "Wolf Man", the religious experience points to an original sacred meaning which indicates that the person cannot possess the "Wholly Other" because He is totally Transcendent; he can only be aware of the "Wholly Other" as He manifests Himself through the world; and even then the "Wholly Other" cannot be possessed. The most man can do is "to be like" the "Wholly Other." Man is negated when he realizes that he cannot possess or be possessed by the "Wholly Other;" but out of the negation man becomes all the more self-conscious or, in other words, "like" the "Wholly Other"—a whole person. "Wolf Man" struggled to grasp reality the way it was; his unconscious conflicts forced him to make use of religious experience which marks the place of his struggle.

With the case of "Little Hans" we are not *directly* dealing with religious experience but we treat his case because of its important

140

relationship with totemism on the cultural level. What is accomplished by the transference of a fear for the father to a fear for an animal? What is most apparent is that by means of the substitution, the child is still able to enter into a relationship with his father. The fact that the animal becomes a substitute indicates the forward drive to maintain the familial relationship intact. At the same time it does aid in the giving up of the "to have" for the father, and still leaves open the possibility of the "to be like." The use of an animal in place of the father will be seen to take place in totemism which is involved in the drama of exchanging the "to have" for the "to be like." Totemism, besides being an effort to annihilate so as to possess the object fully, is also a shadow of the desire "to be like" the "Wholly Other." We will deal with this problem more fully when we treat religion on the cultural level.

In Haizmann's religious experience we again see a sublimation of his unconscious feelings for his father; there is a transition from the "to have" to a "to be like." The sexual desires that he had for his father could become transferential and thus his relationships with other persons would be colored by these unresolved conflicts. However, he works out the conflict with two father figures: the Devil (evil) and God (good). The "to have" becomes "to be like" in that he does not desire the Devil but rather wishes to be at his service or, in other words, to be like a devil. The same transformation takes place in regard to the fathers of the church who are God's representatives; they are like God because they are father figures and are called "Father." He gives up the "to have" in regard to the father and adopts a "to be like" by becoming a monk himself. Thus his religious experience bears witness to the *telos* operating in man's life. The process of sublimation is taking place which is always a sign of a forward movement because a lower drive is being replaced by a higher drive. Sexual libido is being withdrawn from objects and by repression turned into ego-libido and in the ego it is desexualized and sent out as a sublimation having a different aim; what is also achieved is a new identification which is a sign of a forward movement because possession is exchanged for recognition. Therefore, it is apparent that the religious experience analyzed points to or marks a forward movement: identification and sublimation.

We look deeper into this experience because of the employment of religious symbol. Here we have the overcoming of the "return of the repressed" which appears both as an evil father (Devil) and as a good father (God). It is really a God who accuses and a God who consoles and religious symbol, from the direction of genesis, points to these two features in God. Haizmann in his religious experience is struggling to overcome these two notions of God. The "Wholly Other" is outside of these categories which have been revealed, through reduction, as infantile wishes. However, the religious symbol at its teleological horizon points to the sacred. For Haizmann struggles to overcome and go beyond these infantile categories. He reaches out to a "Wholly Other" who will not only cease from accusing but who is not there for consolation. As he is engaged in the struggle, he has faith. Haizmann does not succeed. Therefore he is left with the religious symbols. But the moment of struggle to overcome the archaic and the religious gave us a glimpse of the sacred symbol which in turn shows us that the "Wholly Other" has approached. Faith is seen in Haizmann's struggle to reject the archaic religious forms; the rejection is not something completely negative; it is the negation of the infantile in himself. The rejection is really rooted in a movement toward something positive—the "Wholly Other."

With Dostoevsky we see his unconscious ambivalent feelings (murderous and loving) toward his father being transformed by an identification with Christ. What Dostoevsky accomplishes at least in part is a sublimation and identification. Some of the murderous impulses for the father are seen in his own self-inflicted sufferings (the neurotic symptoms). However, the feminine attitude toward his father is overcome by sublimating the original impulse into a love for Christ. This sublimation is aided through an identification; he gives up the "to have" and replaces it by a "to be like" and sees that he is identified with Christ because of their common sufferings. Christ was willing to suffer for the sake of the Father and Dostoevsky was really now accepting the same thing.

The only further point, which was not mentioned in the other cases, is the acceptance of the "Wholly Other" who allows us to *suffer*. Dostoevsky was not looking merely for a God of consolation. The moment of the acceptance of suffering is a yea saying to the "Wholly Other." It is an acceptance of creation as it reveals: life giving and death imparting. In the act of faith in the life and death forces of the universe, the symbol of the sacred emerges. The "Wholly Other" comes near both in the forces of Eros and Thanatos. Man alone in his heightened consciousness can utter acceptance. Through a reductionism of Dostoevsky's religious experience the infantile is seen and the sacred emerges.

Leonardo, the man of science, is important to Freud because he has overcome his neurosis by a perfect sublimation.[298] Thus he is free from neurosis and has thus transcended traditional religion. In place of the religious symptom there is revealed in the sublimation the ever clear emerging telos—the effort to understand reality more and more—reality being a manifestation of the "Wholly Other." He sees in nature, which is ever revealing, the source of all truth. Leonardo is not intimidated by past knowledge (the genetic) but knows it to be inadequate. He has contempt for religious experience which has been objectified or made part of the culture and insists that the "Wholly Other" is known by a continuous examination of creation. Leonardo did not stand before creation with a view clouded with his own wish fulfillment. At his teleological horizon or striving to grasp reality in its fullness ("Wholly Other") the sacred symbol is seen.

The cases we have seen were illustrative of the mechanisms employed by Freud which have an implicit teleology. However, the persons dealt with (except Leonardo) were all suffering from neuroses because the sublimation for one reason or another was not entirely successful. Religion, as we have seen, was reduced to the Oedipal complex; but it also stands as a marker of the struggle between genesis and telos. A further reduction of the religious manifestation revealed a symbol of the sacred. The religious neurosis thus may be seen as a rebirth of that which is archaic in the person—his Oedipal conflict; and at the same time there seems to emerge something which points beyond. The religious neurosis was not seen to be entirely explained in terms of its genesis because sublimation and identification had taken place. Sublimation in itself shows the two sides of the dialectic as it is determined by its past repressive forces in changing object-libido into ego-libido but it is also free in transforming that libido into another aim. The moment of freedom prevents sublimation from reductionism.

3. *Religious Symbol*

The cases we have discussed show the meeting of genesis and telos. We call symbol the point of their intersection. Thus symbol is a *concrete* moment which is seen in the dialectic.[299] The religious manifestation is thus taken as symbolic for it represents the coming together of two different sectors: the past and future. Symbol points in two directions: the past and the future and is captured in the present moment. Thus we see the religious symbol as both "regressive" and "progressive." We have seen in Freud's cases that the religious manifestation conceals what is really going on in our instinctive life but at the same time it can be made to reveal the dialectic of the two movements.

The religious symbol has taken into itself the past. In our cases, the unconscious conflicts are taken from the past and are actively influencing the present but at the same time they are being sublimated into something new. They are pointing beyond their genesis. The religious symbol becomes worn out when it is too much tied to the past—when it only shows a past phase of the dialectic. When we look at Freud's cases, the religious symbol could be seen as only being representative of past struggle. However, there is also the present moment. The person is involved in a psychic drama in himself and with others. As long as the religious symbol sustains the person himself and allows him more satisfactorily to relate to the other, the symbol is alive. True, one side points to the conflicts still raging but it reveals itself also as a progressive and integrating force. Since symbol helps to construct a world to which the person may relate, it is creative. When the symbol can no longer serve this function for the person, then it has become antiquated. It can no longer serve and must be replaced by another which emerges from the continuous dialectic of genesis and telos.

In regard to the religious neurosis seen as a symbol, it may be either taken so as to advance consciousness to a new understanding of itself or it may be merely a projection of one's conflicts. Thus the cases may be reviewed in either of two ways: the reductionist side merely shows us the archaic and the past; but can the religious neurosis be taken as symbol of one's personal synthesis and forward view? We believe that the cases can be seen from both angles. The religious symbol is alive because the cases all point to an attempt to come to terms with reality.

They all involve confrontations and are not so regressive as to have backed away entirely from the world. Rather they show the human response and solution given in the present moment. They are all engaged in the attempt at recovery as they endeavor to reconstruct reality. They therefore point to a need for rebuilding and restructuring. They clearly indicate the inadequacy of clinging to the past which was an escape from reality. The attempt at reconstruction not only shows the effort to face the present and the future but also to recreate it. It is a struggle in creation. The tighter the grip of the past, the less freedom is allowed in creating. The more dependent the persons were upon *genesis*, the more they created reality in their own image. The more they escaped from the past, the less they projected their own conflicts onto the religious symbol. Yet in all cases the symbol in its progressive direction points to creation.

In its transcendent aspect the "Wholly Other" is beyond the sphere of genesis and telos. However, the "Wholly Other" may annihilate its otherness and become immanent. In such event the "Wholly Other" as immanent may be understood in the dialectic of telos and genesis. The "Wholly Other" is seen at the horizon of the person's genesis and the horizon of his telos. "At the horizon of the person's genesis" means in the depths of his own being which goes beyond consciousness. "At the horizon of the person's telos" means the stretching of the mind out toward the infinite beyond. "Horizon is the metaphor for what approaches without ever becoming a possessed object."[300]

4. *Sacred Symbol*

When we come to deal with the *sacred* or that which has direct reference to the "Wholly Other," we go beyond our dialectic of genesis and telos. For our dialectic aimed not at faith but at knowledge which does not have to include a transcendence. The sacred would not be a part of our dialectic because we cannot have complete knowledge of it. Neither can symbol be *totally* understood or captured by our dialectic. Nevertheless, we can approach the sacred at the horizon of telos. Our dialectic is able to understand the meaning of a symbol which indicates a going further and further beyond. But we cannot *understand* the "Wholly Other."

Where we have the religious neurosis we are involved not only with

145

a reductionism but also with symbols of the sacred. In the ordinary neurosis we believe that there emerges a symbol at the point of union of the genesis and telos. The neurotic symptom is a symbol of suffering and struggle. It is the person struggling to be free from the past so as to grasp the present moment in its full revelation. The neurotic symptom points to the struggle: in one direction, (genesis), it shows the unconscious conflicts; in another direction (telos) it shows us a forward movement or effort to achieve self-consciousness. However, when we have a religious neurosis, we have an added dimension not found in the ordinary neurosis. We have a potential symbol of the sacred veiled by the religious. The symbols of the sacred are seen mixed in with the whole mechanism of the neurosis. These symbols of the sacred are something beyond what is contained in the neurosis. For they speak of God or the "Wholly Other." It is through our understanding of the dialectic of the neurosis that we have here become involved in sacred symbol.

In the cases we have examined we have always seen the movement toward an attempt at recovery. But it is interesting to note that at the intersection of the horizon of telos and genesis (i.e., where we look in both directions, the past and the future) we found not only a symbol of a forward movement but much more a religious symbol. We call it religious because it has been seen before and *used* before by many people. However, may we dare to call it a sacred symbol? Sacred symbol points to the "Wholly Other" as present and alive. Sacred symbol is viable; it is living; it has the ability to evoke faith; it is in the present moment taking us beyond. We would have to say that where the past was merely being relived and old solutions were being acted out again, we had only a religious symbol; religion marks the place where the "Wholly Other" long ago once came.

In our cases we have called the symptom religious and justifiably. For we find the persons entering into various relationships with God and sundry identifications with Christ. The degree of their dependence upon the past (regression) manifested itself in the degree of employment of the more archaic religious symbols. In the hierarchy of the religious symptoms we saw activated the various religious cultural forms of the *past*. These religious symbols have lost their relevance for contemporary man. However, their archaism is not to be ignored for there is meaning to be found in origins.

146

In regard to the gradual "return of the repressed," there is a gradual revealing of a past episode ever more clearly. However, the "return of the repressed" (Oedipal conflict), where it takes on the character of religious symbolism, is still a symbol to be overcome. It is only when that which was concealed is revealed that there is opportunity for overcoming it. The hierarchy of the religious neuroses shows a gradual revelation. The Oedipal conflict acted out in terms of a religious drama which in a way is analogous to the primal crime (murder of God the Father) may be taken as a religious symbol but not as a sacred symbol. It is religious because it is tied tightly to the past. It is solving a present problem by means of the employment of an archaic symbol. Where the person attempts to overcome the "return of the repressed" clothed in religious symbol, he has gone beyond religion to faith.

In the case of Leonardo, we need not engage in a reductive interpretation for his sublimations are complete. Also he has escaped from being a victim of the past i.e., he is not neurotic. His religious experience does not employ any of the *religious* symbols of the past but rather he confronts the universe with a faith which he does not allow to become objectified into religious form. In the very examination of creation he believed God to be revealed. Thus it would seem that the act of faith or yea saying to the cosmos as revelatory is a symbol of the sacred. To be able to see that creation is a sacred symbol of the "Wholly Other" who becomes immanent requires faith. If we could understand and know this teleological horizon, we would have knowledge; where it transcends us we have the sacred which is best approached by faith.

We are not able to see the signs of the coming of the "Wholly Other" unless we engage in a reductive interpretation.[301] Thus to understand the full significance of the cases dealing with religious neuroses, we must look in two directions. The religious symbol which is employed by the neurotic may seem archaic or the past resurrected. It is only through a reductionism that we see the religious symbol as the forward movement in the person's effort to solve the problem of coming to grips with reality—his affirmation of life—his yea saying to the cosmos. When the religious symbol was new and while it was bearing witness to the struggle of the person, it was sacred. The sacred points to the approach of the "Wholly Other" and faith is the "yea"

147

saying to that approach. Religion does not tell us of a coming approach but only a past visitation.

5. *Evolution in Awareness of "Wholly Other" as Other*

When the cases are seen in hierarchical order rather than individually, an evolution of the idea of the "Wholly Other" as other is revealed. With the American Physician the "Wholly Other" is not seen as distinct from himself but is rather a product of hallucination (a voice speaking to him). He and the "Wholly Other" are indistinguishable. There is no object-libido sent out to the other because the other is not seen as another. In the case of Schreber the "Wholly Other" is merely a projection of his own unconscious ideas. The "Wholly Other" can be seen as distinct from the self but not as different. The "Wholly Other" is merely another self. He is not seen as other.

With "Rat Man" and "Wolf Man" the "Wholly Other" can be seen distinctly as other but like the "American Physician" and Schreber they have not *fully* accepted the autonomy of the other. They still see the other in terms of possessing Him themselves. Thus they are not able to perceive completely that He is "Wholly Other."

In the case of Haizmann the "Wholly Other" is seen as distinct. But he seeks from the "Wholly Other" accusation and consolation. Thus he has not fully grasped that the "Wholly Other" is entirely other than a God of consolation and accusation. With Dostoevsky the "Wholly Other" is still the other to whom we look in order to be rewarded for our sufferings. The "Wholly Other" is not seen as other than a rewarder.

Finally, Leonardo has a fuller grasp of other as other and appreciates most the "Wholly Other." He looks at the "Wholly Other" as One who is neither to be possessed nor incorporated, and who is neither One who accuses nor consoles. He sees the "Wholly Other" as a Being who speaks through the World and to this vision he gives assent.

Thus our arrangement of the cases in this order shows how there is a gradation of difference in the person's experience of the "Wholly Other." With a greater ability to see other as other, one is better able to experience the approach of the "Wholly Other." One has the greater assurance that what has approached has not been self but other. In these cases there is also revealed the conflict of the reality principle and the pleasure principle; this conflict runs parallel to the emerging experience of other as other. Thus it is only when reality is seen as it is, without the distortion of illusion (which is a product of the pleasure principle), that one can grasp the approach of the "Wholly Other." The "Wholly Other" can approach clothed only in the garments of reality and not in the rags of illusion.

In this chapter we have seen Freud's reductive interpretation of religious experience which was principally of a neurotic type. At the core of the experience was the unresolved Oedipal conflict. An analysis of Freud's methodology shows that essentially his hypothesis is correct. Freud's reductionism prepares the way for the passing of religion seen as a projection of conflict and wish fulfillment. The hierarchy of the neuroses treated shows the gradual resolution of the conflict. We see a teleology in these neuroses; as taken together they mark a gradual victory of the reality principle over the pleasure principle. The religious neuroses taken separately and subjected to a reductive interpretation reveal a religious symbol which indicates that at one time the "Wholly Other" may have approached. However, since the neurotic is much influenced by the past (more or less dominated by the "return of the repressed") then his religious experience is a re-enactment of the archaic. He is not totally free to encounter the "Wholly Other" here and now because of his fixation to the past.

NOTES

[1]Chapter I

[2]Chapter II

[3]Freud (1912), "Types of Onset of Neuroses," XII, 236-37.

[4]We will not distinguish technically between neuroses and psychoses as Freud saw a continuity rather than a sharp break between the two.

[5]Freud (1911), "Psychoanalytic Notes on an Autobiographical Account of a Case of Paranoia," XII, 77.

[6]Freud, "Extracts from the Fliess Papers," Letter 125, 9 Dec. 1898, I, 280.

[7]Freud (1911), "Psychoanalytic Notes," p. 77.

"The most extreme type of this turning away from reality is shown by certain cases of hallucinatory psychosis which seek to deny the particular event that

149

occasioned the outbreak of their insanity." Freud (1911), "Formulations on the Two Principles of Mental Functioning," p. 218.

[8]Freud (1915), "The Metapsychological Supplement to the Theory of Dreams," XIV, 235.

[9]*Ibid.*

[10]*Ibid.*, p. 232.

[11]Freud (1927), "A Religious Experience," XXI, 170.

[12]*Ibid.*, XXI, 169.

[13]*Ibid.*

[14]*Ibid.*, p. 170.

[15]*Ibid.*, p. 171.

[16]*Ibid.*

[17]*Ibid.*, p. 171.

[18]*Ibid.*, p. 172.

[19]Freud (1913), "The Disposition to Obsessional Neurosis," XII, 318.

[20]Freud, "Extracts from the Fliess Papers," Letter 46 (30 May 1896), I, 231.

[21]Freud (1911), "Psychoanalytical Notes on an Autobiographical Case," XII, 68.

[22]Freud (1911), "Psychoanalytic Notes," XII, 62.

[23]*Ibid.*

[24]*Ibid.*, p. 72.

[25]Freud (1914), "On Narcissism: An Introduction," XIV, 76.

[26]Freud (1911), "Psychoanalytical Notes," XII, 71.

[27]Freud, "Extracts from the Fliess Papers—Draft K, The Neuroses of Defense (A Christmas Fairy Tale)," 1 Jan. 1896, I, 227.

[28]Freud (1896), "Further Remarks on the Neuro-Psychoses of Defense: An Analysis of a Case of Paranoia," III, 184.

[29]Freud (1911), "Psychoanalytical Notes," XII, 71.

[30]Freud, "Extracts from the Fliess Papers—Letter 125," (9 Dec. 1899), I, 280.

[31]Freud (1911), "Psychoanalytic Notes on an Autobiographical Account of a Case of Paranoia," XXI, 3-82.

[32]*Ibid.*, p. 13.

[33]*Ibid.*, p. 14.

[34]*Ibid.*, p. 38.

[35]*Ibid.*, p. 40.

[36]*Ibid.*, p. 14.

[37]*Ibid.*, p. 17.

[38]*Ibid.*, p. 19.

[39]*Ibid.*, p. 20.

[40]*Ibid.*, p. 22.

[41]*Ibid.*, p. 24.

[42]*Ibid.*, p. 25.
[43]*Ibid.*, p. 27.
[44]*Ibid.*, p. 28.
[45]*Ibid.*, p. 29.
[46]*Ibid.*, p. 30.
[47]*Ibid.*, p. 31.
[48]*Ibid.*, p. 32.
[49]Freud (1911), ''Psychoanalytical Notes,'' XII, 34.
[50]*Ibid.*, p. 42.
[51]*Ibid.*, p. 43.
[52]*Ibid.*, p. 44.
[53]*Ibid.*, p. 47.
[54]*Ibid.*, p. 48.
[55]*Ibid.*, p. 49.
[56]*Ibid.*, p. 50.
[57]*Ibid.*, p. 51.
[58]*Ibid.*, p. 52.
[59]*Ibid.*, p. 53.
[60]*Ibid.*, p. 54.
[61]*Ibid.*, p. 73.
[62]*Ibid.*, p. 77.
[63]Freud, *Inhibitions, Symptoms and Anxiety*, XX, 113.
[64]*Ibid.*, p. 113.
[65]Freud, *Introductory Lectures*, XVI, 344.
[66]Freud, *Inhibitions, Symptoms and Anxiety*, p. 114.
[67]*Ibid.*, p. 115.
[68]*Ibid.*, p. 128.
[69]Freud, *The Ego and the Id*, XIX, 54.
[70]Freud, *Inhibitions, Symptoms and Anxiety*, p. 117.
[71]*Ibid.*, p. 118.
[72]Freud (1896), ''Further Remarks on the Neuro-Psychoses of Defense,'' III, 170.
[73]*Ibid.*, p. 172.
[74]*Ibid.*, p. 173.
[75]Freud, *Totem and Taboo*, XIII, 30.
[76]Freud, *Inhibitions, Symptoms and Anxiety*, XX, 119.
[77]*Ibid.*, p. 116.
[78]Freud (1907), ''Obsessional Actions and Religious Practices,'' IX, 117.
[79]*Ibid.*, p. 118.
[80]*Ibid.*, p. 119.
[81]*Ibid.*

[82]*Ibid.*, p. 120.
[83]*Ibid.*, p. 123.
[84]*Ibid.*, p. 124.
[85]*Ibid.*, p. 125.
[86]*Ibid.*, p. 126.
[87]*Ibid.*
[88]*Ibid.*, p. 127.
[89]Freud (1909), ''Notes Upon a Case of Obsessional Neurosis,'' X, 163.
[90]*Ibid.*
[91]*Ibid.*, p. 226.
[92]*Ibid.*, p. 302.
[93]*Ibid.*, p. 236.
[94]*Ibid.*, p. 191.
[95]*Ibid.*, p. 193.
[96]*Ibid.*, p. 242.
[97]*Ibid.*, p. 243.
[98]Freud (1909), ''Notes Upon a Case of Obsessional Neurosis,'' X, 249.
[99]Freud (1914), ''An Infantile Neurosis,'' XVII, 61.
[100]*Ibid.*
[101]*Ibid.*
[102]*Ibid.*, p. 17.
[103]*Ibid.*, p. 62.
[104]*Ibid.*, p. 63.
[105]*Ibid.*
[106]*Ibid.*, p. 64.
[107]*Ibid.*
[108]*Ibid.*
[109]*Ibid.*, p. 65.
[110]*Ibid.*
[111]*Ibid.*
[112]*Ibid.*, p. 66.
[113]*Ibid.*
[114]*Ibid.*
[115]*Ibid.*, p. 87.
[116]*Ibid.*, p. 66.
[117]*Ibid.*, p. 67.
[118]*Ibid.*
[119]*Ibid.*, p. 68.
[120]*Ibid.*
[121]*Ibid.*, p. 117.
[122]*Ibid.*, p. 114.

[123] *Ibid.*, p. 115.

[124] Freud (1914), "An Infantile Neurosis," XVII, 115.

[125] *Ibid.*, p. 116.

[126] *Ibid.*, p. 117.

[127] *Ibid.*

[128] *Ibid.*, p. 70.

[129] *Ibid.*

[130] *Ibid.*, p. 71.

[131] *Ibid.*, p. 70.

[132] Freud (1894), "The Neuro-Psychoses of Defense," III, 54.

[133] Freud (1915), "The Unconscious," XIV, 183.

[134] Freud, *Inhibitions, Symptoms and Anxiety*, XX, 122.

[135] Freud, *Totem and Taboo*, XIII, 129.

[136] Freud (1909), "Analysis of a Phobia in a Five-Year-Old Boy," X, 8.

[137] *Ibid.*, p. 22.

[138] *Ibid.*, p. 24.

[139] *Ibid.*, p. 29.

[140] *Ibid.*, p. 42.

[141] *Ibid.*, p. 51.

[142] Freud, *Totem and Taboo*, XIII, 129.

[143] Freud, *Inhibitions, Symptoms and Anxiety*, XX, 106.

[144] *Ibid.*, p. 105.

[145] *Ibid.*, p. 106.

[146] *Ibid.*, p. 108.

[147] *Ibid.*, p. 109.

[148] Freud (1914), "From the History of an Infantile Neurosis," XVII, 16.

[149] *Ibid.*, p. 29.

[150] *Ibid.*, p. 40.

[151] *Ibid.*, p. 46.

[152] *Ibid.*, p. 112.

[153] *Ibid.*, p. 113.

[154] Freud (1915), "Repression," XIV, 155.

[155] Freud (1926), "Inhibitions, Symptoms and Anxiety," XX, 107.

[156] *Ibid.*, p. 108.

[157] Freud (1893), "On the Psychical Mechanism of Hysterical Phenomena: Case Histories," II, 31.

Freud (1893), "The Psychotherapy of Hysteria," II, 257.

[158] Freud, "Fliess Papers," Draft K: The Neuroses of Defense (A Christmas Fairy Tale), I, 228.

[159] Freud, "Sketches," I, 152.

[160] *Ibid.*, p. 153.

[161] *Ibid.*, p. 154.

[162] Freud, "Hysterical Phantasies and Their Relation to Bisexuality," IX, 163.

[163] Freud, "Fliess Papers," Letter 46 (30 May 1896), I, 230.

[164] Freud, "Neuro-Psychoses of Defense," III, 184.

[165] Freud, "The Psycho-Therapy of Hysteria," II, 297.

[166] Freud (1908), "Some General Remarks on Hysterical Attacks," IX, 233.

[167] Freud, "Psychical Mechanism of Hysterical Phenomena," II, 6.

[168] Freud, *Inhibitions, Symptoms and Anxiety*, XX, 93.

[169] Freud, *Introductory Lectures on Psycho-analysis*, XVI, 395-96.

[170] Freud, *Inhibitions, Symptoms and Anxiety*,, XX, 133.

[171] Freud, "Remembering," p. 150, n. 1. [Cf. Case of Dora (hysteric)].

[172] *Ibid.*

[173] *Ibid.*, p. 151.

[174] Freud, *The Interpretation of Dreams*, V, 544.

[175] Freud, "Fliess Papers," Letter 125 (9 Dec. 1899), I, 280.

[176] Freud (1931), "Libidinal Types," XXI, 220.

[177] Freud (1913), "Disposition to Obsessional Neurosis," XII, 319.

[178] Freud, *Introductory Lectures, XVI, 343.*

[179] *Freud, Inhibitions, Symptoms and Anxiety,* XX, 122.

[180] Freud, (1922), "A Seventeenth Century Demonological Neurosis," XIX, 79. ". . . we have good cause to be grateful to the clergy for having preserved the document [second part] although it added nothing to support the tenor of their views and, indeed, may rather have weakened it."

[181] *Ibid.*, p. 73.

[182] *Ibid.*, p. 74.

[183] *Ibid.*, p. 75.

[184] *Ibid.*, p. 76.

[185] *Ibid.*, p. 101.

[186] *Ibid.*

[187] *Ibid.*, p. 77.

[188] *Ibid.*, p. 78.

[189] *Ibid.*, p. 72.

[190] *Ibid.*, p. 79.

[191] *Ibid.*, p. 81.

[192] *Ibid.*, p. 82.

[193] *Ibid.*, p. 83.

[194] *Ibid.*, p. 84.

[195] *Ibid.*, p. 85.

[196] *Ibid.*, p. 86.

[197] It would seem that this division is more characteristic of paranoia rather than hysteria.

[198]Freud (1922), "A Seventeenth Century Demonological Neurosis," XIX, 86.

[199]*Ibid.*, p. 88.

[200]*Ibid.*, p. 90.

[201]*Ibid.*

[202]*Ibid.*, p. 91.

[203]*Ibid.*, p. 103.

[204]*Ibid.*, p. 104.

[205]*Ibid.*, p. 105.

[206]Freud (1927), "Dostoevsky and Parricide," XXI, 179.

[207]*Ibid.*, n. 2.

[208]*Ibid.*, p. 182.

[209]*Ibid.*

[210]*Ibid.*, n. 1.

[211]*Ibid.*

[212]*Ibid.*, p. 182.

[213]*Ibid.*, p. 183.

[214]*Ibid.*, p. 185.

[215]*Ibid.*

[216]Freud (1927), "Dostoevsky and Parricide," XXI, 187.

[217]*Ibid.* , p. 188.

[218]Freud (1910), "Leonardo da Vinci and a Memory of His Childhood," XI, 131.

[219]*Ibid.*, p. 87.

[220]*Ibid.*, p. 80.

[221]*Ibid.*, p. 90.

[222]*Ibid.*, p. 80.

[223]*Ibid.*, p. 122.

[224]*Ibid.*, p. 123.

[225]*Ibid.*

[226]*Ibid.*, p. 73.

[227]*Ibid.*, p. 124.

[228]*Ibid.*, p. 73.

[229]*Ibid.*, p. 75.

[230]*Ibid.*, p. 124.

[231]*Ibid.*, p. 125.

[232]Heintz Hartmann, "Psychoanalysis as a Scientific Theory," *Psychoanalysis, Scientific Method and Philosophy,* ed. by Sidney Hook (New York: New York University Press, 1959), p. 27.

[233]Wesley C. Salmon, "Psychoanalytic Theory and Evidence," *Psychoanalysis, Scientific Method and Philosophy,* p. 252.

[234]Ernst Kris, "The Nature of Psychoanalytic Propositions and Their Validation," *Freedom and Experience,* ed. by Sidney Hook and Milton R. Konvitz (New York: Cornell University Press, 1947), p. 249.

[235]*Ibid.,* p. 246.

[236]Leopold Bellak, "The Unconscious," *Conceptual and Methodological Problems in Psychoanalysis,* ed. by L. Bellak, *Annals of the New York Academy of Sciences,* LXXVI, Art. 4, (Jan. 1959), 412.

[237]Jacob A. Arlow, "Psychoanalysis as a Scientific Method," *Psychoanalysis, Scientific Method and Philosophy,* p. 203.

[238]Hartmann, "Psychoanalysis as a Scientific Theory," p. 21. Lawrence S. Kubie, "Psychoanalysis and Scientific Method," *Psychoanalysis, Scientific Method and Philosophy,* p. 66.

[239]Hartmann, "Psychoanalysis as a Scientific Theory," p. 22.

[240]Kubie, "Psychoanalysis and Scientific Method," p. 68. Kubie, "Problems and Techniques of Psychoanalytic Validation and Progress," *Psychoanalysis as Science,* ed. by Pumpian-Mindlin (New York: Basic Books, 1952), p. 123.

[241]Benjamin B. Rubinstein, "On the Inference and Confirmation of Clinical Interpretations," Presented in abbreviated form to the New York Psychoanalytic Society (28 May 1968), p. 2.

[242]Hartmann, "Comments on the Scientific Aspects of Psychoanalysis," *The Psychoanalytic Study of the Child,* XIII (New York: International Universities Press, Inc. 1958), 134.

[243]J. O. Wisdom, "The Criteria for Psychoanalytic Interpretation," *The Aristotelian Society Supplement,* No. 36 (London: Harrison and Sons, Ltd., 1962), p. 21.

[244]Hartmann, "Psychoanalysis as a Scientific Theory," p. 32.

[245]Rubinstein, "On the Inference and Confirmation of Clinical Interpretations," p. 3.

[246]*Ibid.,* p. 7.

[247]Fritz Schmidl, "The Problem of Scientific Validation in Psychoanalytic Interpretations," *International Journal of Psychoanalysis* (1955), p. 106.

[248]Roland Dalbiez, *Psychoanalytical Method and the Doctrine of Freud,* trans. by T.F. Lindsay, II (London: Longmans Green & Co., 1941), 106.

[249]Salmon, "Psychoanalytic Theory and Evidence," p. 256.

[250]Dalbiez, *Psychoanalytical Method and the Doctrine of Freud,* p. 109.

[251]*Ibid.,* p. 112.

[252]Ernest Hutten, "An Explanation in Psychology and in Physics," *British Journal for the Philosophy of Science,* VIII (1956-57), 74.

[253]Robert Waelder, "Psychic Determinism and the Possibility of Prediction," *Psychoanalytic Quarterly* (1963), p. 29.

[254]*Ibid.*, p. 40. Raphael Demos, "Psychoanalysis: Science and Philosophy", *Psychoanalysis, Scientific Method and Philosophy*, p. 330.

[255]Robert E. Silverman, "Psychoanalysis and Scientific Method," p. 306.

[256]Rubinstein, "On the Inference and Confirmation of Clinical Interpretations," p. 31.

[257]*Ibid.*, p. 15. Rudolf Ekstein, "Thoughts Concerning the Nature of the Interpretive Process," *Readings in Psychoanalytic Psychology*, ed. By Morton Levitt (New York: Appleton-Century-Crofts, Inc., 1959), p. 230.

[258]Hartmann, "Psychoanalysis as a Scientific Theory," p. 22.

[259]*Ibid.*

[260]Hutten, "An Explanation in Psychology and in Physics," p. 73.

[261]*Ibid.*, p. 77.

[262]J. O. Wisdom, "Testing a Psychoanalytic Interpretation," *Ratio*, VIII, No. 1 (June 1966), 65.

[263]*Ibid.*, p. 66.

[264]*Ibid.*, p. 67.

[265]Wisdom, "Psychoanalytic Technology," *British Journal for the Philosophy of Science*, VII, No. 25 (May 1956), 23.

[266]John Hospers, "Philosophy and Psychoanalysis," *Psychoanalysis, Scientific Method and Philosophy*, p. 342.

[267]Joseph Nuttin, *Psychoanalysis and Personality* (London: Sheed and Ward, 1954), p. 67.

[268]Freud (1912), Totem and Taboo, XIII, 100. Freud (1907), "Obsessive Actions and Religious Practices," IX, 119.

[269]Freud (1927), *The Future of an Illusion*, XXI, 43.

[270]Nagel, "Methodological Issues in Psychoanalytic Theory," p. 53.

[271]Nagel, "Methodological Issues in Psychoanalytic Theory," p. 53. Edwin G. Boring, *A History of Experimental Psychology* (New York: Appleton-Century-Crofts, Inc., 1950), p. 713.

[272]Kris, "The Nature of Psychoanalytic Propositions and Their Validation," p. 248.

[273]Nagel, "Methodological Issues," p. 49. Kennedy, "Psychoanalysis: Protoscience and Metapsychology," p. 272.

[274]Leopold Bellak and M. Brewster Smith, "An Experimental Exploration of the Psychoanalytic Process," *Psychoanalytic Quarterly*, XXV, (1956), 386.

[275]*Ibid.*

[276]Kennedy, "Psychoanalysis: Protoscience and Metapsychology," p. 274.

[277]Kubie, "Psychoanalysis and Scientific Method," p. 70.

[278]*Ibid.*, p. 71.

[279]Nagel, "Methodological Issues," p. 49. Michael Martin, "The Scientific

Status of Psychoanalytic Clinical Evidence," *Inquiry,* VII (Spring 1964), 16.
Markus Reiner, "Causality and Psychoanalysis," *Psychoanalytic Quarterly,* I (1932), 714.

[280]Bjorn Christiansen, "The Scientific Status of Psychoanalytical Clinical Evidence III," *Inquiry,* VIII (Spring 1964), 55.

[281]Kubie, "Psychoanalysis and Scientific Method," p. 71.

[282]Philip Rieff, *Freud: The Mind of the Moralist,* p. 293.

[283]Ernest Van den Haag, "Psychoanalysis and its Discontents," p. 113. It is to be noted that we do not take this criticism to apply to the cases of "Rat Man" or "Wolf Man" who were live patients.

[284]Ida Macalpine and R.A. Hunter, "The Schreber Case," *Psychoanalytic Quarterly,* XXII (July-October 1953), 328-371.

[285]William G. Niederland, "Further Data and Memorabilia Pertaining to the Schreber Case," *International Journal of Psychoanalysis,* XLIV, No. 2 (April 1963), 201.

[286]Macalpine and Hunter, *Schizophrenia 1677* (London: William Dawson & Sons, Limited, 1956), p. 104.

[287]Freud (1922), "A Seventeenth Century Demonological Neurosis," XIX, 87.

[288]*Ibid.,* p. 88.

[289]Macalpine and Hunter, *Schizophrenia 1677,* pp. 94, 102, 110, 115.

[290]Freud (1910), "Leonardo," XI, 135.

[291]*Ibid.*

[292]Meyer Schapiro, "Leonardo and Freud," *Journal of the History of Ideas,* XVII, No. 2 (April 1956), 177.

[293]*Ibid.,* p. 178.

[294]*Ibid.*

[295]T. W. Gervais, "Freud and the Culture-Psychologists," *British Journal of Psychology,* XLVI (Nov. 1955), 294.

[296]Literally made into a *thing.*

[297]Cf. Chapter II, p. 72 for philosophical discussion of "to have" and "to be like."

[298]Cf. Supra, Chapter II, p. 73.

[299]Ricoeur, *Freud and Philosophy,* p. 495.

[300]*Ibid.,* p. 526.

[301]*Ibid.,* p. 530.

Chapter IV

The Origins of Religion: Genesis and Telos

In this fourth chapter we trace the *origins* of religion. To show the continuity with Chapter Three, we first discuss briefly Freud's own analogy of the early trauma (Oedipus complex) in the life of the neurotic and the prehistoric trauma of the race (the primal crime). Then we trace the "return of the repressed" as it shows itself in pre-animism, animism, taboo, totemism, monotheism, and finally the race acting out (like the hysteric) what it cannot remember having done: deicide (the crucifixion of Christ). To appreciate *fully* the analogy the work of Chapter Three will need to be borne in mind, as its development runs parallel to Chapter Four. After the exposition of Freud's ideas, we will make a philosophical critique of the methodology employed and then a philosophical analysis of the underlying principles involved. Both of these analyses will be from the perspective of the philosophy of science.

In this study we will again find a certain reductionism: man's religious experience is traced back to the primal crime just as we saw individual religious experience traced back to the Oedipus complex. Again a reduction to origins is only a preliminary step to seeing a deeper meaning in the experience. There is the teleological side of Freud, too; the evolution we trace is a movement from the "pleasure principle" to the "reality principle." We must not fail to remember that the evolution of religion is a history of man's attempt to come to grips with reality. Religion expresses man's attempt to explain the ultimate meaning of the cosmos as it reveals itself to him. Thus while Freud may show, by means of reductionism, that man has been incorrect in his perceptions and motivated by infantile wishes (reaction to the primal crime), we are still left with man trying to integrate his previous experiences with the reality that stands before him. Man comes to that reality with his own tragic history (the primal crime) and his limitations in psychic development due to the particular stage of human evolution at which he lives. However, we go on to develop the notion that the evolution of the race's religious experience still bears witness to man's struggle to encounter that which is "Wholly Other." From the history of mankind we see a less and less distorted view of the "Wholly Other" emerge. We accept Freud's reductionism only to go on to develop the implicit teleology of his thought. Engaging in a negative theology we remove the inadequate and anthropomorphic ideas which have surrounded the "Wholly Other." The gradual evolution of less distorted views we see as teleological.

A. *Analogy of the Development of Neurosis (Individual) and Religion (Race)*

1. *The Analogy*

Freud maintains that ". . . religious phenomena are only to be understood on the pattern of the individual neurotic symptoms familiar to us—as important events in the primaeval history of the human family—and that they have to thank precisely this origin for their compulsive character and that accordingly, they are effective on human beings by force of the historical truth of their content."[1] In early religion the religious phenomenon is bound up with the ancient history of the family. Religion shows the return of the events of the past after an interval of time in which the events were forgotten.[2]

a. *Trauma.* Freud attempts to draw an analogy between the primal crime with its resulting religious manifestations (a group phenomenon) and neuroses (an individual phenomenon); and he feels the analogy approaches an "identity." In both phenomena there is a traumatic event which is forgotten, a latency period, and the appearance of "unintelligible manifestations" which are compulsive. He states that "We shall see that this analogy is not so surprising as might at first be thought—indeed it is more like a postulate." A trauma is an experience which produces an abnormal reaction in some but not in others (the normal) who adjusted to it satisfactorily.[3] We are

160

not restricting traumatic to a particular extraordinary experience but to any experience that could not be handled in the normal way. The experiences relate to matters of sex and/or aggression[4] which usually occur up to the age of five. The effects of traumas are of two kinds: positive and negative. The positive reaction is to bring the trauma into action anew—to repeat the original relationship which is described as a fixation to the trauma or "compulsion to repeat."[5] The negative but more common reaction to the trauma is to forget which leads to avoidances, inhibitions and phobias.[6]

b. *Latency.* The trauma is usually followed by a latency period during which the defenses usually control the situation but a scar is left. Freud feels that the neurosis, which is the *manifest* effect of the trauma, is only rarely completely interrupted. It seems to be latent aided by physiological latency but at puberty the neurosis usually erupts. The instincts have been intensified again and take up the fight against the defenses. There is really an attempt at cure: the ego tries to reunite those portions that have been split off by the original trauma.[7] Where the defenses fail we have the "return of the repressed." According to the type of personality and the strength of the defenses, the "repressed" will appear in various disguises. The "return of the repressed" may reappear as an hallucination (dementia praecox), projection (paranoia), compulsion (obsessions), fear (phobia), or acting out of the very memory (hysteria).

c. *Return of the Repressed.* In the neuroses we have seen the trauma, a defense made, a latency period, the outbreak of neurosis and finally a "return of the repressed" with some distortion. We are now asked by Freud to "suppose" that what has taken place on the individual level took place in the human race i.e., an episode of either a sexual or aggressive nature (specifically the murder of the father) which left behind its effects and was forgotten and then after a time (latency) returned in the form of symptoms. These symptoms would serve the same purpose as those of the neuroses; namely, protection against the "return of the repressed." "We believe that we can guess these events and we propose to show that their symptom-like consequences are the phenomena of religion." Evolution shows that man has a pre-history which is unknown or forgotten.[8] It was in the pre-history of man that the primal crime occurred and on the analogy of the neurosis it was forgotten. Freud based his "construction" of a

161

forgotten primal crime on a "statement" of Darwin and an "hypothesis" of Atkinson. "We must also accept the hypothesis that the events to be described 'occurred to all primitive men. . . .' "[9] Freud remarked that since primitives are like children, they would have had very intense Oedipal wishes.

> The essential point, however, is that we attribute the same emotional attitudes to these primitive men that we are able to establish by analytic investigation in the primitives of the present day—in our children. We suppose, that is, that they not only hated and feared their father but also honoured him as a model, and that each of them wished to take his place in reality.[10]

After the primal crime the event was forgotten; there was a period of latency in which the event was not recalled. However, Freud claimed the memory of the event was "inherited" by all mankind and the inherited memory could be awakened by events that might occur in subsequent generations. Man's history shows the gradual "return of the repressed." As neurosis marks the distorted attempt of the return of the trauma, religion marks the distorted return of the repressed memory of the primal crime. We see the return through pre-animism, animism, taboo, totemism and finally monotheism.

2. Difficulties in the Analogy

Freud considered some difficulties in the analogy. He felt that the analogy between neurotic behavior and religious events might seem inadequate because he considered only one case (monotheism) from "the copious phenomenology of religions." He has not explained the others. However, he believed that the founding of the Mohammedan religion was like a shortened form of the Jewish religion. "The recapture of the single great primal father brought the Arabs an extraordinary exaltation of their self-confidence, which led to great worldly successes but exhausted itself in them." But the interior spirit of the Mohammedan religion came to an end perhaps because it lacked the depth of the Jewish religion whose founder was murdered.[11] The religions of the East are essentially ancestor worship and terminate at "an early stage of the reconstruction of the past." Primitives today whose only religion seems to be the acknowledgement of a supreme being, we regard as an "atrophy of religious development."[12]

Freud pointed to another problem in his analogy: the way in which a tradition operates among a people. He maintained that the memory of the primal crime had left its trace upon humanity and each generation inherited the memory. Given the proper event this past memory could be activated for a whole group of people.[13] Freud was aware of the biological view which was opposed to the theory of acquired characteristics.

> My position, no doubt, is made more difficult by the present attitude of biological science, which refuses to hear of the inheritance of acquired characteristics by succeeding generations. I must, however, in all modesty confess that nevertheless I cannot do without this factor in biological evolution.
>
> If we assume the survival of these memory-traces in the archaic heritage, we have bridged the gulf between individual and group psychology: we can deal with peoples as we do with an individual neurotic. Granted that at the time we have no stronger evidence for the presence of memory-traces in the archaic heritage than the residual phenomena of the work of analysis which call for a phylogenetic derivation, yet this evidence seems to us strong enough to postulate that such is the fact. If it is not so, we shall not advance a step further along the path we entered on, either in analysis or in group psychology. The audacity cannot be avoided.[14]

Freud believed that a memory became part of the archaic heritage if the experience connected with it was significant enough and repeated frequently. The forgotten memory of the primal crime could have been revived as in the murder of Moses and Christ. "It seems as though the genesis of monotheism could not do without these occurrences." No mere simple event of the past could give to religion its compulsive quality.[15] Freud justified his methodology involved in the questionable *analogy* between neurosis and mankind's religion by saying that certain factors must be accepted without sufficient evidence because of the "outcome" to be achieved in the study.[16]

If we are clear in our mind that a procedure like ours of accepting what seems to us serviceable in the material presented to us and of rejecting what does not suit us and of putting the different pieces together in accordance with psychological probability—if we are clear that a technique of this kind can give no certainty that we shall arrive at the truth, then it may justly be asked why we are undertaking this work at all. The answer is an appeal to the work's outcome. If we greatly tone down the strictness of the requirements made upon a historico-psychological investigation, it will perhaps be possible to throw light on problems which have always seemed to deserve attention and which recent events have forced upon our observation anew."[17]

Freud's analogy between the individual's reaction to the Oedipus complex and the race's reaction to the primal crime allows us to see the evolution of religious form as a gradual "return of the repressed." We will trace the various forms of religion as they have seemed to evolve from the earliest days of man. Since "in the beginning was the deed," the religious phenomena would be man's reaction to this primal crime; the religious manifestation will vary over the course of time because of the variation in man's cultural and mental development. Yet these developments show similar variation as do the neuroses i.e., with time man has given up his initial belief in the omnipotence of his own thoughts; he has gradually sacrificed the pleasure principle (illusions) for the reality principle. The hierarchy of the neuroses, moving from the most to the least severe, has given greater prominence to the reality principle ("the normal") to the diminution of the pleasure principle. As we traced the neuroses, we saw ever more clearly (lesser distortion) the "return of the repressed." As we trace the origins of religion, we should not be surprised to find that over the course of time, the "return of the repressed" manifests itself ever more clearly unto its very acting out. (What the neurotic refuses to remember, he feels compelled to act out.) We should not be surprised, for "ontogeny recapitulates phylogeny."

B. *Exposition of the Evolution of Religion From Its Origins: Genesis*
In tracing the origins of religion, Freud made use of contemporary

164

primitives as having the same mentality as man in his beginnings; he indicated that contemporary primitive men are direct heirs of pre-historic man and that savages have a "well-preserved picture of an early stage of our own development." If this is so, then the psychology of primitive peoples and the psychology of neurotics will have many points of agreement.[18] Later he questioned ". . . whether we should regard the present state of things as a true picture of the significant features of the past or as a secondary distortion of them."[19]

If we may regard the existence among primitive races of the omnipotence of thoughts as evidence in favour of narcissism, we are encouraged to attempt a comparison between the phases in the development of men's view of the universe and the stages of an individual's libidinal development. The animistic phase would correspond to narcissism both chronologically and in its content; the religious phase would correspond to the stage of object-choice of which the characteristic is a child's attachment to his parents; while the scientific phase would have an exact counterpart in the stage at which an individual has reached maturity, has renounced the pleasure principle, adjusted himself to reality, and turned to the external world for the object of his desires.[20]

1. *Animism*

Freud saw the development of civilization as moving away from narcissism to a fuller cognizance of the real world. "Omnipotence of thoughts" is the phrase which he used to indicate man considering his thoughts more powerful than the real world. Primitive man (like the neurotic) paid too much attention to his thoughts at the cost of lacking an awareness of external reality.[21] In the evolution of world views (animistic, religious, scientific) there has been a progressive decrease in the "omnipotence of thoughts." In the animistic phase men attributed omnipotence to themselves. In the religious phase some of the omnipotence was given to the gods. In the scientific phase there is no longer any room for the omnipotence of man because he realizes his smallness and submits to the way of nature. Still a little of man's omnipotence remains even here, where he believes he can master the laws of reality.[22] According to Freud, in primitive men the process of thinking was to a great extent sexualized which gave rise to their belief in "omnipotence of thoughts" and their confidence in controlling the world regardless of reality. And this primitive attitude has continued in neurotics. "Where libido has not been cathected around objects, it remains attached to the ego."[23]

a. *Pre-animism*

Magic is analogous to autoerotism and hallucination. Both the stage of pre-animism and *magic* are somewhat analogous to the auto-erotic phase because the ideas which are imagined have escaped reality testing; they are like hallucinations. The earliest cultural display of the "omnipotence of thoughts" is seen in the primitive assumptions of magic which are older than animism. Magic clearly shows the intention of imposing the laws of mental life upon external reality[24] for ideas are taken for reality. Magic makes use of special procedures and not psychological methods of placation as in sorcery. Thus it seems that magic could have been used before the spiritualization or personification of Nature. Magic must subject natural phenomena to the will of man[25] and an *ideal* connection is taken for a *real* one[26] e.g., certain acts are performed which are *similar* to the expected results as in rain dances.[27] "Relations which hold between the ideas of things are assumed to hold equally between the things themselves. Since distance is of no importance in thinking—since what lies furthest apart both in time and space can without difficulty be comprehended in a single act of consciousness—so, too, the world of magic has a telepathic disregard for spacial distance and treats past situations as though they were present."[28]

It seems that primitive man had great belief in the power of his wishes; what comes to be is due to his will. The primitives, in their magic, made use of an "analogous" psychical situation which children employ[29]; for infants satisfy their wishes through "hallucination."[30] ". . . whatever was thought of (wished for) was simply presented in a hallucinatory manner, just as still happens to-day with our dream-thoughts every night. It was only the non-occurrence of the expected satisfaction, the disappointment experienced, that led to the abandonment of this attempt at satisfaction by means of hallucination."[31]

b. *Animism Proper*

In animism the world view constructed is analogous to paranoia;

however, a greater awareness of reality is seen. "Animism is, in its narrower sense, the doctrine of souls, and, in its wider sense, the doctrine of spiritual beings in general."[32] Primitives regarded spirits and demons as the cause of natural phenomena; both animals, plants and inanimate objects were possessed.[33]

Animism is a system of thought. It does not merely give an explanation of a particular phenomenon, but allows us to grasp the whole universe as a single unity from a single point of view. The human race, if we are to follow the authorities, has in the course of ages developed three such systems of thought—three great pictures of the universe: animistic (or mythological), religious and scientific. Of these, animism, the first to be created, is perhaps the one which is most consistent and exhaustive and which gives a truly complete explanation of the nature of the universe. The first human *Weltanschauung* is a psychological theory.[34]

Spirits are projections of our inner psychic life. At the animistic stage there was not one supreme spirit that created and maintained the lesser spirits. One could turn for help and protection to any one particular spirit. The way primitive man experienced his own self or being, he pictured the outside world to be. Thus he imposed the structure of his own mind upon the outside world. We can understand what the workings of the primitive mind were by taking the external reality they created and putting it back into the human mind.[35]

There is an intellectual function in us which demands unity, connection and intelligibility from any material, whether of perception or thought, that comes within its grasp; and if, as a result of special circumstances, it is unable to establish a true connection, it does not hesitate to fabricate a false one. Systems constructed in this way are known to us not only from dreams, but also from phobias, from obsessive thinking and from delusions. The construction of systems is seen most strikingly in delusional disorders (in paranoia), where it dominates the symptomatic picture. . . . Thus a system is best characterized by the fact that at least two reasons can be discovered for each of its

167

products; a reason based upon the premises of the system (a reason, then, which may be delusional) and a concealed reason, which we must judge to be the truly operative and the real one.[36]

In point of fact I believe that a larger part of the mythological view of the world, which extends a long way into the most modern religions, is nothing but psychology projected into the external world. The obscure recognition (the endopsychic perception, as it were) of psychical factors and relations in the unconscious is mirrored—it is difficult to express it in other terms, and here the analogy[37] with paranoia must come to our aid—in the construction of a supernatural reality, which is destined to be changed back once more by science into the psychology of the unconscious. One could venture to explain in this way the myths of paradise and the fall of man, of God, of good and evil, of immortality, and so on, and to transform metaphysics into metapsychology. The gap between the paranoic's displacement and that of the superstitious person is less wide than it appears at first sight. When human beings began to think, they were, as is well known, forced to explain the external world anthropomorphically by means of a multitude of personalities in their own image; choice events, which they interpreted superstitiously, were thus actions and manifestations of persons. They believed, therefore, just like paranoics, who draw conclusions from insignificant signs given them by other people, and just like all normal people, who quite rightly base their estimate of their neighbors' characters on their chance and unintentional actions. It is only in our modern, scientific but as yet by no means perfected *Weltanschauung* that superstition seems so very much out of place; in the *Weltanschauung* of pre-scientific times and peoples it was justified and consistent.[38]

Projection played the important part in the way the primitive mind functioned. The projecting outwards of internal perceptions is a primitive mechanism and plays a big part in determining the form of the *external* world. ". . . internal perceptions of emotional and thought processes can be projected outwards in the same way as sense perceptions; they are thus employed for building up the external world, though they should by rights remain part of the internal world."[39] When contemporary man as well as the primitives project something into external reality the following happens. First, there are two states—that which is directly given to the senses (conscious material) and that which is *capable* of appearing (unconscious material).[40] Spirits then are something remembered and imagined after perception of them is terminated and then projected outwards;[41] spirits and demons are projections of man's own inner impulses.[42] The thought that the first spirits were evil ones is explained by the idea of outwardly projecting the internal evil impulses toward someone; and upon that person's death, we might be frightened because they could return to threaten us as hostile spirits.[43] With the creation of spirits man has given up some of his omnipotence and freedom of action. Thus animism, in spite of its basic narcissism, would be a step in man's acknowledgement of ANANKE (Necessity) or the reality principle.[44]

2. *Taboo*

a. *Taboo analogous to obsessional neurotic and anal stage.* The race of man, at one phase, had a psychic development which resembled that of the *obsessional* neurotic and the child's *anal* phase.[45] "It [Folklore] also demonstrates the persistent and indeed ineradicable nature of coprophilic interests, by displaying to our astonished gaze the multiplicity of applications—in magical ritual, in tribal customs, in observances of religious cults . . . by which the old esteem for human excretions has found new expression . . . the human infant is obliged to recapitulate during the early part of his development the changes of the attitude of the human race . . ."[46] It is characteristic of primitives also to be influenced by narcissism in their object-choice. However, the object chosen is not themselves, as in primary narcissism, but an object seen as another self.

Corresponding to the obsessional neurosis we have the primitive phenomenon of *taboo* which refers to something as being sacred and also forbidden. ". . . 'taboo' has about it a sense of something unapproachable, and it is principally expressed in prohibitions and restrictions."[47] Certain people are said to have 'mana' or power surrounding their person e.g., priests and chiefs. They are therefore taboo.[48] "The taboos on animals, which consist essentially of prohibitions against killing and eating them, constitute the nucleus of *Totemism*."[49] A violation of a taboo usually enacted an internal and automatic punishment on the part of the violator. The dangers arising out of the prohibition's violation might be avoided by atonement and purification ceremonial; the transmissiblity of the taboo accounts for the attempts to remove it by purificatory rites.[50]

People have created for themselves "taboo prohibitions" and adhere to them as strictly as the savages obey the taboos of their society. Thus the name "obsessional" and "taboo sickness" could be used for the obsessional neurotic. Having explored obsessional neurosis psychoanalytically (Chapter III), one might be tempted to apply this knowledge to the "parallel sociological phenomenon."

A warning must be uttered at this point. The similarity between taboo and obsessional sickness may be no more than a matter of externals; it may apply only to the forms in which they are manifested and not extend to their essential character. Nature delights in making use of the same forms in the most various biological connections: as it does, for instance, in the appearance of branch-like structures both in coral and in plants, and indeed in some forms of crystal and in certain chemical precipitates. It would obviously be hasty and unprofitable to infer the existence of any internal relationship from such points of agreement as these, which merely derive from the operation of the same mechanical causes. We shall bear this warning in mind, but we need not be deterred by it from proceeding with our comparison.[51]

b. *Comparison of taboos and obsessional prohibition.*

The *first* point of agreement between taboo and obsessional neurosis is that the prohibitions are lacking in "assignable motive." The origin of the prohibitions is unknown. The *second* point of agreement is that the prohibitions *presently* are maintained by an internal necessity as there is no threat of external punishment. The *third* point: ". . . the prohibitions are easily displaceable and that there is a risk of infection from the prohibited object . . ."[52] Physical touching is prohibited but more—even the thinking about the object in question is taboo. The *fourth* point: the prohibitions give rise to commands for the carrying out of ceremonial acts. Obsessional neurotics impose upon themselves prohibitions, renunciations and restrictions

170

to a similar extent as those involved in taboo. But the prohibitions may be removed if certain actions are carried out.[53] Because of the apparent similarity between taboo and obsessional neurosis, Freud proposed the "experiment" of treating a taboo *as if* it were of the same nature as an obsessional prohibition. Since taboos may have suffered from displacement and distortion, we must be satisfied with only a little insight into them. "Moreover, the difference between the situation of a savage and of a neurotic are no doubt of sufficient importance to make any exact agreement impossible and to prevent our carrying the comparison to the point of identity in every detail."[54] Freud indicated that it would be worthless to ask the savages for reasons why they have specific prohibitions or taboos. They cannot answer because, according to psychoanalytic postulates, the reasons are unconscious. Freud mentioned that he could demonstrate that taboo began as a primaeval prohibition given by an external authority; instead he tried to confirm the psychological factors which determine taboo.

He indicated that the mechanisms of neurosis were arrived at through the analytical study of symptoms, obsessional acts, defensive measures and obsessional commands.[55] These factors came about as a result of both a wish and counter-wish or ambivalent impulses. What he proposed was a demonstration of *ambivalence*—or simultaneous expression of both currents in taboo phenomena. Then "we should have established the psychological agreement between taboo and obsessional neurosis in what is perhaps their most important feature."

Freud selected certain taboos for his investigation which were taken from Frazer: taboos attaching to the dead chiefs, and enemies.[56] There is emotional ambivalence toward the enemy for while he may be killed, he is also mourned.[57] The savage considered his chief as possessing great power to be guarded and guarded against[58] and therefore ceremonials associated with kings display an ambivalence. Through the ceremonial the king is exalted but at the same time intense discomfort is brought to him. In obsessional neurosis "suppressed impulse and the impulse that suppresses it find simultaneous and common satisfaction."[59] "In exactly the same way, the ceremonial taboo of kings is *ostensibly* the highest honour and protection for them, while *actually* it is a punishment for their exaltation, a revenge taken on them by their subjects."[60]

171

The savages had a taboo upon names because they regarded the name as the essence of the man's personality. They treat words as things; this is also true of neurotics.[61] Therefore the savages avoid using the name of the dead person and perform ceremonials to keep his ghost at a distance.[62] This same sort of ambivalence is characteristic of obsessional neurotics.[63] Projection may be at play here also: unconscious hostile feelings that a person has toward the dead are projected out so that it appears that the dead are out to do harm.[64] "Accordingly, there follow the repression of the unconscious hostility by the method of projection and the construction of the ceremonial which gives expression to the fear of being punished by demons."

At this point, Freud was satisfied with showing the ambivalent attitude of the primitives toward enemies, rulers and the dead and the protective measures taken to ward off the impulses. Here he claimed we had a feature which marks the life of the obsessional neurotic most clearly.

"... *the psychical impulses of primitive peoples were characterized by a higher amount of ambivalence than is to be found in modern civilized man. It is to be supposed that as this ambivalence diminished, taboo (a symptom of the ambivalence and a compromise between the two conflicting impulses) slowly disappeared.* Neurotics, who are obliged to reproduce the struggle and the taboo resulting from it, may be said to have inherited an archaic constitution and an atavistic vestige."[65]

Ambivalence indicates a lack of resolution of some complex and we have seen clearly that this was the Oedipal conflict for neurotics. It is only in the study of totem that it will become apparent that the same psychic forces are at work in the savage as in the neurotic. It remains to be shown that the *ambivalent* attitude toward the tribal totem—worship and destruction—is an acting out on the conscious level of the unconscious attitudes towards the father. Ceremonial and ritual, both in neurotic and savage, serve the purpose of alleviating the guilt coming from unconscious hatred. When the hostility goes beyond the unconscious and savage taboos are violated (or self-imposed prohibitions broken as in the neurotic) expiatory ceremonial and ritual again follow.

3. Gods and Their Surrogates

a. *Totemism.* Freud was interested in the two taboo prohibitions of totemism; namely, not to kill the totem animal and not to marry (exogamy) within the totem clan for these phenomena will be directly related to the primal crime. But first we must understand totemism. Freud believed that totemism was a transitional stage between the time of primitive man and the time of heroes and gods. In totemism, certain animals are neither killed nor eaten. If the animal accidentally dies it is mourned like a clan member. If necessity forces the animal to be killed, expiation is made to it; it is bewailed when it is a ritual sacrifice. Skins of the animal are worn and the clan takes the name of the animal which protects the clan that believes it is related to the animal by common ancestry.[66] In the study of totemism Freud warned that there might be problems in the collection of data by travellers and missionaries and the subsequent interpretation by students who are already set in what they are looking for. Also, savages do not always tell all; we are not sure if the material gathered is really ancient or rather recent distortions and modifications.[67]

If we seek to penetrate to the original nature of totemism, without regard to subsequent accretions or attenuations, we find that its essential characteristics are these: *Originally, all totems were animals, and were regarded as the ancestors of the different clans. Totems were inherited only through the female line. There was a prohibition against killing the totem* (or—which, under primitive conditions, is the same thing—against eating it). *Members of a totem clan were forbidden to practice sexual intercourse, with one another.*[68]

Where we find totemism there is usually a prohibition of marriage for members of the totem to each other.[69] Savage life is also marked by the "horror of incest"; much time and effort is spent in setting up measures of defense against incest. Freud believed that a satisfactory explanation of totemism should embody both historical and psychological elements which indicate the circumstances under which the institution developed and the psychical needs it expresses.[70] Freud mentioned that almost any generalization about totemism and exogamy is open to question; he admitted that he could also be

173

criticized for selecting Frazer's account as expressing "the present writer's arbitrary preferences." Further, Frazer changed his original account and it was the original which Freud continued to use believing that if one got to the genesis of the two institutions (totemism and exogamy) then one would have a better idea of their essential nature.[71] However, he realized that primitive peoples might not have retained the *original forms* of these institutions; the *conditions* which gave rise to them may be gone ". . . so that we have nothing whatever but hypotheses to fall back upon as a substitute for the observations which we are without."[72]

Some of the attempted explanations seem, in the judgment of a psychologist, inadequate at the very outset: they are too rational and take no account of the emotional character of the matters to be explained. Others are based on assumptions which are unconfirmed by observation. Yet others rely upon material which would be better interpreted in another way. There is generally little difficulty in refuting the various views put forward: the authorities are as usual more effective in their criticisms of one another's work than in their own productions. The conclusion upon most of the points raised must be a *non liquet*. It is not surprising, therefore, that in the most recent literature on the subject (which is for the most part passed over in the present work) an unmistakable tendency emerges to reject any general solution of totemic problems as impracticable.[73]

Freud examined the various theories explaining the origin of totemism: the nominalist, the sociological, and the psychological. In regard to the *nominalist* theory, its proponents claim that totemism arose as a need for each clan to distinguish itself from every other; later the clan developed a kinship with the totem.[74] Freud maintained that this reason did not explain the importance that has become attached to the names as a totemic system. With the *sociological* theory its advocates believe that a clan might have traded in a particular animal which became associated with them. Then they took more interest in that animal as time went on. Freud felt that this is a too "rational" explanation for savages were not that dependent upon one animal as they were omnivorous.[75] It is also hard to understand how this became a religious devotion to the point of abstaining from eating that animal. Freud next considered what he called *psychological* theories. The theory that the totem was responsible for conception might have begun by the woman selecting an object nearby as the responsible agent for the first stirrings of life she felt within her. A man would not eat this animal later because he would be eating himself. Yet, at times, he would eat so as to identify with it. Therefore it would seem that the ultimate source of totemism was savage ignorance of human reproduction.[76] However, Freud maintained that there is no way of establishing the savage ignorance of conception.

Thus Freud concluded that there is no clear and conclusive agreement on the origin of totemism. Also, there is no adequate explanation for the fact that exogamy is found along with totemism. In fact, authors disagree on their relationship. "Into this obscurity one single ray of light is thrown by psychoanalytic observation."[77] The insight into totemism and exogamy is found in the analysis of childhood phobias which deal with animals onto which the unconscious forces of the Oedipus complex are displaced. Freud stated that the following points are in agreement with totemism: the boy identifies with the totem and there are ambivalent feelings toward the totem. Freud felt justified in substituting the father for the totem animal. Primitives, too, call the totem their ancestor and primal father.[78]

> If the totem animal is the father, then the two principal ordinances of totemism, the two taboo prohibitions which constitute its core—not to kill the totem and not to have sexual relations with a woman of the same totem—coincide in their content with the two crimes of Oedipus, who killed his father and married his mother, as well as with the two primal wishes of children . . .[79]

With regard to a case involving fear of being eaten by an animal, Freud stated: "This fear of his father, too, was silent on the subject of castration: by the help of regression to an oral phase, it assumed the form of a fear of being eaten by his father. At this point it is impossible to forget a primitive fragment of Greek mythology which tells how Kronos, the old Father God, swallowed his children and sought to swallow his youngest son, Zeus, like the rest and how Zeus was saved by the craft of his mother and later on castrated his father."[80] What the sons feared from the father, they inflicted upon him.

b. *Monotheism*

Freud quoted the work of William Robertson Smith who put forward the hypothesis that the "totem meal" was from the beginning a part of totemism. Herein is re-enacted the primal crime: the sons killed and devoured their father.[81] Smith indicated that sacrifice was an act of unity between the deity and his worshippers.[82] "The oldest form of sacrifice . . . was the sacrifice of animals . . ." A special bond arises between those who share in the totem meal;[83] the strongest bond between men is kinship i.e., sharing in a common substance and to share a meal with a god implies that they are related.[84] "There cannot be the slightest doubt, says Robertson Smith, that the slaughter of a victim was originally among the acts which *'are illegal to an individual, and can only be justified when the whole clan shares the responsibility of the deed.'*" Freud thus concluded: ". . . *the sacrificing community, the god and the sacrificial animal were of the same blood and members of one clan.*"[85]

After the animal has been slaughtered and eaten, it is mourned which event is necessary because of fear of retribution. Freud felt that Robertson Smith gave an analogous situation showing that mourning served the purpose of disclaiming responsibility for the killing. After the mourning there are festivities when everything is allowed.[86] Psychoanalysis shows that the totem animal is a father substitute with the same ambivalent attitudes expressed toward it: festivity and mourning just as in a father-complex we find love and hostility.[87] Freud believed the brothers, after the murder, felt the same ambivalence as children with father-complexes and neurotics. The sons were filled with guilt; they then prohibited the same things which the father had forbidden. The mechanism operative is called "deferred obedience." They revoked their murder by not allowing the killing of the totem and did not take the father's women now set free i.e., the two rules of totemism which correspond to the repressed wishes of the Oedipus complex.[88] "Thus psycho-analysis, in contradiction to the more recent views of the *totemic system* but in agreement with the earlier ones, requires us to assume that *totemism* and *exogamy* were intimately connected and had a simultaneous origin."[89]

The totemic system was also a covenant: while the brothers promised to respect the totem's life, he promised them the answer to their infantile longings—protection and care.[90] There was also some self-justification. If the father had been as generous as the totem, the deed would not have happened.

Features were thus brought into existence which continued thenceforward to have a determining influence on the nature of religion. Totemic religion arose from the filial sense of guilt, in an attempt to allay that feeling and to appease the father by deferred obedience to him. All later religions are seen to be attempts at solving the same problem. They vary according to the stage of civilization at which they arise and according to the methods which they adopt; but all have the same end in view and are reactions to the same great event with which civilization began and which, since it occurred, has not allowed mankind a moment's rest.[91]

Freud insisted that his analysis of totemism was not imaginary because totemism and the male confederacies are historically founded; the old totem meal is still preserved in Holy Communion; Legends, fairy-tales, and the psychic development of children provide missing material in this study; the work on animal phobias, the son's fear of being eaten by the father, and fear of castration; all these lend support to the study.[92]

In totemism we have the beginnings of what we recognize to be religion. The form in which religion appears is dependent upon the culture and the structure of the community.[93] A further development of totemism shows a clan *deity* emerge in whose presence the sacrifice is performed. To survive, the totem meal had to find relevance to the new system involving a deity.[94] Freud was concerned with the fact that the father is represented two times in the primitive sacrifice as god and as victim. Freud examined the many relationships between the god and the sacred animal: gods usually had one animal sacred to them; in sacred sacrifice the animal sacred to the god was used; the god was worshipped in the form of an animal; and in myth the god changes into the animal sacred to him. Thus Freud concluded that the god and the totem animal are really one and the same with the god developing as a

177

result of subsequent religious feeling. "Thus, while the totem may be the *first* form of father surrogate, the god will be a later one, in which the father has regained his human shape." This happens, perhaps, because of a change in man's relation to animals or fathers or both.[95]

Where the father is represented twice in the sacrifice as god and victim, the scene must not be seen as an allegory but rather as historical.[96] It is an expression of the ambivalent attitude toward the father: the father is triumphant in that he is remembered and the sons are affectionate to him; the father is also vanquished as the victim. With the passage of time the animal was no longer considered sacred but was a simple offering to the god. God was so transcendent that he was only approached through a priest. The sons relieved themselves of guilt because they were not responsible for the sacrifice; it was God Himself who demanded it. "This is the phase in which we find myths showing the god himself killing the animal which is sacred to him and which is in fact himself." This is the most extreme denial of the primal crime which was the beginning of society and the sense of guilt. There is also satisfaction in the replacement of the original father substitute in favor of a superior idea of God.[97]

In the religion of Mithras, we have a youthful god slaying a bull which indicates a son sacrificing his father and redeeming his brothers from the guilt of the primal crime; the crime of parricide "must" have left a permanent trace on the history of man, and where the event was not brought to consciousness, it emerged in mythology.[98] In the Greek theatre there are resemblances to the totem meal and just as many differences according to Freud.[99] The Hero took on the "tragic guilt" which was founded in revolt against a divine or human authority and he took on the guilt of the Chorus. It was necessary that he suffer because he was the primal father. Then he was mourned by the Chorus which tried to make it seem that the Hero was responsible for his own suffering. "In the remote reality it had actually been the members of the Chorus who caused the Hero's suffering."[100] Thus it would seem that men were acting out, even though in a somewhat distorted fashion, the primal crime.

When something returns from oblivion it asserts itself with great force. This is a phenomenon in mass psychology, too. No logical explanation can be used against its insistent truth. This phenomenon can only be explained on the model of delusions of the psychotic where there is an element of truth which has been distorted. What the person is insisting upon is a basic truth now encrusted with errors. Neurotic symptoms all in some way show the "return of the repressed," subjected to distortion. "We must grant an ingredient such as this of what may be called *historical* truth to the dogmas of religion as well, which is true, bear the character of psychotic symptoms but which, as group phenomena, escape the curse of isolation.[101] The "mnemic image" of the primal father has been imprinted on the minds of the human race to be later changed into a god.[102] (We feel that Freud's description of the hysteric as one who acts out what he cannot remember comes closest by way of analogy on the individual level to what we see on the cultural level: the race's acting out the primal crime through the murder of Moses and Christ.)

When Moses brought the people the idea of a single god, it was not a novelty but signified the revival of an experience in the primaeval ages of the human family which had long vanished from men's conscious memory. But it had been so important and had produced or paved the way for such deeply penetrating changes in men's life that we cannot avoid believing that it had left behind it in the human mind some permanent traces, which can be compared to a tradition.[103]

We have learned from the psycho-analyses of individuals that their earliest impressions produce at some time or another effects of a compulsive character without themselves being consciously remembered. We believe we have a right to make the same assumption about the earliest experiences of the whole of humanity. One of these effects would be the emergence of the idea of a single great god—an idea which must be recognized as a completely justified memory, though, it is true, one that has been distorted.[104]

The murder of Moses and Christ can be viewed as a "return of the repressed" memory analogous to hysteria. In the course of the development of civilization the "repressed" returned; the Jews rejoiced when their God appeared to them on Mt. Sinai.[105] In the Monotheism of the Jews we see further the re-emergence of the primal crime which was repressed. It is probable that the world-empire of the Egyptians under the one Pharoah may have led to the "emergence" of the monotheistic idea which Moses took to the Jews who cherished with pride the notion of the one God whose chosen people they were.[106] The Mosaic prohibition against image-making elevated God to a higher degree of intellectuality and the way was opened to further alterations in the idea of God. Here we have an advance of intellectuality over sense perception and sensuality as the higher intellectual processes, namely memories, reflections and inferences, are now used.[107] "Thus we are faced by the phenomenon that in the course of the development of humanity sensuality is gradually overpowered by intellectuality and that men feel proud and exalted by every advance."[108] This advance implies some degree of renunciation with a victory of the reality principle over the pleasure principle.[109] The Jews as a group aimed in their renunciation to please Moses—the father surrogate.[110]

Moses, rather than the Egyptian influence, was probably the chief factor influencing the Jews to adopt the monotheistic notion of God. Moses was an excellent prototype of a father who bent down to the Jews as if they were his children. The Jews probably did not distinguish clearly between Moses and God. Therefore, their killing of Moses was a repeating of the killing of the primal father.[111] "It was a case of 'acting out' instead of remembering, as happens so often with neurotics during the work of analysis.[112] The original primal father had left his trace on the mind of man.[113] "An idea such as this has a compulsive character: it *must* be believed. To the extent to which it is distorted, it must be described as a *delusion*; in so far as it brings a return of the past, it must be called the *truth*."[114]

Freud claimed that the world at the time of Christ was plagued by a growing sense of guilt as an omen of the "return of the repressed." St. Paul called this sense of guilt "original sin," which was a crime against God to be made up only by a death. The crime was the murder of the primal father.[115] But the Jews refused to recognize what they had done; Paul told them to admit their guilt and thus he continued the primal history.[116] If they would admit their crime, they would be

180

redeemed (freed from guilt). "But the murder was not remembered: instead of it there was a phantasy of its atonement, and for that reason the phantasy could be hailed as a message of redemption (evangelium)."[117]

Historically, the redeemer would have to be the most guilty one—the ringleader of the primal crime concerning which we do not know if there was one specific ringleader but we know every brother had the wish. "If there was no such ringleader, then Christ was the heir to a wishful phantasy which remained unfulfilled; if there was one, then he was his successor and his reincarnation."[118] "And the intermediate step between the delusion and the historical truth was provided by the assurance that the victim of the sacrifice had been God's son. With the strength which it derived from the source of historical truth, this new faith overthrew every obstacle."[119] Man felt he was now redeemed from original sin for Christ sacrificed his own life to save the brothers from original sin.[120] If we draw some further inferences on Freud's own principles, we can gain further insight into the primal crime which he considers was the murder of the father. In *Genesis* the original sin was a crime against the father. Displacement frequently takes place in the myth (as it does in dreams) and we find that Eve ("the mother of all things") might have been the Mother and Adam the Son. Here we would have the classic Oedipal situation. In *Genesis*, God the Father returns in the evening to discover the crime of Adam and Eve. Further the son, Christ (the "New Adam" so named by St. Paul) offers himself as a sacrifice to his father in payment for the sins of mankind against the Father. At the same time as he pays for the primal crime by his death, he relinquishes his mother Mary (the "New Eve" so named by the Church Fathers). Thus it would seem that the "return of the repressed" has appeared.

Freud stated that there was no doubt that in Christianity the original sin was against God the Father. If Christ gave his life in payment for the original sin, then, according to the law of talion, the original crime was murder.[121] "The law of talion, which is so deeply rooted in human feelings, lays it down that a murder can only be expiated by the sacrifice of another life: self-sacrifice points back to blood guilt." Yet there was the usual ambivalence in the case of the sacrifice of the son. While the son offered the greatest atonement to the father, he also

181

triumphs over him; he became God not alongside the Father but by replacing Him. "A son-religion displaced the father-religion." That this substitution is evident, we need only consider the revival of the totem meal in which the brothers eat the flesh and blood of the son and thereby identify with him.[122]

Thus we can trace through the ages the identity of the totem meal with animal sacrifice, with the anthropic human sacrifice and with the Christian Eucharist, and we can recognize in all these rituals the effect of the crime by which men were so deeply weighed down but of which they must none the less feel so proud. The Christian communion, however, is essentially a fresh elimination of the father, a repetition of the guilty deed. We can see the full justice of Frazer's pronouncement that 'the Christian communion has absorbed within itself a sacrament which is doubtless far older than Christianity.'[123]

Freud concluded:

To this day I hold firmly to this construction. I have repeatedly met with violent reproaches for not having altered my opinions in later editions of my book in spite of the fact that more recent ethnologists have unanimously rejected Robertson Smith's hypothesis and have in part brought forward other totally divergent theories. I may say in reply that these ostensible advances are well known to me. But I have not been convinced either of the correctness of these innovations or of Robertson Smith's errors. A denial is not a refutation and innovation is not necessarily an advance. Above all, however, I am not an ethnologist but a psycho-analyst. I had a right to take out of ethnological literature what I might need for the work of analysis. The writings of Robertson Smith—a man of genius— have given me valuable points of contact with the psychological material of analysis and indications for its employment. I have never found myself on common ground with his opponents.[124]

Conclusion: Gradual "Return of the Repressed"

In tracing the origins of the religious phenomenon, we began with the primal crime. After the crime man was filled with guilt, fear of

182

retaliation and longing for the father who had been the protector in man's helplessness. The way man brought back the father or the way the father returned varied according to man's own psychical development. Religion as a cultural institution was influenced in its form by the stage of man's psychic development. Thus in early man (pre-animism) he handled his fear and longings by *hallucinating* (magical thought); he could remove the threat by thinking it away; he could have the longed-for person by thinking the person present. Later, man by *projecting* his internal fears and longings saw them as outside himself in the forms of spirits (animism) which could be benevolent or malevolent to him. Further, man by *displacing* showed ambivalent feelings (taboo) toward particular beings (totemism). These beings invoked in him feelings of hostility and love. Finally, by *acting out* (murder of Moses and Christ) man brings back clearly the forgotten memory which long ago had been repressed (the primal crime). Thus we have seen the gradual "return of the repressed." Man's religious experience has been a story of overcoming the primal crime or *the* event of the past. Man has been trying to free himself from the past. From the viewpoint of genesis, man's religious forms can be reduced to the primal crime.

C. *Philosophical Critique of the Reductive Analysis of the Origins of Religion*

1. Methodology Employed

a. *Use of Analogy.* We will make a philosophical critique of the methodology employed in the treatment of the hypothesis that the origin of religion is to be found in the primal crime. Then we will make a philosophical analysis of the *underlying* principles involved in the presentation. It may be objected that sufficient evidence was not presented by Freud to show that he could equate the child, the neurotic and the savage (past and present).[125] However, Freud does point out the dangers of identifying these three categories and maintains that he is dealing with *analogies.*[126]

> We are not entitled, in view of the current state of knowledge of genetics and heredity, especially mental heredity, to affirm positively that infantile psychology reflects accurately the

prehistoric vicissitudes of human life. We are entitled to say that the course of infantile development seems to exhibit a certain parallel to reconstructions of the course of racial development, and that this assumption makes many infantile strains and stresses more intelligible. We are most fully justified by our clinical experience in asserting that Oedipal and pre-Oedipal conflicts operating in the individual are of an importance which can hardly be exaggerated in the development of personal religion and, therefore, presumably also in the historical development of the great religions.[127]

b. *Field Work.* It has been pointed out that Freud did not do field work nor did he read primary accounts of primitive ritual behavior. Rather, he read secondary sources which were the *speculations* of Atkinson, Darwin, Frazer, Wundt, and Lang. Ritual behavior was set up according to the schema of these authors' interests.[128] The answer to this objection is that although the authors he read may have contained their own speculations, this does not mean that they did not contain descriptive accounts of human behavior. Frazer's work, for example, is used as a vast source book for primary data.

c. *Primal Crime as Historical.* There is a more serious objection brought by anthropologists with reference to the occurrence of the "primal crime." Where Freud speaks of the "primal crime" as a "typical" event, he seems to mean a recurrent one. However, from an historical standpoint some believe there is insufficient evidence to show that it occurred even once as Freud describes.[129] Freud has inadequate evidence to show that the murder of the primal father was the practice for primitives and that these episodes occurred over thousands of years. However, we may answer this objection by stating that even if a primal crime cannot be established as an *historical* event (which possibility Freud allows),[130] each individual still must face the Oedipal conflict. And it is possible with the similarity of early experiences of individuals that the group, which is made up of individuals, would show similar needs and responses.

The primal crime is for Freud the beginning of culture with its institutions, e.g., religion. It is objected that Freud's description of the crime shows that there was already some degree of culture.[131] For according to Freud, after the crime the sons imposed laws and reli-

184

gious taboos, i.e., cultural forms to be handed on. But to hand things on presupposes there was something existing to be handed on. If there was not something already available, then there would be no customs to hand on. [132] We believe this objection may be answered. Let us first take the primal crime as *historical*. It is still possible that there may have been quite a difference in the laws and taboos that were passed on as a result of the crime as compared with the regulations in the period before the crime. Although we observe that customs are inherited from a previous generation, Freud is asking how does custom itself begin. If the primal crime is taken as an *individual* psychic event, then it is possible that man may reflect his reaction to this conflict through his cultural institutions.

d. *Archaic Heritage.* "No part of Freud's theory has been more strongly rejected than the idea of the survival of the archaic heritage— his reconstruction of the prehistory of mankind from the primal horde through patricide to civilization." [133] The inheritance of memory traces from the past does not find unanimous support among geneticists. [134] We answer that it would have been a better scientific procedure had the archaic heritage been defended *first*, perhaps, by means of natural selection, then *second* as a type of unconscious communication between the unconscious of parents and children. [135] It is not impossible according to some biologists that there could be the inheritance of acquired characteristics. [136] If the primal crime is not taken as historical, then we may find ourselves involved in an experience unique to each man—the Oedipal conflict.

Freud has been accused of taking advantage of the lack of concord among anthropologists and biblical scholars in order to select data which would fit his theory. [137] In regard to the murder of Moses as a re-enactment of the primal crime, Freud bases his construction on uncertain views which in some cases were later totally rejected by their authors. [138] While it is true that at present there are few, if any, biblical scholars who maintain that Moses was murdered, Freud's ideas on the "return of the repressed," as operative in culture, still find support in the death of Christ.

It has been pointed out that Freud only accounted for the origins of monotheistic religion; but all religions are not monetheistic. There are some religions which are not theistic at all e.g., Buddhism, Jainism, and Advaita-Vedantism. It would seem that Freud's analysis

185

would not apply to the godless religions. "None the less they are religions, because they represent an attitude of life which is distinct from other attitudes like the moral, aesthetic, and secular."[139] It is not our purpose in this work to defend Freud's analysis of oriental religions; his study may not be adequate. However, we feel that his theory may illuminate aspects of these religions e.g., Freud points out that the practice of Yoga bears some resemblance to the "ego-feeling" of the child's early development.[140]

2. Underlying Principles Involved

a. *Causes.* To see deeper into the type of explanation which Freud gives with reference to religious phenomena, we must consider the matter of causality further. In the traditional explanation of a phenomenon we are involved in the four causes:[141] formal, material, efficient and final. To account fully for a phenomenon it would be necessary to call upon, in some way, each of the four causes. Where we would eliminate any particular cause, we would not be explaining fully the phenomenon under study. Where we take a final cause as that for the sake of which something is done, we would find final causality in Freud. Difficulties arise when we attempt to consider *all* the reasons or causes which go to explain the purpose for which something is done or the purpose for the existence of a particular phenomenon. When a phenomenon is explained or accounted for at the *present* moment all four causes must be taken into consideration to explain the phenomenon here and now existing. We can immediately realize that something is wrong when we leave out totally one of the causes in our attempt to account for that phenomenon. Thus with Freud's explanations we are not immediately jarred by his accounting for phenomenon.

However, difficulties arise with reference to the genetic explanation which by definition is explanation in terms of the *past* or origins. To say that this is the way it began or this is *why* it came about does not exclude entirely the teleological element. We would have to find out if we have considered *all* the reasons why it began or came about. Freud tends to overlook some of the factors which might have been at the origin of a phenomenon because of his method which was designed to investigate material of psychoanalytic interest.

Now the problem becomes compounded when we account for a

present phenomenon in terms of past causes. We will grant that the four causes were considered (although *each* may not have been totally adequate or exhaustive) in accounting for a past phenomenon. But do these *past* causes explain what is before us here and now? Does the genesis (including the four causes) account for the *present*? The reason we ask this quesiton is because of the fact that the present is not the past; however, we realize that past and present are intimately related. Also, the fact that we carry the past explanation as an accounting for the present without a re-examination of the present phenomenon only increases the possibility of incompletion. Freud has a tendency to examine the purpose of a phenomenon in terms of purpose for which it was done in the past. Then that past purpose is brought up to the present moment intact. This is the problem: the past purpose may not be the present purpose. Much has happened in time.

If for further elucidation we locate this same problem in terms of our dialectic, we find that we are in process but at the same time man, in confronting the present moment, comes with the *same* archaic past over and over again. For Freud, man comes to the present with an experience made up of the reasons and purposes for which he did something in the past; in the present moment past experience meets with the present. But in the next moment of confrontation we should realize that it is not the same past of the previous moment in confrontation with the present. Synthesis becomes the thesis of the next moment. It is Freud's conflict—his trying to break with the past—which causes him at times to fall victim to a heavy reliance upon genetic explanation. There are several moments in Freud; he is not completely stuck to the past but also sees a whole new future opening. The genetic moment serves to highlight the teleological moment.

In viewing the *underlying* principles in Freud's presentation we must consider an important passage at the beginning of one of his explanations bearing on the religious phenomenon.

There are no grounds for fearing that psycho-analysis, which first discovered that psychical acts and structures are invariably overdetermined, will be tempted to trace the origin of anything so complicated as religion to a single source. If psycho-analysis is compelled—and is, indeed, in duty bound—to lay all the emphasis upon one particular source, that does not mean it is claiming either that that source is the only one or that it occupies first place among the numerous contributory factors. Only when we can synthesize the findings in the different fields of research will it become possible to arrive at the relative importance of the part played in the genesis of religion by the mechanism discussed in these pages. Such a task lies beyond the means as well as beyond the purposes of a psycho-analyst.[142]

By "overdetermination" we mean that there may be causes from other systems involved in the phenomenon under examination. It is true that at times Freud's approach is basically reductionistic. Nevertheless, we maintain that the reductionism does not totally explain away the phenomenon in question. Freud's reductionism is a necessary moment on the way to a deeper understanding of the religious phenomenon. We must bear this thought in mind in the discussion which follows.

b. *Genetic Explanation.* We will now engage in a philosophical analysis of the underlying principles involved in Freud's tracing religion to its *origins.* ". . . the characteristic mental habit of the nineteenth century was translating 'essence' into 'origin', so that the statement 'This is the essence of the situation' becomes 'This is how it began.' We need only translate back, and Freud's origin theory transforms into 'culture and society have the sort of defensive emphases they might have had had they originated in a prehistoric parricide and incest.' "[143] What Freud is giving us is a genetic explanation of religious phenomena; he is accounting for the religious phenomena in terms of its origins and history. For Freud, to understand the present phenomenon one must go back to its genesis.[144]

The question arises with the genetic explanation of religion as to whether sufficient conditions are given to account for the occurrence of the *explicandum.*[145] Some claim that Freud committed the general fallacy of believing that the origin of a thing determined its end or purpose.[146] Thus if religion originated from fear and longing, then the whole purpose of religion is a response to these two emotions. Freud would say that this may not be the whole purpose of religion but according to *psychanalytic* investigation, these fears and wishes are bound to be at the core of the religious experiences of mankind as he studies it.

It may also be objected that those using a genetic explanation may select according to their own inclination the events which they think are causally relevant in accounting for the phenomenon. [147] Here Freud made events dealing with parricide central to his explanation of religion; [148] this he did because of his special interest in the Oedipus complex which led to a limitation on possible factors involved in the phenomenon under examination. However, Freud did admit that there might be other factors explaining the religious phenomena but he believed that the contribution of psychoanalysis did have something to say in providing a plausible explanation for its origins.

    c. *Evolution and Unilinear View.* From evolutionary theory, Freud saw that since the beginning of life one biological form has evolved into the other forms found throughout nature. Thus Freud, saw religion as an institution with a unique beginning and in the process of evolving from one form to another. It is objected that he applied his evolutionary principles indiscriminately to religion wherever it manifested itself in culture and at whatever period in history it was seen. He presumed that the primal crime was the beginning of religion and was universal in its influence. Evolution was taken to be *unilinear* and uniform for all mankind; present-day institutions were seen as survivals of the primitive types of long ago. With the unilinear view, Freud believed he could move from one culture to another and could take from each what he needed for a unified theory. [149] Thus he selected from various cultures the religious manifestation which would fit his schema. Freud never considered making comparisons between different social institutions as evolutionary theory showed this not to be a necessity. He believed the Oedipal conflict was universal and thus imagined that institutions had no influence on its origin. Therefore, he made the Oedipal conflict the center of social structure; institutions arose as derivatives of this fight against incest. [150] When Freud wrote *Totem and Taboo* in 1912, he was not cognizant of the fact that the evolutionary way of thinking was not the methodology being used in anthropology. [151]

    However, when Freud took the primal crime to be a universal phenomenon, he believed that the Oedipal conflict was something which all mankind experienced as part of being human. Thus within this substrate of common experience he saw religion evolve. Freud realized that religious forms and functions might vary from culture to culture and according to time. What he is saying is that the basic underlying motivations (fear and longing for the father) leading to the religious phenomena are the same for all cultures. Although it may be the case that anthropologists do not use evolutionary theory to explain religious phenomena, Freud is maintaining that the religious phenomena can be viewed in an evolutionary light if his hypothesis of the Oedipal origin of religion is adopted. In answer to the anthropologists, Freud maintains that religious phenomena will fit in an evolutionary scheme at least in some of its aspects.

Against Freud it is argued that the anthropological mode of explaining by origins is incomplete i.e., this mode will not give us the complete picture from a primitive to a later religion. Examination of an earlier form cannot tell us *why* we have a later form arising. ''The mud hut does not explain the skyscraper, even if there is in some sense an evolution with the contemporaneous conditions, whatever light may be thrown on them from the knowledge of earlier conditions.''[152] Freud admits that an earlier form of religion does not explain *why* we have a later form; yet the possibility that there could have been similar motivation for both is not ruled out. Further, there may be a common feeling which brings man to religion; one religion may be more complex than another but the function which they fulfill may be similar. In the case of the skyscraper, it is more complex than the mud hut; yet there is still similarity in functions in so far as they are both shelters.

The discovery of origins is often elusive. The beginnings of many things cannot be dated. We cannot strictly say that they begin at a certain stage of culture or of civilization. They emerge rather than begin. This is what evolution properly means. If so, it may be vain to look for a *specific* origin or original form. If a thing evolves it cannot be dated. We can date events or laws or constitutions, the collapse of power systems, and so forth. Within limits we can date specific fashions, modes, styles, customs, and the rise of power systems. But we cannot date custom itself or ceremony or the family or the state. And we cannot, without arbitrary discrimination, derive such undatable and permanent phenomena from any one of their manifestations, however early or primitive these may be.[153]

190

It is for this type of objection that Freud left the possibility open for a non-*historical* interpretation of the primal crime. We may not be able to date the primal crime because like the family it is undatable. But the primal crime was probably closely connected with the family (Oedipal feelings) and thus the origins of religion, too.

d. *Monocausality.* We will now examine the objections of those who see Freud as a monocausalist. Institutions which have lasted a long time are not influenced by merely *one* emotion which can be singled out from the people who have them. A single motive like "fear" can have myriad meanings among children and savages. Freud attributes the origins of religion to guilt and fear which seem to be limited factors in view of the universality of religion. To say that the religious phenomenon is strictly related to a sexual origin is to violate the principle of sufficient reason: a cultural phenomenon (the greater) is being derived from a lesser cause. To accept the view that the greater can be derived from the lesser would mean that the qualities inherent in religion *qua* religion would appear as an illusion.[154]

However Freud did not claim to exhaust all the factors which account for religion. What he claimed was that he revealed the infantile factor at the basis of religion. It is not contradictory that the same motives be operative whenever we come upon a particular phenomenon. Further, while Freud held libido to be the source of all activity, he did allow for other mechanisms. Particularly, we recall that *sublimation* played a part in the transformation of the sexual in order that we might have the artistic and religious. Therefore, religion is not derived from libido, although they may be closely related. If it could be shown that the origin of religion was directly sexual, there are still other factors which could be propounded for religion's continued existence, e.g., a way of holding the community together. Freud allowed for these other factors but he insists that the factors psychoanalysis has discovered must be considered, namely, the infantile wishes.

The critics of Freud maintain that a particular drive or complex which may be related to religion does not explain the variations and changes seen in the religious phenomenon. The fact that primal drives are seen to be operative in the process of change does not account for the change itself. "Recurrence and recapitulation cannot explain

191

change but only the unchanging element within it." Where Freud *may* show that the fear of incest was the origin of taboo, he has not accounted for the wide variation in taboo systems. To reduce the complicated to the simple will still leave the complicated unexplained. Where a reduction is made there is the implicit acceptance of the original Freudian hypothesis from which the conclusion (in regard to phenomenon to be explained) was derived. The family shows a variation in structure under various conditions and thus "instincts" alone would not account for the variety;[155] so too with religion and its endless variation.

On the other side, Freud never ruled out other cultural factors which might come into play thus giving religion its various forms. Also, after the Freudian reductionism, it may quite well be that the complicated factor is still left unexplained. That is the precise point we wish to make. Freudian reductionism can only work upon those factors which its psychoanalytic methodology is designed to investigate. It reveals, by reductionism, the genetic side of these factors which may turn out to be infantile; with the exposure of the infantile, a teleology may be revealed.

   e. *Methodological Individualism.* Having discussed the problem of explaining religion in terms of its cultural origins, we discuss the problem of explaining religion in *culture* in terms of *individual* experience. Some object to Freud's "methodological individualism" which maintains the reducibility of statements about social phenomena (e.g., religion) to psychological statements about human behavior.[156] Thus, according to Freud, the cultural phenomenon of religion is explained by examining the religious behavior of the individual. However, the critics point out that there is immense difficulty in understanding the complex social behavior from a study based upon the model of individual behavior. This is so because of the great number of possibilites involved when so many social variables are brought together in combination.[157] Further, they argue that a social institution cannot be conceived to be only a "direct expression" of the unconscious and conscious desires of those in the society. Otherwise the institution would be a mere "wish fulfillment." They maintain that the institutions first impose themselves upon the growing individual. Tradition, too, makes an impact upon a social institution. There is great variety among individuals in their attitude toward the institution and the way in which they are in turn affected by it. To not consider these factors but only to see the social institution as a product of the individual psychology is a limitation in outlook.[158]

However, the reason for the difficulty in seeing only a strict methodological individualism in Freud is due to the fact that in Freudian theory we find two modes of explanation of phenomena. He tries to give an accounting in terms of libidinal impulse (instincts) and yet he wishes to account for object-relations (Oedipal situation).[159] The first mode ignores man as social.[160] Thus there seems to be a certain ambivalence in Freud's approach to phenomena. From the standpoint of id psychology, Freud seems to be more the determinist or geneticist; from the standpoint of ego psychology he allows more current interaction. He did leave enough room for the interaction with environmental factors. For the parents who represent social forces are internalized early in the life of the person.[161] There are other social forces operative during the whole course of the person's development influencing him.

Thus we see that there is a give and take between the individual and society. One cannot be separated from the other. The individual incorporates into his own psyche what society has to offer and he in turn influences society. With regard to religion, the individual's solution to his desires are brought into the stream of society in the form of his personal religion. Society in turn provides the individual with the way the community solves the desires of its members by means of cultural religion. While this process of interaction of the many allows for wide variation, the needs and desires which lead to religion stem from a basic source.

Against Freud it is argued that a social phenomenon (e.g., religion) is kept in existence by the attitudes and interests of the group perduring with the phenomenon. When a group attitude or group interest changes, the social phenomenon undergoes change, too. Group attitudes and interests, in response to the conditions of the environment, go to make up the religion. "Present social institutions therefore depend on the interplay, *in the present*, of these complexly cooperating determinants, and are expressive alike of their continuity and their change."[162]

In answer, Freud would certainly admit that the attitude of the group

193

would determine the *form* that religion takes in the community. However, he would maintain that since each member of the group was in a relationship with a mother and a father for a certain period of time, then it is probable that these early feelings could be activated later on as the infantile needs might arise for both individual or group. Thus religion may very well be a response to a group need felt here and now; and the causes for the activation of the need could be numerous depending upon culture and time.

We have seen the Freudian reductionism operative in our study. Religion has been reduced to its origin—the primal crime; religious cultural phenomena have been explained on the model of individual religious experience; and finally, fear and longing have been seen to be at the core of religion. Thus we find summed up in the following comments a critique of Freud's reductionism: Reductive explanations run the risk of "explaining away" what they set out to take an accounting of. There may be an insight into basic motivation but they tell us little about the "values" involved in the phenomenon to be explained.[163] Thus for Freud "there is no distinctly religious need—only psychological need."[164] It seems that Freud explains the higher forms of psychic life in terms of the lower forms.[165] "Thus Freudianism has entered into our mores as the prototype of descending explanation, of the reduction of the higher to the lower; nothing hinders us any longer from going to the very end of a total explanation of man in terms of this repressed and repressing unconscious, sexual and autopunitive, infantile and ancestral."[166]

Nevertheless, having defended Freud's reductionism, it will be our task to show that his procedure is a necessary stage in preparation for the emergence of a teleology. It was necessary to expose the *infantile* at the core of religion in order to allow for the appearance of that which points beyond. Without the reductionism or purification, we will not be able to appreciate that which is revealed in the process.

D. *Reductive Analysis of Religious Phenomena in Culture Allows for Possible Emergence of Sacred: Telos*

We will examine now the deeper meaning of the cultural forms which religion has taken from the early beginnings of mankind. We have seen Freud's reductionism to a primal crime, which event all do not agree upon as historical. However, it is possible that the reductionism might be defended on the basis that *each* person commits a primal crime in his own inner psyche. Thus religion in culture may be seen to be influenced in some way by the group whose members share a similar psychical experience. We have seen pre-animism, animism, taboo, totemism, and monotheism.

1. *Evolution in Awareness of "Wholly Other" as Other*

The cultural forms which religion has taken mark the locus of man's struggle to come to grips with reality. The religious forms are a record of man's psychic development with the gradual victory of the reality principle over the pleasure principle. The clear view of the "return of the repressed" points to a firmer grasp of reality. For what was concealed has been revealed and may now be overcome. The evolution of the religious forms shows a movement toward a greater awareness of the "Wholly Other" as other. We will examine Freud's reductionism of the various religious forms in order to see what they may be made to reveal. In the meeting of the genesis and telos there is symbol and the religious forms are symbols of a past dialectic; they may once have been sacred symbols pointing to the "Wholly Other." By looking at the genesis of the religious forms we see man as infantile and at the same time we see a gradual emergence of a telos. When we look over the long history of religious forms, there seems to appear an ever clearer view of what man was trying to express. It was his attempt to reach out to the "Wholly Other."

Freud has shown that in *pre-animism* or magic man has relegated to himself the structuring of the cosmos through hallucination. Here man's omnipotence of thoughts are at their height; he has little appreciation of the other which he hardly recognizes as outside himself. He takes the whole of reality merely to be a reflection of his own mind because he is still deeply involved with himself and is unable to come to the point of wanting "to have" the other as other. Man in confrontation with reality soon becomes aware that a correspondence between his hallucination and the real world does not always follow. He becomes aware of the other i.e., that which is not himself. Therefore, man knows that there are beings and he is one among them. He begins to also realize his dependency upon the other. Therefore, the passing of the stage of magic marks man's awareness of his contingency and the awareness of other as other.

Freud points out that in the stage of *animism* man gives to the world a form and populates it with spirits. When we, with Freud, engage in a reductionism, we find that these spirits who rule nature are none other than the projections of unconscious wishes and conflicts. However, while the reductionism reveals the infantile and neurotic origin of these projections, we maintain that there is still something more. To man the spirits which inhabit nature are more than the longings for father or Oedipal conflicts. The spirits indicate more. They clearly show man in confrontation with the other. It is true that the spirits are like him (his projections), but they are also *distinct* from him. Because of spirits, he becomes aware of his lack of omnipotence, his contingency and dependency on the other.

The role of the spirits involves something much different from the things a father or any other can do. The spirits are different from any *other* he knows. To consider them merely as an exalted father does not exhaust their meaning. For they are not father and their task in sustaining nature is beyond the role of a father who sustains the child. With the belief in spirits we see man in awareness of something outside of himself upon whom he is dependent. But the other and the dependency are different than any of his infantile experiences. The moment of faith in the spirits, although it is limited in depth because of the narrowness of the view of other, is a symbol which points beyond to the ''Wholly Other.''

In examining the phenomenon of *taboo* we find that primitive man considered certain objects or persons to be both ''sacred'' and ''forbidden,'' at the same time. If we engage in a reductionism, we find that this ambivalent attitude toward an object is a displacement of unconscious hostility and admiration for a parental figure. However, after we have seen the infantile origin for such feelings we are still faced with objects which have something ''uncanny'' about them; they have a supernatural power; they are above the realm of ordinary profane objects and people. Man can distinguish these things as distinct from his parents and possessing far superior powers. While the present feelings may have an infantile origin, their infantile genesis does not exhaust the present experience. Man is in confrontation with something entirely different from himself and any other thing in his experience. He does not see his own contingency in regard to these objects in the same way that he realized his contingency with reference to his father. He realizes his contingency now in confrontation with a whole universe. These objects, especially when seen in their "sacred" aspect, point beyond themselves to something transcendent.

In *totemism* we see that the "return of the repressed" comes closer to consciousness as the only disguise for its true meaning is the use of an animal. The feelings toward the animal are a combination of many things: "to have" and "to be like." However, the only way man achieves the "to be like" is to orally incorporate the other. Thus other, while seen as distinct, can not yet truly be encountered as other. Other is not yet allowed to have its own autonomy. It is the force of the "repressed" which still prevents man from seeing the other as other. When we, with Freud, engage in a reductionism of totemism, we realize that the animal is a substitute for the father who is being sacrificed and adored. Thus at the origin of totemism are found the infantile features. However, we maintain that in totemism more is expressed than just the infantile feelings for the father. The totem is seen to be superior to any of the persons or things that we meet in our ordinary experience. Worship which is not given to any other human is given to the totem which represents something more than ordinary human interrelationships. It is a relationship with something which transcends the human.

In *monotheism*, the "return of the repressed" appears without distortion. It also marks the time for mankind to see the other as other. He is able to see the other as transcendent or "Wholly Other." With Christianity the opportunity to overcome the "to have" is given, for by identifying with Christ we accept the "to be like." Yet the "to have" is not fully overcome. Part of man's archaic past still remains and interferes with his present encounter. Man still sees God as having the qualities of the longed-for father. In monothesim much distortion has been removed and the reductionism is more easily made. The worship of the one God may be reduced so as to reveal its infantile longings for the father. However, the monotheistic God is not exhausted in a reductionism to the father for He is seen as transcendent. Not only are we, because of our contingency, dependent upon Him but also the whole hierarchy of beings.

In our examination of the reduction of religious forms, it becomes more and more apparent that some form of *telos* emerges. When we come to monotheism, we see more clearly man reaching out by faith to

197

a "Wholly Other" who is other. In the evolution of psychic life and its corresponding evolution of religious forms there is a gradual emergence of this "Wholly Other." In the early life of mankind the "Wholly Other" is most concealed. There is the greatest amount of distortion. Man takes himself to be the whole world. Only gradually there emerges the other. In the beginning the other as other is not very significant. In animism the other was something nebulous which inhabited nature and gave power to the forces of nature. In taboo there is something uncanny ("sacred" and "forbidden") surrounding the other. In totemism the other is worshipped as being far above ordinary man. In monotheism, the other emerges as Transcendent and "Wholly Other." In spite of the reductionism to the father and infantile wishes, the other continues to emerge and to confront us in a way which makes the father only a shadow of this "Wholly Other."

In our tracing of mankind's religious forms, we see a genesis and a teleology. The genesis is what is revealed about the religious form when it is reduced to its origins. The teleology is that which emerges or escapes reductionism. Where the genesis and telos meet we have a symbol. Thus the religious forms of animism, taboo, totemism, and monotheism are symbols which are the "concrete moments" of the dialectic between genesis and telos. They are the resultant of man's infantile past ("return of the repressed") and his struggle to move forward in comprehending a revealing cosmos—a cosmos as other than himself and other than an image of the primal father. Thus the evolution of religious forms shows the presence of the archaic but at the same time the emergence of the new. The religious symbol for man shows both the revival of the past and the thrust forward. Mankind in religion projects its infantile desires but these are sublimated in a new form which points beyond the past to a common faith in the "Wholly Other."

2. *Religious Forms Seen as Symbols of "Wholly Other"*

The *religious* symbols of animism, taboo, totemism and monotheism have become common-place; they point to a *past* drama of man attempting to encounter the "Wholly Other." The religious symbols all capture archaic phantasies. To understand these symbols they have to be grasped in the creative moment or subjected to a reductionism; but a reductionism which is more than an immediate going from the synthesis to the thesis. There is the moment of anti-thesis which must be considered; the moment of confrontation, alienation, striving, and struggle must also be seen. The anti-thetical moment saves us from equating the present experience with the past. The forementioned religious forms do not show their power today because their symbols are worn out. They were once signs of faith, subject to all the distortions which burden man's darkened intellect. To try to resurrect them today would be like an attempt to restore idols.

The religious forms should not only be examined separately, but rather collectively with the components seen as stages. The fact that the religious forms which mankind experienced had their regressive side does not prevent us from also seeing the progress that has been achieved. The progress is seen from what emerges. A better view of what is emerging is only seen when we step back or look at the past from the proper perspective. When we are engaged in the experience in the present, we may tend to lose sight of the past moment. Only when the past and present moment are compared can we grasp the movement or telos that is emerging. The religious forms that mankind developed through his culture are not private expressions; there is something more to be communicated. There is always the risk that the religious form will be merely a projection of unconscious conflicts and in such event man would not arrive at a greater understanding of himself by participating in that religious form. However, at the time when the religious symbols were new, they did represent something more for the community than neurotic projection. They represented the drama of man and the "Wholly Other." They were symbols of the community effort to go beyond the profane activities of the group to something which was beyond themselves.

Men did not merely express their longing for their father as the child and neurotic would; they sought to enter into a relationship with that which was totally other. With the evolution of consciousness, as witnessed by the religious forms, man's coming to the idea of a "Wholly Other" who was really entirely the other was a gradual process. Man saw the "Wholly Other" as part of this world: first as inhabiting nature, then by a special presence in certain things, later in objects to be worshipped, and finally as transcendent. As in the individual, mankind's religious experience bears witness to a movement from the "to have" to the "to be like." Man wanted to have the "Wholly Other." Therefore, he located Him in nature, in special objects and finally in sacred things which he could consume. Mankind has grown to see that the "Wholly Other" is not grasped through His annihilation but by an encounter between man, as one, and the "Wholly Other" as the other. Going beyond the "to have" in a relationship with the "Wholly Other" shows a movement of a greater grasp and understanding of the "Wholly Other." Our reductionism to the infantile allows us to see man going beyond the infantile.

Thus as we see new solutions to the dialogue emerging, as witnessed by changing religious symbols, we realize that mankind is not engaged in regression to the infantile but is rather taken up into a forward movement. This may be seen as an experience in encounter with being. Man in his various religious forms is involved with being in various ways. He at first sees everything as part of himself, then as he realizes being as other he tries to capture it and take it into himself. There is a gradual realization of being as really distinct from oneself or as other. The evolution of religious forms shows the gradual emergence of being as other. Mankind is in a continuous dialectic with its past—the "return of the repressed" or the drama of fear and longing. Man has gradually learned to give up his hold on the "to have" for the primal father. And thus man has allowed himself no longer to see the "Wholly Other" as that which one incorporates ("to have") but as one distinct and as other. Mankind in giving up the "to have" accepts the "to be like"; but in the process he becomes more aware of himself as a distinct person. Through his encounter with the other as other, he arrives at a more heightened sense of self-consciousness. He also identifies with that which is other and at the same time realizes his own unique self-identity. He now can stand before the "Wholly Other" as a complete person; he can more freely make an act of faith in the "Wholly Other." He is free because he no longer projects his own longings onto the "Wholly Other."

In one respect the religious symbols are seen to represent the culture of a particular time i.e., they mark the place of man bearing his past in confrontation with the present. However, the religious symbol really has much more; it has something which is not contained in the culture. The religious forms of mankind, when reduced, reveal that man by faith has moved beyond the cultural in an endeavor to reach the "Wholly Other." Going beyond cultural limitation makes it impossible to engage in a reductionism to culture. When we examine the religious symbols in a culture, they represent the intersection of genesis and telos. It is at this locus—where we realize the horizon of the telos of cultural forms. At this point where culture points beyond itself we cannot understand the "Wholly Other." However, we can know the place that points beyond. In the various cultural forms of religion we have objectifications of what was once an experience of faith or man striving to encounter the "Wholly Other." Where we are involved in the immanent (the world), we see its genetic and teleological side. But man is in a state of tension; he can only try to go beyond himself by placing himself solidly in the culture. Whatever he experiences he can only attempt to express in terms of the culture albeit inadequately. But faith expressed by means of the culture is religion—faith reified.

When we speak of the forms of religion, we are really speaking about an objectifying process that has taken place. The various religious forms are seen to be in the world of objects alongside the other cultural institutions. However, we must see them not as sacred objects but rather as signs of the sacred. The religious forms of the past show us a group of idols. The horizon of the telos has been objectified. Faith that has been reified gives birth to idols which religion presents to us. Alienation takes place for man because the sacred object is still in the category of other cultural objects. When something was only viable in the past we cannot adequately relate to it at present. It seems out of place in our times. An idol cannot bear witness to the "Wholly Other."

Thus on the analogy of the neurosis we have traced the "return of the repressed" on a cultural level. We have seen the evolution of man's reaction to the primal crime. Philosophy of science points to the possibility that Freud's methodology did not justify the positing of an historical event; but room is still left for the possibility that each man commits a primal crime (Oedipus complex) and manifests his reaction to it through religion which varies according to the time, place and psychic development. Freud's reductionism of religious experience has unmasked its infantile roots. With this revelation we were able to look beyond to a purified meaning of man's religious experience; namely, an evolution in encounter with the "Wholly Other."

NOTES

[1] Freud (1938), *Moses and Monotheism*, XXIII, 58.
[2] *Ibid.*, p. 84.
[3] *Ibid.*, p. 72.
[4] *Ibid.*, p. 73.
[5] *Ibid.*, p. 75.
[6] *Ibid.*, p. 74.
[7] *Ibid.*, p. 77.
[8] *Ibid.*, p. 80.
[9] *Ibid.*, p. 81.
[10] *Ibid.*, p. 82.
[11] *Ibid.*, p. 92.
[12] *Ibid.*, p. 93.
[13] *Ibid.*, p. 100.
[14] *Ibid.*
[15] *Ibid.*, p. 103.
[16] *Ibid.*, p. 105.
[17] *Ibid.*
[18] Freud (1912), *Totem and Taboo*, XIII, 1.
[19] *Ibid.*, p. 4.
[20] *Ibid.*, p. 90.
[21] *Ibid.*, p. 86.
[22] *Ibid.*, p. 88.
[23] *Ibid.*, p. 90.
[24] *Ibid.*, p. 91.
[25] *Ibid.*, p. 78.
[26] *Ibid.*, p. 79.
[27] *Ibid.*, p. 81.
[28] *Ibid.*, p. 85.
[29] *Ibid.*, p. 83.
[30] *Ibid.*, p. 84.
[31] Freud (1911), "Formulations on the Two Principles of Mental Functioning," XII, 219.
[32] Freud (1912), *Totem and Taboo*, p. 75.
[33] *Ibid.*, p. 76.
[34] *Ibid.*, p. 77.
[35] *Ibid.*, p. 91.
[36] *Ibid.*, p. 96.
[37] Freud (1901), *The Psychopathology of Everyday Life*, VI, 258.
[38] *Ibid.*, p. 259.

[39]Freud (1912), *Totem and Taboo*, p. 64. Freud (1915), "The unconscious," XIV, 171.

[40]Freud (1912), *Totem and Taboo*, p. 93.

[41]*Ibid.*, p. 94.

[42]*Ibid.*, p. 92.

[43]*Ibid.*

[44]*Ibid.*, p. 93.

[45]Freud, *Three Essays on Sexuality* (footnote added 1915), VII, 146.

[46]Freud (1913), "Preface to Bourke's *Scatalogic Rites of All Nations*," XII, 335.

[47]Freud (1912), *Totem and Taboo*, XIII, 18.

[48]*Ibid.*, p. 19.

[49]*Ibid.* p. 23.

[50]*Ibid.*, p. 20.

[51]*Ibid.*, p. 26.

[52]*Ibid.*, p. 28.

[53]*Ibid.*

[54]*Ibid.*, p. 31.

[55]*Ibid.*, p. 35.

[56]*Ibid.*, p. 36.

[57]*Ibid.*, p. 41.

[58]*Ibid.*, p. 48.

[59]*Ibid.*, p. 50.

[60]*Ibid.* p. 51.

[61]*Ibid.*, p. 56.

[62]*Ibid.*, p. 57.

[63]*Ibid.*, p. 60.

[64]*Ibid.*, p. 61.

[65]*Ibid.*, p. 66.

[66]*Ibid.*, p. 101.

[67]*Ibid.*, p. 102, n. 1.

[68]*Ibid.*, p. 107.

[69]*Ibid.*, p. 4.

[70]*Ibid.*, p. 110.

[71]*Ibid.*, p. 113.

[72]*Ibid.*, p. 114.

[73]*Ibid.*, p. 109.

[74]*Ibid.*, p. 109.

[75]*Ibid.*, p. 108.

[76]*Ibid.*, p. 118.

[77]*Ibid.*, p. 126.

[78]*Ibid.*, p. 131.
[79]*Ibid.*, p. 132.
[80]Freud (1938), "Splitting of the Ego in the Process of Defense," XXIII, 277.
[81]Freud (1912), *Totem and Taboo*, XIII, 132.
[82]*Ibid.*, p. 133.
[83]*Ibid.*, p. 134.
[84]*Ibid.*, p. 135.
[85]*Ibid,*, p. 136.
[86]*Ibid.*, p. 140.
[87]*Ibid.*, p. 141.
[88]*Ibid.*, p. 143.
[89]*Ibid.*, p. 146.
[90]*Ibid.*, p. 144.
[91]*Ibid.*, p. 145.
[92]Freud (1938), *Moses and Monotheism*, XXIII, 84.
[93]*Ibid.*, p. 83.
[94]Freud (1912), *Totem and Taboo*, XIII, 147.
[95]*Ibid.*, p. 148.
[96]*Ibid.*, p. 149.
[97]*Ibid.*, p. 150.
[98]*Ibid.*, p. 155.
[99]*Ibid.*, p. 155.
[100]*Ibid.*, p. 156.
[101]Freud (1938), *Moses and Monotheism,* XXIII, 85, 127.
[102]Freud (1915), "Thoughts for the Times on War and Death," XIV, 292.
[103]Freud (1938), *Moses and Monotheism*, p. 129.
[104]*Ibid,*, p. 130.
[105]*Ibid.*, p. 133.
[106]*Ibid.*, p. 85.
[107]*Ibid.*, p. 115.
[108]*Ibid.*, p. 118.
[109]*Ibid.*, p. 115.
[110]*Ibid.*, p. 117.
[111]*Ibid.*, p. 110.
[112]*Ibid.*, p. 89.
[113]*Ibid.*, p. 129.
[114]*Ibid.*, p. 130.
[115]*Ibid.*, pp. 86, 135.
[116]*Ibid.*, p. 89.
[117]*Ibid.*, p. 86.
[118]*Ibid.*, p. 89.

[119]*Ibid.*, p. 135.

[120]Freud (1912), *Totem and Taboo*, p. 153.

[121]Freud (1912), *Totem and Taboo*, p. 154.

[122]*Ibid.*, p. 155.

[123]*Ibid.*

[124]Freud (1938), *Moses and Monotheism*, p. 132.

[125]Margaret Mead, "*Totem and Taboo* Reconsidered with Respect," *Bulletin of the Menninger Clinic*, XXVII (July 1963), 185. Freud (1927), *The Future of an Illusion*, XXI, 43.

[126]Meyer Fortes, "Malinowsky and Freud," *Psychoanalysis and the Psychoanalytic Review*, XLV, Nos. 1 & 2 (1958), 135.

[127]M. Brierley, *Trends in Psychoanalysis* (London: Hogarth Press, 1951), p. 210.

[128]Mead, "*Totem and Taboo* Reconsidered," p. 188.

[129]A. L. Kroeber, "*Totem and Taboo* in Retrospect," *American Journal of Sociology*, XLV (Nov. 1939), 447.

[130]Freud (1912), *Totem and Taboo*, XIII, 161.

[131]Branislaw Malinowski, *Sex and Repression in Savage Society* (London: Routledge & Kegan Paul, 1953), p. 153.

[132]*Ibid.*, p. 155. F. D. Klingender, "Palaeolithic Religion and the Principle of Social Evolution," *British Journal of Sociology*, V (June 1954), 150.

[133]Herbert Marcuse, *Eros and Civilization* (Boston: Beacon Press, 1955), p. 59.

[134]Gail Kennedy, "Psychoanalysis; Protoscience,"p. 277.

[135]*Ibid.*

[136]E. Roy John, "Studies in Learning and Retention in Planaria," *Brain Function* II, *RNA and Brain Function, Memory and Learning*, ed. by Mary Brazier (Berkeley: University of California Press, 1964), pp. 161-182.

[137]Salo W. Baron, "Book Review of *Moses and Monotheism*," *American Journal of Sociology*, XLV (Nov. 1939), 472.

[138]*Ibid.*, p. 476. Trude Weiss Rosmarin, *The Hebrew Moses: An Answer to Sigmund Freud* (New York: The Jewish Book Club, 1939), p. 5.

[139]S. C. Chatterjee, "Freud on the Future of Religion," *Indian Journal of Psychology*, XV, No. 4 (Oct. 1940), 143. Terrence W. Gervais, "Freud and the Culture-Psychologists," *British Journal of Psychology*, XLVI (Nov. 1955), 294.

[140]Freud (1927), *The Future of an Illusion*, XXI, 72.

[141]We are using the four causes in the Aristotelian sense.

[142]Freud (1912), *Totem and Taboo*, XIII, 100; Freud (1927), *The Future of an Illusion*, XXI, 37, 43.

[143]Stanley Hyman, *The Tangled Bank—Darwin, Marx, Frazer and Freud as Imaginative Writers* (New York: Atheneum, 1962), p. 366.

[144]Nathaniel Ross, "Psychoanalysis and Religion," *Journal of the American Psychoanalytic Association*, V (New York: International Universities Press, 1958), 525.

[145]Ernest Nagel, *The Structure of Science* (New York: Harcourt, Brace and World, Inc., 1961), p. 25.

[146]Philip Rieff, *Freud: The Mind of the Moralist* (New York: Viking Press, 1959), p. 292.

[147]Nagel, *The Structure of Science*, p. 25.

[148]R. M. MacIver, *Social Causation* (Boston: Ginn and Co., 1942), p. 110.

[149]Abram Kardiner, "Social and Cultural Implications of Psychoanalysis," p. 82. Rieff, "The Meaning of History and Religion," p. 114.

[150]Kardiner, *The Individual and His Society*, p. 409. Ellis, "An Introduction to the Principles of Scientific Psychoanalysis," p. 177.

[151]Kardiner, "Social and Cultural Implications," p. 84.

[152]MacIver, *Social Causation*, p. 111.

[153]*Ibid.*, p. 112.

[154]Roland Dalbiez, *Psychoanalytical Method and the Doctrine of Freud*, II (London: Longmans Green & Co., 1941), 290.

[155]MacIver, *Social Causation*, p. 218. Else Frenkel-Brunswik, "Psychoanalysis and the Unity of Science," p. 332.

[156]Nagel, *Structure of Science*, p. 542.

[157]Friedrich A. Hayek, *The Counter Revolution of Science* (New York: Free Press of Glencoe, Inc., 1952), p. 41.

[158]Heinz Hartmann, "The Application of Psychoanalytic Concepts to Social Science," *Psychoanalytic Quarterly* (1950), 391. Gregory Zilboorg, *Mind, Medicine and Man* (New York: Harcourt, Brace & Co., 1943), p. 300.

[159]Fairbairn, "A Critical Evaluation," p. 50.

[160]*Ibid.*, p. 52.

[161]Ernest Van den Haag, "Psychoanalysis and its Discontents," p. 106.

[162]MacIver, *Social Causation*, p. 111. Alex Inkeles, "Psychoanalysis and Sociology," *Psychoanalysis, Scientific Method and Philosophy*, p. 127. Kardiner, "Social and Cultural Implications," p. 85.

[163]W. R. D. Fairbairn, "A Critical Evaluation of Certain Basic Psycho-analytic Conceptions," *British Journal for the Philosophy of Science*, VII, no. 25 (May 1956), 49. Ricoeur, *Freedom and Nature*, p. 404.

[164]Rieff, *Mind of the Moralist*, p. 27.

[165]Robert Waelder, *Basic Theory of Psychoanalysis* (New York: International Universities Press, 1960), p. 59. Carl G. Jung, *Collected Works*, XI, trans. by R. F. C. Hull (London: Routledge & Kegan Paul, 1961), 349.

[166]Ricoeur, *Freedom and Nature*, p. 402. Jung, "Sigmund Freud in his Historical Setting," *Character and Personality*, I (Sept. 1932-June 1933), 49.

Chapter V
Contemporary Religious Experience: Genesis and Telos

In this *fifth* Chapter we are concerned with Freud's analysis of contemporary religious experience; he points out the prevalence of wish fulfillment in religious ideas. The source of this wish fulfillment or illusion is found in the infantile longing for consolation and fear of accusation. The desire for consolation in a world to come takes man away from his commitment to the world here and now. The commands and prohibitions of religion are too demanding upon man; they stand over against him as an accusation. In discussing the arguments given by believers who support religious ideas, Freud indicates the superficiality of evidence given for beliefs in the past and present along with the weakness in the argument from individual religious experience; he further objects to the approach which philosophers make to the problem of God.

In view of the lack of evidence for the validity of religious experience and religion's detrimental effects (especially in distorting reality), Freud opts for a religionless education. Science is not founded upon illusion and thus offers man the best opportunity for grasping reality as it is, science is still young but shows great promise of being able to comprehend the cosmos and psychoanalysis as a part of science shares its goals.

We discuss the various objections to Freud's position and then attempt to answer them. These objections revolve around the value of religion, and the relationship of philosophy, reason and science to each other. We then examine the effects of Freud's reductive interpretation: Freud makes way the path for a God beyond accusation

207

and consolation. We look to Freud's contribution to the philosophy of religion and finally, we summarize the argument of our work.

A. Exposition of Contemporary Religion: Genesis
1. Religious Ideas and Infantile Foundations

a. *Illusions.* Freud is concerned with the role of illusion (wish fulfillment) in religious ideas. He maintains that "Religious ideas are teachings and assertions about facts and conditions of external (or internal) reality which tells one something one has not discovered for oneself and which lay claim to one's belief."[1] These things which are given out as religious teachings are not the results of the thinking process or experience but " . . . they are illusions, fulfillments of the oldest, strongest and most urgent wishes of mankind." It is a human wish that there be a Providence to allay our fears, a moral world-order to fulfill the demands of justice, and a future life for all desires to be fulfilled.[2] In an *illusion*, we attempt to make ourselves independent of the external world by obtaining fulfillment through the internal processes of the mind. Illusions have their origin in the imagination; when we were growing to understand reality, this one area was left exempt from reality testing.[3] An illusion is not the same as an error nor need it be an error.[4] Illusions are derived from human wishes and in this respect come close to psychiatric delusions which contradict reality while illusions need not. "Thus we call a belief an illusion when a wish-fulfillment is a prominent factor in its motivation, and in doing so we disregard its relations to reality, just as the illusion itself sets no store by verification."[5] All religious doctrines are illusions and incapable of proof. Some of them are so out of harmony with reality that they could (if we take into account psychological differences) be compared to delusions. We cannot judge their "reality value." They cannot be proved or disproved. They might be true. Our knowledge is still limited so that we cannot make a critical evaluation of these illusions. Science is the only hope in leading to the truth of the matter.

To assess the truth-value of religious doctrines does not lie within the scope of the present inquiry. It is enough for us that we have recognized them as being in their psychological nature, illusions. But we do not have to conceal the fact that this

208

discovery also strongly influences our attitude to the question which must appear to many to be the most important of all. We know approximately at what periods and by what kind of men religious doctrines were created. If in addition we discover the motives which led to this, our attitude to the problem of religion will undergo a marked displacement. We shall tell ourselves that it would be very nice if there were a God who created the world and was a benevolent Providence and if there were a moral order in the universe and an after-life; but it is a very striking fact that all this is exactly as we are bound to wish it to be. And it would be more remarkable still if our wretched, ignorant and down-trodden ancestors had succeeded in solving all these difficult riddles of the universe.[6]

b. *Consolation.* Freud examines the sources of religious illusion namely, *consolation* and *accusation* and points out their infantile origins along with their incapacitating features which prevent man from facing reality the way it is. He reduces religion, seen as a source of *consolation*, to the infantile longings for protection that the child felt toward its father. Man is subject to all types of injury from the powers of nature: he calls these forces "Fate." Civilization, through religion, may console man in the face of Fate by attempting to take some of the terror out of the universe. There begins the process of the "humanization of nature" i.e. the impersonal forces of the universe are given passions similar to man.[7] With this change, man is not so defenseless; he can now adjure, appease and bribe these an-thropomorphic forces. This humanization of nature has an infantile prototype as it is a setting up of the same relationship that existed between the child and the parents. Nature, like the father, is to be feared but it also protects. Man gives to natural forces the exalted character of a father. "He turns them into gods, following in this as I have tried to show [*Totem and Taboo*], not only an infantile prototype but a phylogenetic one." The regularity in the order of nature resulted in a decrease of man's anthropomorphic view. However, in spite of this, man still remains helpless with a longing for the father and the gods who still maintain their threefold task of driving out the terrors of the universe, reconciling man to Fate and compensating man for his privations due to civilization.[8]

The gods ruled over nature and intervened (in miracles) to keep men aware of their presence. In the realm of destiny, man's helplessness did not seem to be remedied. Therefore, it seemed that Fate or Moira stood above the gods. As nature became more autonomous, and Fate was over the gods, the latter's task became that of rectifying the defects and evils of civilization. The gods supervised the commands of civilization which were seen to be of divine origin.[9] In the course of time the attributes of the gods were "condensed" into a single being.

We find in religion a combination of "instruction, consolation and requirements." These are the very things involved in the father-child relationship. The fact that all religions deal with a cosmogony which usually involves the activity of a being similar to man but of great power, wisdom, passion, makes us think of the child exalting or magnifying its own father. (Where we have animals creating the universe we see the influence of totemism.) This Creator is "always" a single being even in the presence of other gods; this being is "usually" a man. Mythologies show creation beginning with a male god removing a female deity;[10] in myth this Creator is called "father." Psychoanalysis claims that this superman is truly the father appearing with all the grandeur that the child conferred on its own father. Accordingly, as Freud remarks, "a religious man pictures the creation of the universe just as he pictures his own origin." It is true that when the child grows up he realizes that he is stronger but he also sees the greater dangers of life. Thus correctly he concludes that he is still helpless and "unprotected" but realizes also that his own father has limitations and imperfections.

> He therefore harks back to the mnemic image of the father whom in his childhood he so greatly overvalued. He exalts the image into a deity and makes it into something contemporary and real. The affective strength of this mnemic image and the persistence of his need for protection jointly sustain his belief in God.[11]

When he is confronted with the overwhelming problems of life, the person may engage in "a regressive revival of the forces which protected his infancy."[12] Religion is thus the adult's seeking for a defense against "childish helplessness."[13]

Man is limited in his making of choices because the way to

happiness and avoidance of suffering is already pointed out by religion. The individual is not allowed to face life without a crutch. Religion achieves its aim by placing little emphasis on the value of this life to the point of creating a delusional world.[14] Man is thus kept in a state of "psychical infantilism." It is true that some (witness the escape to monasticism of the past)[15] are spared an individual neurosis by entering into a "mass-delusion." But often, even in this, the believer finds that religion cannot answer the problems of life and leaves the answer to the nebulous idea of "God's inscrutable decrees." The only way then for consolation in suffering is submission to these decrees. Freud maintains that man could have saved himself the trouble of the religious detour.[16]

Freud believes that the person who only dwells on his insignificance and impotence in the face of the universe and who gives in to the idea of the little part man plays in the wide universe is "irreligious." The person who takes the next step—seeks a remedy to the present plight of man—that person sees the very essence of the religious attitude.[17] Christianity, by placing little estimate upon life here and now, is responsible for some of the hostility the masses feel toward civilization and the consequent lack of full commitment to the world.[18] Looking to the heavens for explanations and consolation takes man away from finding solutions to the problems of earth.[19] Man's energies should be concentrated on the betterment of this world and not expended on hopes of consolation in the next. "We leave Heaven to the angels and the sparrows."[20] Man is not to turn away from the world but is to become a part of the "human community" in which he pledges himself to make use of the techniques of science in an attack upon nature bending her to the will of man. As Freud says, "Then one is working with all for the good of all."[21]

And now, I think, the meaning of the evolution of civilization is no longer obscure to us. It must present the struggle between Eros and Death, between the instinct of life and the instinct of destruction, as it works itself out in the human species. This struggle is what all life essentially consists of, and the evolution of civilization may therefore be simply described as the struggle for life of the human species. And it is this battle of the giants that our nursemaids try to appease with their lullaby about Heaven.[22]

Those who find escape in religion are seeking consolation in a "narcotic."[23]

c. *Accusation.* Freud reduces religion, seen as a source of accusation, to the infantile fears that the child felt toward his father. The same father who gave him life and protected him also gave him commands with rewards and punishments. It is important for the child to believe that the parents love him and that he loves them. These parental relations are brought into religion which has its system of rewards and punishments. The individual feels himself protected and happy when he fulfills the ethical demands. Knowing that he loves God and is loved by God, enables him to face the perils of the world. In prayer, he can influence God and, at the same time, have some part in the power of the Divinity.[24] It is possible that what were at one time external commands may have become internalized in the form of what we call the "super-ego."[25] Man does not easily give up his infantile stage of conscience even after he has formed a super-ego. Fate is seen as a disguise for the parents. A man who does not do well feels he is no longer loved by the powers that be. He feels guilty; he must have done wrong and so he bows before the parental substitute—the super-ego. This is now the time for self-imposed abstinences and penances. He punishes himself as his parents once did when he was a child. As Freud points out, "This becomes especially clear where Fate is looked upon in the strictly religious sense of being nothing else than an expression of the Divine Will."[26]

Just as the individual has a superego, a particular civilization at a particular time may have its own unique super-ego which was derived from the impressions of its outstanding leaders who may have been ill-treated and even murdered. For even the primal father was not seen as divine till long after his murder.[27] Civilization, like individuals, can suffer from feelings of guilt which may be unconscious. What the culture does experience is a type of "*malaise.*"[28] Religion has always been interested in the guilt that civilization experiences. Accordingly, mankind makes use of religion because it offers to save humanity from this guilt. Christianity shows that the death of one man took away the guilt of everyone.[29]

Freud believes that the requirements of religion, which can be reduced back to the commands of the father, are too severe. The moral ideal that religion set before man was too difficult for him to attain and

212

psychologically unhealthy. Some people, who are constitutionally capable, and who have taken seriously the commandment of Christ ("Love thy neighbor as thyself") engage in aim-inhibited love. They give up the sexual aim and thus are in a general state of affectionate feeling. Freud maintains that of all the historical figures known to him, St. Francis of Assisi was best able to arrive at this state: at the same time he also received the benefit of inner happiness which gives man a share in the pleasure principle. Religion makes sure of this principle by telling its advocates to neglect the distinction between the ego and object or object and object i.e., religion tells us to love our neighbor as ourself and that all men are brothers and sons of the same Father. Thus we would have a condition of "universal love of mankind." However, Freud feels that a love that does not discriminate loses its own value: an object may not receive its true value and a person unworthy of love is given the same worth.[30]

To propagate the commandment of "universal love" and to hold the organization together the church makes use of the "illusion" that Christ loves all the members equally. Freud quotes Christ: "In as much as ye have done it unto one of the least of these my brethren, ye have done it unto me." Christ is likened to an elder brother or father substitute. The demands made by religion flow from the love of Christ and the Christian community is likened to a family. The bond which holds the individual to Christ is the same bond that holds all the members together: Christ is said to have more concern for the individuals than any human being.[31] Each individual has a "libidinal tie" with Christ and the other members at the same time. "If each individual is bound in two directions by such an intense emotional tie, we shall find no difficulty in attributing to that circumstance the alteration and limitation which have been observed in his personality." There is a curtailment of freedom: there is the prohibition against injuring members of the group but at the same time the person's own individuality suffers.[32]

> Every Christian loves Christ as his ideal and feels himself united with all other Christians by the tie of identification. But the Church requires more of him. He has also to identify himself with Christ and love all other Christians as Christ loved them. At both points, therefore, the Church requires that the position of

the libido which is given by group formation should be supplemented. Identification has to be added where the object-choice has taken place, and object-love where there is identification. This addition evidently goes beyond the constitution of the group. One can be a good Christian and yet be far from the idea of putting oneself in Christ's place and having like him an all embracing love for mankind. One need not think oneself capable, weak mortal that one is, of the Saviour's largeness of soul and strength of love. But this further development in the distribution of libido in the group is probably the factor upon which Christianity bases its claim to have reached a higher ethical level.[33]

Freud points out that St. Paul, who advocated a universal love as the foundation for the Christian community, was unknowingly laying the foundation for intolerance toward those outside this community. One has only to recall the massacres of the Jews in the Middle Ages to see this working out in history.[34] Those who do not love Christ and are not loved by Christ stand outside the community and are thus subject to intolerance. This seems to be the "natural" outcome in every religion. Yet, in a way, believers are to be pitied. For the unbeliever is better off psychologically in the matter of cruelty and intolerance. If there is less intolerance found today, it is not that men have become better, but rather religion and the libidinal ties that it establishes have been weakened.[35] But intolerance is not at an end. If Socialism and even Science could have the same meaning for the group that religion has, cruelty to outsiders would be the order of the day.[36]

With regard to "Love thy neighbor as thyself," Freud asks: "What is the point of a precept enunciated with so much solemnity if its fulfillment cannot be recommended as reasonable?"[37] "The commandment, 'Love thy neighbor as thyself,' is the strongest defense against human aggressiveness and an excellent example of the unpsychological proceedings of the cultural super-ego. The commandment is impossible to fulfill; such an enormous inflation of love can only lower its value, not get rid of the difficulty."[38] Because of man's inhumanity to man (witness the atrocities of the Huns, Mongols, Crusaders, World War I), Christianity is proposing another "*credo quia absurdum*" when it asks us to love our enemies.[39] Freud does not believe that men were more moral at the time of religious domination, people only obeyed the external commands of religion but their intentions were not pure. Frequently, the priests had to mitigate the commands which were too difficult to be carried out. After sin, there was the opportunity for sacrifice and penance only to be followed by more sin.[40] "In every age immorality has found no less support in religion than morality has." Thus if religion has not brought men happiness, acceptance of culture and morality, the questions arise as to whether it is needed and whether the demands of civilization should be based upon it.[41]

Freud contends that the construction of a God of accusation leads man to belittle himself all the more; man has taken the good things of earth and projected them out into some transcendent entity, leaving himself and earth impoverished. "Thus it was agreed: God alone is strong and good, man is weak and sinful."[42] In the course of time men have made instinctual renunciations which they offered to God as a sacrifice. These offerings were declared sacred.[43] Man formed the ideals of omnipotence and omniscience and gave these qualities to the gods along with everything that seemed unattainable or forbidden to himself. In the matter of cultural prohibitions, we tend to think of them as being given by God but they come from our own will.[44] The sacred character attached to prohibitions seems strange when the regulations change from time to time, on the other hand, the reluctance to make change ignores legitimate demands of the civilization. God should be left out of the matter and the origins of the precepts seen in the light of their human beginnings.[45] An ethical system based upon religious promises of reward or punishment in an afterlife is a futile attempt because ethics cannot succeed unless the virtuous life is rewarded here on earth.[46] Civilization remains in greater danger if it maintains a religious foundation for its precepts than if it were to abandon this basis.[47]

Freud goes on to say that the masses, for the most part, base their conduct in society upon a religious foundation. The problem will begin to arise when they discover that people no longer believe in God. The masses are willing to accept what scientific thinking has brought to civilization but they do not have the same motivations as the educated who maintain culture from secular motives. As Freud indicates " . . . either these dangerous masses must be held down

215

most severely and kept most carefully away from any chance of intellectual awakening, or else the relationship between civilization and religion must undergo a fundamental revision."[48] Therefore, Freud insists that man understand that the God of accusation is reducible to the father of our infancy. With knowledge of this revelation we must then abandon this idol which has been unmasked.

2. *Reason For Religious Beliefs*

Having maintained that religious doctrines, from the psychological aspect, are illusions with an infantile foundation, Freud embarks on the task of examining the reasons given by believers as proofs for the validity of the doctrine. Freud will attempt to refute these reasons. In ordinary experience, when we are asked to believe something, there are some grounds given for the claim. The conclusion comes as a result, perhaps, of a long process of thought based upon observations and inferences. What is more, one can go through the process oneself. Proofs are given. We are aware of the possibility that through our own experience we could acquire our own personal conviction. However, when we ask for the foundation of religious belief, we are given the following three answers: *one*, the doctrines are worthy of belief because our ancestors believed them; *two*, we have proofs which have been handed down from primaeval time; *three*, to raise such a question is not even permitted. In olden times, punishment was given for those who asked these questions; and even today people do not like these questions to be asked.[49]

a. *Tradition.* However, Freud notes that our ancestors were more ignorant than we are. What they believed could not be given credence today. Proofs given for the validity of religious belief are found in documents marked by contradictions, revisions and falsifications. Religionists consider it impertinent on the part of science to make religion a part of its study. They claim that religion is in a category above the categories of which the human mind is capable of operating. The reason given for the special place of religion is its divine origin. Freud points out that this is the very issue in question.[50] "Whatever may be the value and importance of religion, it has no right in any way to restrict thought—no right, therefore, to exclude itself from having thought applied to it."[51] However, the situation is different today. Religion no longer has the same influence, people find its promises less believable, natural science has exposed its errors and comparative

216

religion shows the similarity between religious ideas held sacred and the ideas of primitive peoples.[52]

The scientific spirit brings about a particular attitude towards worldly matters; before religious matters, it pauses for a little, hesitates, and finally there too crosses the threshold. In this process there is no stopping; the greater the number of men to whom the treasures of knowledge become accessible, the more widespread is the falling-away from religious belief—at first only from its obsolete and objectionable trappings, but later from its fundamental postulates as well.[53]

Science, with its foundation in observation, began to treat religion like any other natural phenomenon. Under this critical scrutiny religion was not able to bear up. Tales of miracles were seen to be products of imagination and in contradiction to what is observed in the world, e.g. the origins of the universe, proposed by religion, were in contradiction to scientific explanation.[54] Scientific investigation went further into the matter of reward or punishment for ethical behavior. Supposedly there is a Being who looks to the well-being of people and brings their activities to a providential ending. However, the fact shows that what has happened to mankind is neither in harmony with a "Universal Benevolence" or "Universal Justice." For it is evident that disasters in nature show no preference for the good or the evil person. Impersonal forces determine the fate of man.[55]

Freud maintains that it is not a new discovery that religious doctrines are impossible to prove. Our ancestors felt this and they also had doubts about their religious belief. However, they were under pressure from their peers; they thought it was their duty to believe and brilliant minds have suffered from this conflict.[56] Since the evidence authenticating religious doctrine happened in the past, we look for the same evidence in the present which we can better understand. If we could just prove a single point of religious doctrine, freeing it from doubt, the whole of religion would be benefited.[57]

b. *"Credo Quia Absurdum."* Freud challenges another argument used for the authenticating of religious belief—the *"credo quia absurdum"* of the early Church Fathers. The proponents of this belief maintain that religious doctrines are above reason, their truth is *felt*

217

interiorly, and it is not necessary to understand them rationally. Freud states that these arguments are weak because they raise the problem of which absurdities to believe and which not to. If the truth of religion is based on inner experience, then what becomes of the doctrine for those who do not have the experience? If the doctrine were based on reason, then all could come to understand the issue, because reason is common to all. Since the religious experience is unique to those who have it, their belief may easily be founded on a wish fulfillment. The doctrine may command belief because reality is too disturbing without it. "If one man has gained an unshakable conviction of the true reality of religious doctrines from a state of ecstasy which has deeply moved him, of what significance is that to others?"[58] The same is true for those who claim to have the sensation of eternity or limitlessness or the "oceanic feeling" which is supposed to bring promise of future immortality. What is the value for those who do not experience these? The "oceanic feeling" is described as being one with the whole world. Freud sees this experience as reducible to an intellectual perception with an accompanying feeling; it does not seem to be especially significant. He also questions whether the "oceanic feeling" should be regarded as the origin for the whole need for religion and he is moved to look for a psycho-analytic explanation for such a feeling. Ordinarily (except for the height of love) the ego maintains clear lines of demarcation between itself and the outside world.[59] In its beginning, the ego included everything, but later the external world was distinguished from it. Therefore in the normal person, "ego-feeling" is only a condensed version of what the original feeling was. In some people the *original* "ego-feeling" may still persist along with the reduced "ego-feeling." In such event, they could easily experience limitlessness and a union with the universe or what we spoke of as the "oceanic feeling."[60]

In regard to the origin of religion, Freud will not give primacy to the "oceanic feeling" (which resembles limitless narcissism) because the infant's helplessness and longing for the father (continued to adult life) seems closer to the origin of the religious attitude than the "oceanic feeling." The "oceanic feeling" probably came later as an attempt at "religious consolation" on the part of the ego escaping the threats of the external world. The practices of Yoga seem to induce these primordial states of mind. There seems to be a physiological foundation for these states and an insight into mysticism, trances and ecstasies can also be seen here.[61]

Another reason given for a belief in religion is that there is *purpose* operative in the world:[62] and it is an essential part of being human to ask about the purpose of life. However, Freud thinks it may *not* even be valid to ask whether there is any purpose to life as the question is presumptuous. To ask the question of the purpose of life is for Freud to presuppose already a religious position. " . . . the idea of life having a purpose stands and falls with the religious system." The purpose of life for Freud is the "pleasure principle"—man wants to be happy.[63]

> The moment a man questions the meaning and value of life, he is sick, since objectively neither has any existence; by asking this question one is merely admitting to a store of unsatisfied libido to which something else must have happened, a kind of fermentation leading to sadness and depression.[64]

Act "As If." Another attempt to justify the validity of religious ideas is the philosophy of "as if." The proponents of this position proceed to say that in our thinking activity we realize that we employ a great number of hypotheses which are groundless and absurd. We refer to these as "fictions," for practical reasons we act "as if" the fictions were true. We do the same with religious doctrines because of their great importance in maintaining society.[65] Freud points out that it seems strange that for such important activities so little certitude is required. We would ask for more certitude on ordinary activities. He believes that, since the "as if" position implies that religion is false, people will soon behave to the stories of religion as children behave to fairy stories which they discover to be false.[66]

Philosophy. Freud also rejects the philosophical[67] attempt to handle the problem of God.

> Philosophers stretch the meaning of words until they retain scarcely anything of their original sense. They give the name of "God" to some vague abstraction which they have created themselves; having done so they pose before the world as deists, as believers in God, and they even boast that they have rec-

219

ognized a higher, purer concept of God, not withstanding that their God is now nothing more than an insubstantial shadow and no longer the mighty personality of religious doctrines.[68]

However, this God of the philosophers is not the God of the common man who cannot think of God except as a great father knowing the needs of his children, listening to their prayers and forgiving their transgressions. The whole thing is grossly infantile. And there really is no way to rescue the situation. At the same time the philosophers attempt to save the God of religion with an "abstract principle." In this they are guilty of blasphemy.[69] If religious ideas are purified and belief is restricted to a superior being whose characteristics are "indefinable" and whose designs are incomprehensible, then those ideas will be invulnerable to the attack of science. However, these religious ideas will have no hold on mankind.[70]

3. *Religionless Education*

Because Freud finds that religion can be reduced to illusion, he advocates a non-religious education with the consequence that religion would more easily come to its inevitable demise. The age of science with its aim of understanding reality as it reveals itself will replace the efforts of religion. Psychoanalysis as part of science shares the same aim. Freud feels that religious education may hamper the development of the intellectual powers of the child.[71] Before the child is able to use its own mind, the religious doctrines have been implanted. Weakness of intellect, extending to all activities of the person, results because the child becomes accustomed to accepting things uncritically.[72] If the child was not given the religious education, he would not bother thinking about God and the after-life.[73] Yet Freud could also bring himself to write of Professor Hammerschlag: "Religious instruction served him as a way of educating towards love of the humanities, and from the material of Jewish history he was able to find means of tapping the sources of enthusiasm hidden in the hearts of young people and making it flow out far beyond the limitations of nationalism or dogma."[74] Therefore, it would seem that Freud is opposed to a particular type of religious education i.e., the type that is intellectually inhibiting and emotionally stifling—the type which speaks of accusation and consolation.

As Freud points out, "Thus I must contradict you when you go on to argue that men are completely unable to do without the consolation of the religious illusion, that without it they could not bear the troubles of life and the cruelties of reality. That is true, certainly, of the men into whom you have instilled the sweet- or bitter-sweet poison from childhood onwards.'' Man will have to admit his helplessness and smallness in the face of the universe. He must see that he is not the center of the universe and that Providence does not watch over him. In this way man will be like the child who has left the comfort of the parental home. Yet it is to be agreed that infantilism is not forever. "Men cannot remain children forever; they must in the end go out into 'hostile life.' We may call this 'education to reality.' ''[75] The things that cannot be overcome, man must learn to accept with resignation.[76] We cannot tell what man would really be like without these religious inhibitions. To find out, Freud advocates experimenting with an "irreligious education.''[77] "Should the experiment prove unsatisfactory I am ready to give up the reform and to return to my earlier, purely descriptive judgment that man is a creature of weak intelligence who is ruled by his instinctual wishes.''[78]

Freud considers the phenomenon of the demise of religion and makes use of a comparison of the child's growth and mankind's development. He points out that the child cannot successfully complete its development to a civilized degree unless it goes through a period of neurosis of greater or lesser intensity.[79] This condition is brought about because the child, faced with numerous instinctual demands, is not able to *suppress* them rationally in the same way as an adult. Instead, motivated by anxiety, he *represses* the instincts. Childhood neuroses, e.g., obsessional neurosis, usually clear up in the course of growth. "In just the same way, one might assume, humanity as a whole, in its development through the ages fell into states analogous to the neuroses . . .'' Man's beginning was a time of ignorance and weak intellect; instincts had to be given up so that community would be possible. The renunciation was done by force. The "precipitates'' of the repressive processes would be the universal obsessional neurosis of humanity—religion. Like the neurosis of childhood it is traced to the Oedipus complex and father-child relationship.[80] If the above analogy is correct, then as humanity grows religion will disappear. Presently, mankind is at this transitional phase.[81]

221

The time has come, as it does in analytic treatment, to allow the intellect to replace the forces of repression which were previously operative.[82] Religion can be compared to a childhood neurosis; we are optimistic that mankind will outgrow this neurotic phase as children outgrow their neuroses.[83] Religion also has a set of wishful illusions and escapes from reality as in the case of insanity—"blissful hallucinatory confusion." "But these are only analogies, by the help of which we endeavour to understand a social phenomenon: the pathology of the individual does not supply us with a fully valid counterpart." "Our analogy does not, to be sure, exhaust the essential nature of religion."[84]

Freud states that if his own wishes are illusions they differ from religious ones in that they are capable of correction. If it is pointed out in the future that we are incorrect, we will give up our expectations.[85] The religious cannot do this or their whole world collapses. Freud has given up infantile wishes and can bear the possibility that some of his expectations are illusions.[86] "The voice of the intellect is a soft one, but it does not rest till it has gained a hearing." The time when the intellect will predominate lies a long way off but not forever. The task of the intellect will be the same as that which the religious give to God i.e., love of one's fellow man and the alleviation of suffering.[87] Reason will be the force which will unify all men, the intellect and the scientific spirit will take over the mental life of man.[88] Thus Freud and the religious want the same thing. But Freud is more patient; the religious want paradise right after death with an emphasis on the individual.[89]

Our God Λόγος, will fulfill whichever of these wishes nature outside us allows, but he will do it very gradually, only in the unforeseeable future, and for a new generation of men. He promises no compensation for us, who suffer grievously from life. On the way to this distant goal your religious doctrines will have to be discarded, no matter whether the first attempts fail, or whether the first substitutes prove to be untenable. You know why: in the long run nothing can withstand reason and experience, and the contradiction which religion offers to both is all too palable.[90]

222

There is little to be said against the Dutch writer Multatuli when he replaces the *Moῖρα* [Destiny] of the Greeks by the divine pair *'Λόγος καὶ 'Ανάγκη*, [Reason and Necessity], but all who transfer the guidance of the world to Providence, to God, or to God and Nature, arouse a suspicion that they still look upon these ultimate and remotest powers as a parental couple, in a mythological sense, and believe themselves linked to them by libidinal ties.[91]

Both neurosis and psychosis are thus the expression of a rebellion on the part of the id against the external world of its unwillingness—or, if one prefers, its incapacity—to adapt itself to the exigencies of reality, to *'Ανάγκη* [Necessity].[92]

Religion, by its promise of a future reward in heaven, makes people renounce the pleasure principle so as to give victory to the reality principle. This is still illusion. Science, however, comes closest in conquering the pleasure principle, for it offers practical rewards here and now for the renunciation.[93] The movement away from religion to science cannot be an immediate process for the common man who has neither science nor art. The charitable thing to do for mankind will be to allow a gradual transition.[94]

a. *Science.* The best grasp of reality is through science which has been accused of being illusory since it gives nothing but subjective results: it is limited by our own mental apparatus. Some maintain that the real nature of things lies outside of ourselves and remains inaccessible to science. But Freud insists that our mental apparatus has been made to examine the external world,[95] this apparatus itself is also open to examination. We do limit science to telling us how the world "appears" to our mind. The findings of science are not only determined by the mental apparatus but also by the things acting upon that apparatus. If the mental apparatus could not work upon the real world, then there would be no practical interest in the world; the world would be an "empty abstraction." "No, our science is no illusion. But an illusion it would be to suppose that what science cannot give us we can get elsewhere."[96]

223

Freud claims that "intuition," "mysticism" and "divination" are illusions which are based upon emotion. Science looks to see the sources of these emotions but does not regard them as true knowledge.[97] Intuition and divination have value and express themselves in art, religion and philosophy but he allows them no place in the realm of knowledge. He claims that he is trying to deal with reality and not with wishes. Religion poses the greatest obstacle to science,[98] at an earlier age, it encompassed everything in the intellectual lives of men and took the place of science with a Weltanschauung which unified all experience. Science and religion come into competition because some of their aims overlap as in giving information on the origin and existence of the universe. However, science cannot make the promises of consolation that religion does.[99] In regard to precepts, both science and religion make them but for different reasons.[100]

Scientific thinking is the same type of thinking a believer or unbeliever uses in his everyday way of living; it does have some special features and is interested in all things even those which do not seem to have an immediate use; it attempts to avoid *subjective* and *emotional* factors in its investigating and scrutinizes carefully the data coming from the senses which will become the basis of further conclusions: it comes upon "new-perceptions" which are beyond everyday experience and by means of specific, varied experiments finds the cause of the former.[101] Scientific thinking attempts to correspond with reality i.e., it wants to know the outside world as that world is. "This correspondence with the real external world we call 'truth'." When religion claims to take the place of science or claims to be true because it helps mankind, it is rejected by science. Religion demands too much when it asks a person, who obeys the rules of experience in his investigation of reality, to accept a body of data which exempts itself from reason.[102]

The question arises for Freud as to why religion does not put an end to the dispute by admitting that it cannot give what man commonly considers "truth" which only science can give. (Freud distinguishes a "material" truth and an "historical" truth in regard to religion. Thus there is no great God in our day—no "material" truth; but there was in primaeval days the primal father—"historical" truth. The latter returns to man's mind as raised to divinity.)[103] Religion should claim that she can give something more beautiful than science—something that is true in a different higher sense. The truth of religion is that which consoles and uplifts. Religion refuses to admit it cannot give "truth" because it would lose its hold over mankind for the common man only knows one truth which does not admit of degrees; and Freud believes the common man to be correct.[104] There is the possibility that a non-religious education may not succeed in bringing in the god of reason.[105] But man will be resigned because he knows that science is able to give him knowledge about reality. Science is not an illusion as can be seen in its success. Science is still young and what is now an approximation to truth will be replaced by a fuller truth.[106] Science has not had the time to show all its potentialities but man can observe its advances in the last century.[107] Science moves slowly; it may be necessary to change its views many times on the way to truth. Only those that expect from science a substitute for the catechism will not be able to understand the necessity of its changing views.[108] Those in the camp outside of science have it easy; they have an immediate Revelation.[109] Freud maintains that "Mediocre spirits demand of science a kind of certainty which it cannot give, a sort of religious satisfaction. Only the real true scientific minds can endure doubt, which is attached to all our knowledge."[110]

As Freud says, "Science, as you know, is not a revelation; long after its beginnings it still lacks the attributes of definiteness, immutability and infallibility for which human thought so deeply longs. But such as it is, it is all that we can have."[111] Science does not consist *in toto* of strictly proven theses; it would be unfair to demand this. "Science has only a few apodeictic propositions in its catechism . . ." The rest of its propositions have varying degrees of probability. It is the way of science to be satisfied with approximations to certitude and to continue in spite of the lack of final certainty.[112] Freud points out that " . . . science has its particular approach to reality but really does not have a complete Weltanschauung; a Weltanschauung is an intellectual construction which solves all the problems of our existence uniformly on the basis of one overriding hypothesis, which, accordingly, leaves no question unanswered and in which everything that interests us finds its fixed place."[113] Science assumes a uniformity in the universe but it awaits the future to see the fulfillments of events. Science is limited to what is knowable at the moment and it works upon observations; there is no place for revelation, intuition or divination.[114]

b. *Psychoanalysis.* A *Weltanschauung* based upon science, placed emphasis on the "real external world," tried to bow before the truth and opposed illusions.[115] Psychoanalysis does not construct its own Weltanschauung but comes under the scientific view and makes a contribution in the mental field,[116] ". . . it engages in careful and laborious investigations, devises hypotheses and scientific constructions . . .,"[117] is aware of the force of human wishes (wish fulfillments—illusions) and the pleasure principle. In order to achieve a small amount of certainty, analysis is willing to give up what appears to be a "flawless theory" or a "comprehensive view of the universe." Rather it searches out more laws in nature which will explain reality to a greater depth.[118]

Psychoanalysis is not like a philosophy which starts out with a few defined concepts and tries from these to understand the whole universe leaving no room for new discoveries. Psychoanalysis stays in contact with the data under investigation and moves forward—aided by experience; it is an incomplete science looking to correct its theories;[119] it does not differ much from chemistry and physics as its general concepts at times are lacking in clarity and its postulates are only provisional. Future work will look to further precision of definition and clarification.[120]

Freud denies that the Weltanschauung of psychoanalysis is directed at the destruction of religion stating, "In point of fact, psychoanalysis is a method of research, an impartial instrument, like the infinitesimal calculus. . . ."[121] Anything that psychoanalysis says against religion was already said sometime in the past. It may be that the psychoanalytic method brings new evidence against religion: that is too bad for religion.[122] The following comment of Freud is quite significant:

> Moreover, it is quite unscientific to judge analysis by whether it is calculated to undermine religion, authority and morals; for, like all sciences, it is entirely non-tendentious and has only a single aim—namely, to arrive at a consistent view of one portion of reality. Finally, one can only characterize as simple-minded the fear which is sometimes expressed that all the highest goods of humanity, as they are called—research, art, love, ethical and social sense—will lose their value or their dignity because

psychoanalysis is in a position to demonstrate their origin in elementary and animal instinctual impulses.[123]

Psychoanalysis as a science is characterized not by the material it treats but by the special technique it employs. Analysis can be applied to the history of civilization, art, philosophy, neuroses, mythology and the "science of religion" or "philosophy of religion."[124] As the Weltanschauung of psychoanalysis was not directed against the destruction of religion, neither does it give any different consideration to religion as distinct from any other phenomenon. Psychoanalysis as a part of science aims to reveal reality ever more fully. It tries, by its reductive technique, to remove distortions which prevent us from seeing reality as it is in itself.

B. *Critique of Freud's Position*
1. *Religious Person as Dependent*
Having seen Freud's critique of contemporary religious experience, we consider the objections to his position and we attempt to answer them. Freud is criticized because his notion of religion is restricted to the feeling of *dependence* one has in relation to God conceived of as father of the human family;[125] the religious person is considered passive and docile;[126] Freud seemed to ignore the other side of religious experience; the heroes or prophets in religion were great individualists who did stand in opposition to the mores of their culture:[127] a decision of faith is not always a pleasant one for a man to make; it is more challenging than "wish-fulfillment."[128] Freud would answer that regardless of what aspect of the religious experience we are involved in, the experience always remains one in which unresolved conflicts *might* be the force behind the action. Each experience would thus have to be scrutinized as a person's overt behavior is not a decisive criterion for Freud in determining neurosis. A neurotic person may exhibit either passivity or activity. Thus heroes, prophets, and men of faith may have infantile motives at the heart of their action.
2. *Future Consolation*
The critics maintain that Freud cannot understand that the consolation of religion is not a mere substitute for earthly values because he

does not fully accept the possibility of a transcendent God,[129] there is no earthly value comparable to this God; man, from the depths of his being, is directed toward this Being as truly as he is directed to the world.[130] Freud would have to admit that man is not satisfied by earthly values alone but he would be closed to the problem of the existence of a transcendent God. Those for whom a transcendent God is meaningful find in religion consolation for earthly misery; therefore, religion is not functioning as a substitute for earthly values. Earthly misery takes on a different meaning when endured in union with God.[131] However, Freud maintains the possibility of the existence of God but not a God made after the image of man.[132] A God above all earthly values is a possibility but He is not without suspicion. Especially is this God called into question when He is the type that merely consoles us amidst our sufferings with promises of heavenly bliss. In this case, as in all cases of religious experience, we must be assured of the absence of the infantile longings before we can affirm such a being.

3. *Value of Individual Religious Experience*

Some raise objections to Freud's treatment of the "credo quia absurdum."[133] Here it is an inner conviction which is experienced. The opponents might maintain that Freud is correct in saying that this experience is limited to individuals who have the experience. However, they claim that Freud does overlook[134] the fact that the leap of faith in the midst of surrounding absurdity has made life a meaningful experience for many and not just a few. Freud would have to consider that (whether there is a God or not) for those who opt for faith, this option does something to change their life; it gives them the resolve to go on living. These are meaningful experiences whether their origins may be reduced to psychological complexes or whether there is no referent (God) with whom they think they are in a relationship (religion).

Freud would maintain that there is psychological truth in religious experience. It does provide for the possibility of maintaining sanity in the midst of absurdity. However, Freud would question whether an experience based on the "credo quia absurdum" has truth value establishing the existence of a Transcendent. Also, he would maintain that such a "leap of faith," like any other religious experience, would have to be scrutinized in order to determine whether there is an infantile foundation to it.

4. "Purpose" in the World

In the matter of the "purpose" of life, Freud's thought is ambivalent. In one instance, he rules out the validity of asking about the purpose of life. In seeking for purpose he claims we enter implicitly the realm of religion. Also he states that there is no meaning (no real referent) to questions about the "purpose of life;" he tries to explain away purpose by saying that questions about it arise only when there is some unsatisfied libido. At Freud's time, scientists believed that there was no purpose in nature; there were only observable causal connections. This same reasoning was extended to life itself—purposeless. Scientists were resigned to the idea. If one looked at the world in order to see purpose operative, one was a philosopher, not a scientist.[135] Thus when Freud returned to Vienna from Paris claiming that the causes of neuroses could be found in psychical experiences, he was called a philosopher. This categorization Freud rejected forcefully.[136]

While Freud saw the scientist as one who was resigned to the forces of the cosmos, he emphasized strongly the continuous and progressive effort of the scientist to grasp more and more of that revealing cosmos. The whole path of man's development in confrontation with the cosmos shows purpose; the scientist in his endeavors acts to understand more and more the purpose of nature. Whatever the *origin*, the question of "purpose" is of human concern[137] and is not that easily dismissed. It is because Freud dislikes discussing "purpose" that his analyses of phenomenon are always limited and incomplete; he only completes himself when he sees the emergence of telos after his reduction; he should have realized that he could not escape from a teleological direction at least implicitly. For his scientific endeavors were for some purpose: to grasp reality more completely and to serve mankind. "Science is inseparable from the rationalist aims of Western culture, which are as utopian as any vision of heaven."[138]

5. "Scientism" Philosophy and Religion

Freud gave science an all-embracing role in explaining the universe because of the "scientism" rampant at the end of the nineteenth century. Haeckel was a prominent supporter of this view which made science supreme.[139] When Freud was attending school, the scientific method (which meant deriving knowledge from empirical observation) was then accepted as the *only* way of coming to knowledge.[140]

Therefore, Freud does not distinguish clearly between science and reason; he used the terms interchangeably. Science was thought to be the solution of all the world's problems.[141] If science could not fathom the phenomenon, then no man could.[142] Thus it is objected that Freud has a limited theory of knowledge.[143] Religion and philosophy are rejected as providing no real knowledge and since they are bound up with the *inner* workings of the mind and their truth cannot be observed experimentally, Freud considered them suspect; religion and philosophy have some value but not true knowledge because they are the products of wish fulfillment.

We will attempt to answer these objections. It should be remembered that Freud considered that true knowledge was derived through sense observation. What religion proposed to speak of was a relationship with some transcendent Being which Freud admits there might be but he questions the means of arriving at the certainty of this Being. Since the relationship of man to this transcendent can be expressed in no other way than by human behavior, and since this behavior can be comprehended by psychoanalysis, the latter feels competent to speak about it. Where psychoanalysis reveals unconscious conflicts and wish fulfillments at the core of the religious experience, it claims that the true value of the experience as telling about the nature or existence of this transcendent is suspect. Freud seriously considered the religious experiences of various sorts as possibly giving some knowledge of a transcendent. However, when he investigated these phenomena and found that wish fulfillment was at their root, he ruled them out as valid approaches to knowledge. Freud was also afraid of giving much credence to mysticism and spiritualism because these phenomena were looked down upon by the scientists of the day. Freud was reluctant to study them carefully because he feared that any association of psychoanalysis with them might endanger the respectability of analysis.[144]

We will explore the fact that Freud used the concepts of science and reason interchangeably.[145] Freud considered that the mind worked in the following manner: it made use of data provided through the senses and then it organized the material obtained so as to arrive at further knowledge. This is the way Freud believed science operated. It observed reality and then organized the material into hypotheses, theories and laws. It was inconceivable to Freud that one could do any scientific work without beginning with observation of the sensible world: and it was equally inconceivable as to how one could reason without first making use of the sensible world. The philosopher ordinarily believes that what he has to say is about the real world. However, in Freud's view the philosopher was not talking about that same world that the scientist observed. When Freud speaks of philosophy he sometimes has in mind a type of rationalism which begins with the conceptual order and tries to derive information about the real world by means of concepts alone;[146] at other times he has in mind Schelling's "philosophy of Nature" which he considered a kind of mysticism. Freud was extremely anxious that psychoanalysis not be associated in any way with "philosophy of Nature" because he feared analysis might lose its scientific respectability.[147] Thus it is conceivable that Freud did not realize there could be a valid philosophical approach to reality, namely, one that began with the world of sense and rose beyond the world of the sensible; it might be that his limited view of what philosophy was did not allow him to see philosophy as a valid discipline for arriving at truth.

We believe Freud's historical limitation in regard to philosophy was one of the reasons that caused him to rule out the possibility of arriving at a philosophical knowledge of God. The fact that Freud despised a God which was part of a philosophical system[148] was due to the fact that God was made merely a cog in a machine. He was there to guarantee that the system would hold together and he rightly believed that this forementioned God was not the God of religious experience.

A critic, using Freud's own technique, could say that science ought to be rejected because here man finds an outlet for his inordinate infantile curiosity; science could be an expression of man's overconfidence in himself. "Such a critic might even assert that science is an infantile, neurotic adaptation which leads us to destroy life while claiming that we aspire to achieve the opposite."[149] In answer to the critic, we maintain that Freud has established the infantile at the foundation of religious behavior. That the infantile is at the source of science and the very desire "to know" has not been established. We do not maintain that the infantile *totally* exhausts faith in the "Wholly Other." Freud, too, admitted there might be a God. We have shown that beyond the infantile and the religious there was a *telos* in man pushing "to know" the other—to comprehend more and more of the cosmos as revealing. Whether it is demonstrated or not that the infantile is at the core of science, a deeper meaning is still found in scientific investigation not unlike that which we find hidden in the religious.

C. *Emergence of a Religion Beyond Accusation and Consolation: Telos*

We now reflect upon the implications of Freud's reductive interpretation for religious thought. From the process of reification of the sacred there comes forth both religion and metaphysics. Religion treats the sacred as a new group of objects alongside other objects of culture. Metaphysics makes God into a "supreme being." Freud's reductive interpretation attempts to bring about the death of the religious and metaphysical object[150] while allowing us to see the *signs* of the approach of the "Wholly Other." "Faith is that region of the symbolic where the horizon function is constantly being reduced to the object-function:" with deification idols are born in religion. Metaphysics also gives birth to concepts of "supreme being," "first substance," "absolute thought."[151]

However, the sacred means distinctness and otherness; the sacred is a sign of that which does not belong to us—the "Wholly Other." But the sacred can also be made a sphere of separate objects in our culture along with the others. The sacred can be a sign of the approach of the "Wholly Other" or it can be an idol set in a special place in our culture. The idol becomes a source of alienation. Psychoanalysis when it had destroyed the idols cannot tell us whether it has explained away faith: it cannot say whether ritual is *entirely* reduced to obsession and whether faith is based on the infantile longing. Psychoanalysis may hold before the religious man his caricature but there is still allowed the possibility of overcoming the distortion.[152] Freud's atheism is not completed merely by his destruction of religion. His atheism prepares for a faith of a post-religious age.[153] The Freudian attack upon religion concentrated upon the two major roles of religion: a source of accusation and consolation. This type of religion must be overcome by faith[154] which would preach a creed of liberation without any prohibition and condemnation.[155] To understand what Being is trying to say to us, we must be free from the fear of accusation. In order to hear the "Wholly Other," there must be silence but the silence is not mere negation. It is a time of receptivity: but to be receptive one must be free of anxiety born of fear. We must be fully ourselves without alienation in the encounter. There is in each person the desire to be—to exist. The desire to be is the movement of effort or "conatus" to use Spinoza's word. Freud's Eros shows the affirmation of the desire to be. Alienation, because of a desire for a God of accusation and consolation, works against the affirmation of the desire to be and the source of alienation must be overcome.

The God of condemnation and consolation is not the only type of God that man can encounter.[156] Freud's atheism means the destruction of God as ultimate source of protection. Reality must be seen as it is; Freud sometimes makes Ananke (Necessity) synonymous with the reality principle and it is the acceptance of reality as it reveals itself that enables us best to grasp it. Being tries to reveal itself as it is; we must give up the pleasure principle which distorts our view of Being. Renunciation of the longing for the father is a necessity before we can encounter Being. The God that is beyond accusation and consolation is a God who allows me to encounter the dangers of life because this is what it means to be human. Only beyond the longing for the God of protection will we find the real meaning of the God of consolation.[157] Where Being is received as totally meaningful, then my narcissism is gone and along with its disappearance there go fear of accusation and desire for consolation. Being is revealed in its fullness and there now remains the opportunity of consent and resignation which can be considered the beginning of consolation which goes beyond the desire of protection.[158]

Reality is not only observable facts and laws that can be verified: reality is the world of things and of men as perceived by a self which has given up the pleasure principle. This means that a person has "subordinated" his point of view to the whole. Being is manifested through the world; man as being is part of the manifestation of Being: consolation is attainable to man in that he belongs to Being. We have moved from resignation to consent; from consent to a way of living upon the earth where there is "love of creation" which is a mode of consolation free of reward or punishment.[159] To have been part of the manifestation of Being is itself consolation.

Atheism shows us that the father image must be overcome as any idol. The father seen as symbol would mark our journey from accusation and consolation to resignation: from resignation to rejoicing in creation. As Ricoeur says, "An idol must die, in order that a symbol of Being may speak."[160] "A path is thus opened, a path of non-narcissistic reconciliation: I give up my point of view: I love the whole: I make ready to say: 'The intellectual love of the mind towards God is a part of that very love of God whereby God loves himself'."[161]

We believe the overcoming of the God of accusation and consolation is best seen in Freud's treatment of Leonardo as scientist and artist. In the latter's idea of love, knowlege is made a pre-requisite to the love-experience. Man ordinarily does not proceed from intellectual reflection to love; our experience shows love to be somewhat impulsive. Leonardo, with reference to the Creator, held that love for the other came forth from great knowledge of the other. In this *first* moment, Leonardo neither loved nor hated the other: he was indifferent to good and evil, beauty and ugliness. He was not without eros but his passion or desire was transformed into a thirst for knowledge. He gathered all of his energy in the effort to encounter the universe as it revealed itself.[162] The "greatness of the Creator" was seen in what was discovered[163] and thus Leonardo does not encounter the Creator with a narcissism which would distort reality.

The postponement of loving until full knowledge is acquired ends in a substitution of the latter for the former. A man who has won his way to a state of knowledge cannot properly be said to love and hate; he remains beyond love and hatred. He has investigated instead of loving.[164]

We mentioned that the person who begins, through investigation, to see the splendor of the universe begins to see less his own insignificance. His ability to reflect upon the whole of being shows that the small is as full of significance as is the great.[165] Leonardo in his research became involved in the whole hierarchy of beings: colors, shadows, plants, animals, the human body. He saw these things from the outside and then proceeded to view their interior. Having gone beyond a providential and accusing God, he encounters the cosmos with an undistorted vision. One can then give up " . . . the pious view of the Universe which Leonardo himself was on the way to overcoming when he wrote that the sun does not move."[166]

234

D. *Freud's Contribution to Contemporary Philosophy of Religion*

1. *Abandonment of Naïveté*

We concern ourselves with Freud's contribution to contemporary philosophy of religion. We consider that he has caused us to scrutinize religious experience more carefully. He makes the philosopher of religion aware of the need to purify the conception of God from its anthropomorphisms. Particularly, we must relinquish a God of accusation and consolation. Freud has brought to our attention the need for greater insight into how much wish fulfillment is at play in one's relation to God. One must be aware, therefore, of what part of the experience is based upon subjective factors and what part upon objective factors. The infantile, and fixated, must be distinguished from the mature and free.[167]

The person who is fully mature is no longer a victim of unconscious infantile longings which seek satisfaction in their beliefs about God; nor is the mature person one who has unconscious hostility toward the father which finds expression in doing away with him, i.e., atheism.[168] The important factor is to examine the *character* of the belief or unbelief. Belief or disbelief, to be considered mature, must be the distillation of a mind which has gone through the infantile stages of development successfully. As the child has had to resolve the relations with the parents, so the mature person has resolved these attitudes toward God.[169]

2. *Committment to the World*

The one who gives to his thought and action "divine guarantees" is one who refuses to accept the human side of thought and conduct. If one is not aware of the *human* character of his thought and action, can he really take them seriously? Freud has pointed to religion's over-emphasis on the consolation of God and happy life hereafter. Man, to be completely human, needs the solace of earth. This is a valid criticism of a religion which is too overbalanced on the spiritual side.[170] With the emphasis that Freud gives to the world here and now, special obligations become apparent to those who claim to be religious. Love for neighbor must include seeing the other as free and involved in the world. One becomes truly a self because of his involvement. This world includes the whole spectrum of human experience. Thus the love for neighbor finds best expression in making this world a place for the neighbor to grow and develop. The religious person becomes involved in the reform of society[171] so that he may make self-realization most accessible.[172] Some religious people seem to think they can use and dispose of God. They act as if they have an insight into the Infinite Wisdom.[173] This view does not allow the person to take all the risks that are meant in life. He really never fully feels the existential plight of man. This false view of reality is derived from our own narcissism and is a distortion of God's transcendence.[174]

As one author says of Freud, '' . . . like an Old Testament Prophet, he overthrew false idols and pitilessly spread out to view the rottenness of the contemporary soul. Wherever he applies a painful reduction (for example, in explaining our God of the nineteenth century as a glorification of 'Papa', . . .), we can be sure that a collective over-evaluation or falsification is called into question''[175] Freud like Moses is making the very difficult demand of asking mankind to give up pride—i.e., what he makes himself appear to be in favor of what he really is.[176]

Freud as a Jew (with a vision, perhaps even mystical)[177] comes to the Christian religious experience, which has become irrelevant, and tries to purify it as Christ tried to purify Judaism of its Pharisaic orthodoxy.[178] Psychoanalysis aims at liberation.[179] Freud unmasks, in the course of his analysis of religion, the God who is a product of "human miseries, aspirations and search after power."[180] If the religious acts and practices of the primitive are abandoned because man can handle his problems by technology, then the God originally worshipped was a pseudo-God. The "presence" of God, in a primitive time, which was affirmed because of man's impotency in the face of the universe, was really a "Pseudo-presence." In cultures with advanced technology it is not easy to affirm that "pseudo-God" as the transcendent God. "For this we owe in part a debt of gratitude to atheism."[181]

"Modern Man, then will not, without more ado, call God back, when the time for it has arrived. Jupiter and Thor, after their fall, have never been restored to their altars, and rightly so. So also will the man of the future not call back a "God" who has to make up as a sort of physical energy, for the loss of energy in the macrocosm, who has to make the poor accept their wretched

236

lot on earth, who must keep the oppressed in their social and political state of degradation. He will not be a God who acts like a French king or a German emperor, who can be inspected as a factor in an Oedipus-complex, who is a kind of 'unstared stare' and pursues man with his threats, who produces man as a kind of utensil, who makes man's cultural activity superfluous. He will not be a God who lets theologians have a look at the maps of His Providence, who lets Himself be invoked as a meteorological and agricultural factor. He will not be a super-economist, a super-physician, a super-psychiatrist who puts all economists, physicians, and psychiatrists in the shade, who so greatly prompts man to forget his fellow-man that charity becomes unimportant. The man of the future will call God back, but this call will be only for the true God. With the heaven above his head empty of pseudo-gods, he will walk through the world and history, calling for a Transcendent God.''[182]

3. Purification

Freud more than any other contemporary thinker leads us through an excruciating purification. No idea is left secret; it must be exposed to brilliant flame. This is not God; that is not God; this is you; that is you. Now we are enlightened: we know all that He is not. Thus man is caught in a dilemma in his search for God. He has had to sacrifice all his idols. "Man frees himself from superstition through atheism . . . only to fall once again into superstition.''[183] Wherever man turns there fall before his path numerous illusions which he must suffer to overcome, if he will attain victory.[184] God must disclose himself to man as "Other." He is unconditional and He is unavailable to be coerced by man. God is hidden but this distinguishes Him from the gods of the tribe whom man has placated over the centuries. Nor is God a part of an ontological system where he may be manipulated along with other concepts.[185]

Thus gods, which are a little beyond the activities of man and which draw their life from the culture, are not transcendent enough to be alive. As one author points out, " . . . every attempt of any age to be religious in this way bestows just enough life upon such deities for them in turn to prove inhumanly oppressive and to suck up into themselves the well-springs of cultural creativity from which they spring by an immanent act of God-creation.''[186] The Transcendent

237

God has a life of his own and is not limited by culture. A Transcendent God allows man to make accomplishments while remaining the Other.[187] God is in the very tension of finding and losing. If reality is revelatory, then we are constantly forming and reforming our ideas and experiences as we become more and more aware of the revelation. Freud tells us that we are mistaken in our old notions; that we have not really known; because of our narcissism, that which we thought we knew about God is dreadfully inadequate. We have been deceived; we have deceived ourselves.

Freud does not come with a challenge to a metaphysical system; he does not point out that the notion of God has been introduced to hold a system together. Neither does he tell the metaphysician that a rational or empirical approach is insufficient. Freud does not come to tell us that a particular factor (a substructure) operative in the civilization is the cause for our views on religion or God. Freud is much more disturbing. He points to the very core of man—the most basic impulses and not even those we are aware of as operative but those which are unconscious! He proclaims that we cannot grasp reality completely unless we are *consciously* aware of what we *unconsciously* would like that reality to be.

Freud more than any other thinker has pointed to the limitation man can have on a grasp of reality because of not knowing himself completely. Thus the contribution of Freud to a philosophy of religion is a radical one. It demands that before one engage in a philosophy of religion he must be purified: he must have gone through a dark night before he can dare to say, "I see a little less darkness." Contemporary man feels most intensely the problem of the death or absence of God because he has come to a more heightened consciousness of himself and the cosmos. He is beginning to understand the significance of unconscious desires being brought to the conscious level. For now we have a greater grasp of reality with all the accompanying responsibility. When Freud was questioned by opponents on his analysis of religious phenomenon, he said that " . . . we are speaking at cross purposes, and our differences will be ironed out only after centuries."[188] He was not aware how quickly a century could pass.

Freud had the obsessive drive "to know" and "to know" ever more deeply. Man in his relationship with himself, to others and to the cosmos intrigued him to no end. To understand reality he looked to the past as providing an insight into the present and at the same time he realized the independence of the present. Around these two poles, his thoughts fluctuated as he endeavored to understand all phenomena. He was acutely aware of the limitations of the human mind— limitations which prevented it from grasping reality in its fullness. He tried to understand that mind; he had available the tools of his own science—psychoanalysis. Perhaps he did not realize fully the inner tension of his invention which reflected the mind of its inventor. No one ever took more seriously the words "Know thyself." He was able to know the mind in a way that no one ever knew it before. His only error was to think, perhaps, that he had captured it totally.

He was obsessed with religion. It haunted him throughout his life. It is in all his writings. Maybe we now know the reason. Could the very thing which intrigued him so much—the thing which he considered blocking the clear vision of reality—could that be the very key he was looking for as opening up a new vision of reality? He compared religious manifestation with neurotic behavior. They seemed both to be escapes from reality; they seemed to rest heavily upon the "pleasure principle" while sacrificing the "reality principle." Yet beyond the symbols of neurosis and religion, there was concealed a struggle: the person endeavoring to meet with reality—to grasp it, to comprehend it, and finally, to come to terms with it. Neuroses and religion point to the various terms the person agreed upon in the struggle. Distortion of reality points to the person's weakness. Freud must have seen himself in this struggle.

We see that the history of mankind has been a continuous battle between the forces of darkness and light. The Fall (primal crime) plunged man into darkness; he would have to labor to enlighten his darkened intellect. Mankind's epic has been one of the slow emergence of the "reality principle." Religion tells the story of the struggle and holds the symbols pointing to the struggle in understanding reality. It has been a continuous story full of hope in spite of illusion. Contemporary man is under few illusions now. He experiences stark reality. The neurotic cannot use the symptom any longer once he discovers its meaning. Man can no longer use religion when the meaning of his actions are revealed. The illusions have gone and he finds in his hands symbols. They are very precious as are all souvenirs of a struggle. But they tell us something of the past and we

239

are in the present. We have nothing else to do but to continue to confront reality leaving as our bequest new and everchanging symbols of our struggle.

E. *Summary*

In this work we have seen a certain ambivalence running through Freud's thought; he has both a genetic and teleological orientation. We traced the source of his ambivalence back to the evolutionary thinkers who had an influence on Freud from the beginning. We have maintained the position that neither a genetic nor teleological explanation *alone* provides an adequate explanation of a phenomenon under study.

In Freud's analysis of the ontogeny of person we have found both genetic and teleological explanations given. However, these explanations, we feel, were not looked at as complimentary by Freud. Rather, his analysis shows at one time an implicit teleology operative in his explanation of growth and regression; and at another time we see only the genetic orientation. We have shown that there is a richer meaning in Freud's analysis of person if we take the two orientations as complementary. For we found that person is not fully understood merely in terms of a determined past but by the freedom, spontaneity, and purpose operative in the present moment. However, the significant point made is that we do not appreciate the present purposeful orientation unless we have engaged first in an endeavor of accounting for person in terms of genesis. *Genesis* in its inadequacy highlights *telos*. Man moves in the direction of grasping the "reality principle" in preference to the "pleasure principle."

Further, investigation showed us that the psycho-analytic concepts have both their genetic and teleological sides. Freud's predominant orientation was to the genetic. The concepts seen from the genetic aspect were seen to be meaningful and valid with reference to what they said about person. However, again we found a deeper understanding of the person when we saw a dialectic of genesis and telos within the concept itself, i.e., the relationship of the genetic side of that concept to its teleological aspect. The teleological aspect of the concepts were seen when they were taken in relation to each other, e.g., conscious and unconscious. The concepts did not fully tell us about person unless we included their teleological orientation.

Having seen Freud's basic orientation in the understanding of person and the richer meaning obtained by juxtaposing genesis and telos, we followed this development into the study of person as religious. Since Freud's discussion of religion is intimately bound up with neurosis, we obtained an understanding of his views on religion through an analysis of his case studies. Freud's analysis was essentially reductionistic or genetic in orientation. We have taken the position that his reduction of religious experience to the Oedipus complex is correct as far as it goes. Since we believe that the reductive moment is correct, we have defended this position by an examination of the methodology employed in Freud's cases. We have seen that the methodology is satisfactory according to the norms of philosophy of science. Further, we believe that Freud's conclusion has some degree of probability.

However, we have seen the reductive moment as not being able to fully explain the religious phenomenon. Rather Freud's reductionism was a preparation for a deeper understanding of religious experience. Therefore we endeavored to develop the implicit teleology in Freud with reference to religion. With an accounting given to the neurotic elements we were still left with man in confrontation with a Being who is not reducible to the father. Beyond the religious symbols we found the sacred symbols which remain concealed till a reductive analysis has taken place. Through our own development the case studies were made to reveal an evolution in awareness of the "Wholly Other" as other. They allowed us to see man less and less under the influence of the "return of the repressed"; we saw the victory of the "reality principle" over the "pleasure principle."

Having seen Freud's analysis of religion on the individual level, we turned to his study of the origins of religion in culture. Again we saw that Freud employed an analysis which reduced religion in culture to the primal crime. While objections were brought against Freud's methodology in this vast study, we have taken the position that even if there were not a primal crime as an historical event, civilization might still react in the same way (religion) to its unconscious Oedipal wishes.

With this reductionism to the primal crime or Oedipal wishes religion in culture has not been totally accounted for. Through our own analysis, we saw that the reductionism was the first moment toward a richer insight into religious experience. There was revealed an evolution in the race's awareness of the "Wholly Other" as other. A reductionism of the religious symbols employed by man from the "beginning" and distorted by time were made to reveal the sacred.

We then discussed Freud's views on contemporary religious experience. At the core of religion we, with Freud, found illusion or wish fulfillment. The God that religion presents to man is a God of accusation and consolation corresponding to two aspects of the Oedipal drama: fear and longing for the father. Freud analyzed the various reasons that believers give for their assent to religious doctrines and he found them inadequate. Because of the spurious grounds upon which religion is based and its detrimental qualities, Freud proposed a religionless education. Replacing religion would be science which seeks in a way to accomplish what religion failed to do: grasp reality as it reveals itself. Psychoanalysis as part of science would share the same role. We have tried to answer the objections which have been brought against Freud's position.

After the reductive interpretation which reveals the God of accusation and consolation as a product of infantile desires and fears, we believe philosophy of religion is offered the option of going beyond this idol. Finally, we looked to Freud's contribution which is a radical purification of all religious experience which claims to bear a relationship to the "Wholly Other." Freud, in a way, is like Moses in that he destroys the false gods and prepares for the advent of the "Wholly Other": "I am the Lord thy God: thou shalt not have strange gods before Me."

NOTES

[1]Freud (1927), *The Future of an Illusion*, p. 25.
[2]*Ibid.*, p. 30.
[3]Freud (1929), *Civilization and Its Discontents*, p. 80.
[4]Freud (1927), *The Future of an Illusion*, p. 30.
[5]*Ibid.*, p. 31.
[6]Ibid., p. 33.
[7]*Ibid.*, p. 16.

[8]*Ibid.*, p. 17.

[9]*Ibid.*, p. 18.

[10]Freud (1932), *New Introductory Lectures on Psychoanalysis*, XXII, 162.

[11]*Ibid.*, p. 163.

[12]*Ibid.*, p. 164.

[13]Freud (1927), *The Future of an Illusion*, p. 24.

[14]Freud (1929), *Civilization and Its Discontents*, p. 84.

[15]Freud (1910), "Future Prospects of Psycho-analytic Therapy," XI, 146.

Freud (1909), "Five Lectures on Psychoanalysis, XI, 50. Freud (1913), "The Claims of Psychoanalysis to Scientific Interest," XIII, 188. Freud (1921), *Group Psychology and the Analysis of the Ego*, XVIII, 142.

[16]Freud (1929), *Civilization and Its Discontents*, p. 85.

[17]Freud (1927), *The Future of an Illusion*, p. 32.

[18]Freud (1929), *Civilization and Its Discontents*, p. 87.

[19]Freud (1921), "Psychoanalysis and Telepathy," XVIII, 180.

[20]Freud (1927), *The Future of an Illusion*, p. 50.

[21]Freud (1929), *Civilization and Its Discontents*, p. 77.

[22]*Ibid.*, p. 122.

[23]Freud (1927), *The Future of an Illusion*, p. 49.

[24]Freud (1932), *New Introductory Lectures*, p. 164.

[25]Freud (1927), *The Future of an Illusion*, p. 11.

[26]Freud (1929), *Civilization and Its Discontents*, p. 126.

[27]*Ibid.*, p. 141.

[28]*Ibid.*, p. 135.

[29]*Ibid.*, p. 136.

[30]Freud (1929), *Civilization and Its Discontents.* p. 102. Freud (1932), *Why War?*, XXII, 212.

[31]Freud (1921), *Group Psychology and the Analysis of the Ego*, XVIII, 94.

[32]*Ibid.*, p. 95.

[33]*Ibid.*, p. 134-35.

[34]Freud (1929), *Civilization and Its Discontents*, p. 114.

[35]Freud (1921), *Group Psychology and the Analysis of the Ego*, p. 98.

[36]*Ibid.*, p. 99.

[37]Freud (1929), *Civilization and Its Discontents*, p. 109.

[38]*Ibid.*, p. 143.

[39]*Ibid* ., p. 112.

[40]Freud (1927), *The Future of an Illusion*, p. 37.

[41]*Ibid.*, p. 38.

[42]*Ibid.*

[43]Freud (1908), " 'Civilized' Sexual Morality and Modern Nervous Illness," IX, 187.

44Freud, (1927), *The Future of an Illusion*, p. 40.
45*Ibid.*, p. 41.
46Freud (1929), *Civilization and Its Discontents*, p. 143.
47Freud (1927), *The Future of an Illusion*, p. 35.
48*Ibid.*, p. 39.
49*Ibid.*, p. 26.
50Freud (1932), *New Introductory Lectures*, XXII, 169.
51*Ibid.*, p. 170.
52Freud (1927), *The Future of an Illusion*, p. 38.
53*Ibid.*
54Freud (1932), *New Introductory Lectures*, p. 166.
55*Ibid.*, p. 167.
56Freud (1927), *The Future of an Illusion*, p. 27.
57*Ibid.*
58*Ibid.*, p. 28.
59Freud (1929), *Civilization and Its Discontents*, XXI, 65.
60*Ibid.*, p. 68.
61*Ibid.*, p. 72.
62Freud (1927), *The Future of an Illusion*, p. 19.
63Freud (1929), *Civilization and Its Discontents*, XXI, 76.
64Freud, *Letters of Sigmund Freud*, ed. by Ernest Freud, "Letter to Marie Bonaparte" (13 Aug. 1939), p. 436.
65Freud (1927), *The Future of an Illusion*, p. 28.
66*Ibid.*, p. 29.
67Freud, "Letter to Weiner Achelis," in *Letters by Sigmund Freud*, ed. by Ernest Freud and trans. by Tonia and James Stern (New York: Basic Books, Inc., 1960) 20 Jan 1927, p. 375.
68Freud (1927), *The Future of an Illusion*, p. 32.
69Freud (1929), *Civilization and Its Discontents*, p. 74.
70Freud (1927), *The Future of an Illusion*, p. 54.
71*Ibid.*, p. 47.
72*Ibid.*, p. 48. Freud (1910), *Leonardo da Vinci and a Memory of His Childhood*, XI, 79. Freud (1908), " 'Civilized' Sexual Morality," IX, 199. Freud (1932), *New Introductory Lectures*, XXII, 171.
73Freud (1927), *The Future of an Illusion*, p. 47.
74Freud (1904), "Obituary of Professor C. Hammerschlag" in "Contributions to the *Neue Freie Presse*," IX, 255.
75Freud (1927), *The Future of an Illusion*, p. 49.
76*Ibid.*, p. 50.
77*Ibid.*, p. 48. Freud (1910), *Leonardo da Vinci*, XI, 79. Freud (1908),

" 'Civilized' Sexual Morality,'' IX, 199. Freud (1932), New Introductory Lectures, XXII, 171.

[78]Freud (1927), *The Future of an Illusion*, p. 49.

[79]*Ibid.*, p. 42.

[80]*Ibid.*, p. 43. Freud (1913), ''The Claims of Psychoanalysis to Scientific Interest,'' p. 185.

[81]Freud (1932), *New Introductory Lectures*, p. 168. Freud (1927), *The Future of an Illusion*, p. 43.

[82]*Ibid.*, p. 44.

[83]*Ibid.*, p. 53.

[84]*Ibid.*, p. 43.

[85]*Ibid.*, p. 53.

[86]*Ibid.*, p. 54.

[87]*Ibid.*, p. 53.

[88]Freud (1932), *New Introductory Lectures*, p. 171.

[89]Freud (1927), *The Future of an Illusion*, p. 54.

[90]*Ibid.*, p. 54.

[91]Freud (1924), ''The Economic Problem of Masochism,'' XIX, 168.

[92]Freud (1924), ''The Loss of Reality in Neurosis and Psychosis,'' XIX, 185.

[93]Freud (1911), ''Formulations on the Two Principles of Mental Functioning,'' XII, 223.

[94]Freud (1929), *Civilization and Its Discontents*, p. 74.

[95]Freud (1927), *The Future of an Illusion*, p. 55.

[96]*Ibid.*, p. 56.

[97]Freud (1932), *New Introductory Lectures*, XXII, 159.

[98]*Ibid.*, p. 160.

[99]*Ibid.*, p. 161.

[100]*Ibid.*, p. 162.

[101]*Ibid.*, p. 170.

[102]*Ibid.*, p. 171.

[103]Freud (1938), *Moses and Monotheism*, XXIII, 129.

[104]*New Introductory Lectures*, p. 172.

[105]*Moses and Monotheism*, p. 129.

[106]Freud (1927), *The Future of an Illusion*, p. 54.

[107]*Ibid.*, p. 55.

[108]Freud (1932), *New Introductory Lectures*, p. 173.

[109]Freud (1920), *Beyond the Pleasure Principle*, XVIII, 64. Freud (1926), *Inhibitions, Symptoms and Anxiety*, XX, 96.

[110]Freud (1932), *New Introductory Lectures*, p. 174. Ernest Jones (quoting Freud to Marie Bonaparte, in *Life and Works of Sigmund Freud*, II, 419).

[111]Freud (1926), "The Question of Lay Analysis," XX, 191.

[112]Freud (1915), *Introductory Lectures*, XV, 51.

[113]Freud (1932), *New Introductory Lectures*, XXII, 158.

[114]*Ibid.*, p. 159.

[115]*Ibid.*, p. 182.

[116]*Ibid.*, p. 159.

[117]Freud (1917), "A Difficulty in the Path of Psychoanalysis," XVII, 142.

[118]Freud (1921), "Psychoanalysis and Telepathy," XVIII, 178.

[119]Freud (1922), "Two Encyclopaedia Articles," XVIII, 253.

[120]*Ibid.*, p. 254.

[121]Freud (1927), *The Future of an Illusion*, p. 36.

[122]*Ibid.*, p. 77.

[123]Freud (1922), "Two Encyclopaedia Articles," p. 252.

[124]Freud (1915), *Introductory Lectures*, XVI, 389. Freud (1918), "On the Teaching of Psychoanalysis in Universities," XVII, 173. Freud (1926), "Question of Lay Analysis," p. 248. Freud (1925). "Psycho-analysis," XX, 268.

[125]Philip Rieff, *Freud, the Mind of the Moralist*, p. 266.

[126]*Ibid.*, p. 268.

[127]*Ibid.*, p. 282.

[128]Will Herberg, *Judaism and Modern Man*, (Philadelphia: Jewish Publication Society of America, 1951), p. 37.

[129]Herdis LeRoy Deabler, "Freud's View of Religion," (Unpublished Ph.D. dissertation, Department of Psychology of Religion, Boston University, 1936), p. 222.

[130]William A. Luijpen, *Phenomenology and Atheism* (Pittsburgh: Duquesne University Press, 1964), p. 153.

[131]*Ibid.*, p. 154.

[132]Freud (1927), *The Future of an Illusion*, p. 30-32.

[133]Karl Stern, *The Third Revolution: A Study of Psychiatry and Religion* (New York: Harcourt-Brace, 1954), p. 122. Erich Fromm, "The Philosophical Basis of Freud's Psycho-analysis," *Pastoral Psychology*, XXIII, No. 121. (Feb. 1962), 26.

[134]*Ibid.*

[135]Fritz Wittels, *Freud and His Time*, p. 52.

[136]*Ibid.*, p. 53.

[137]Dalbiez, *Psychoanalytical Method and the Doctrine of Freud*, II, 319-20. Gabriel Vahanian, *The Death of God* (New York: George Braziller, 1961), p. 166.

[138]Rieff, *Freud, The Mind of the Moralist*, p. 298.

[139]Dalbiez, *Psychoanalytical Method and the Doctrine of Freud*, II, 294.

[140]Andrew Eickhoff, "Freud's Criticism of Religion and the Roman Catholic

Reply" (Unpublished Ph.D. dissertation, Department of Psychology of Religion, Boston University, 1953), pp. 131, 212.

[141]Ernest Jones, *Life and Work of Sigmund Freud*, I, 34.

[142]Fritz Whittels, *Freud and His Time* (New York: Liverright, 1931), p. 49.

[143]H. M. Tiebout, "Freud and Theology," *Religion in Life*, XXVII, (1957-58), 269.

[144]Freud (1921), "Psychoanalysis and Telepathy," p. 178. Freud (1915), *Introductory Lectures*, XIX, 22.

[145]Freud (1932), *New Introductory Lectures*, p. 171.

[146]Freud (1922), "Two Encyclopaedia Articles," p. 253.

[147]Freud (1924), "The Resistance to Psychoanalysis," XIX, 215. Freud (1915), *Introductory Lectures*, XIX, 20.

[148]Freud (1927), *The Future of an Illusion*, XXI, 32.

[149]Gregory Zilboorg, *Mind, Medicine and Man* (New York: Harcourt, Brace and Company, 1943), p. 308.

"Freud exaggerates the psychological difference between scientific hypotheses and religious beliefs. Both satisfy to some extent the will to take power over the object and at the same time the will to give power to the object. Only by denying this can Freud so strictly separate the religious illusions and delusions as will products from the scientific theories as the products of reality-facing intelligence. If there are unbalanced religious beliefs, are there not also scientific theories that imply the taking of too much power or too little?" C. Moxon, "Freud's Denial of Religion," *British Journal of Medical Psychology*, XI (1931), 152.

[150]Ricoeur, *Freud and Philosophy*, p. 530.

[151]*Ibid.*

[152]*Ibid.*, p. 534.

[153]Paul Ricoeur, "Religion, Atheism and Faith," in Alasdair MacIntyre and Paul Ricoeur, *The Religious Significance of Atheism* (New York: Columbia University Press, 1969), p. 59.

[154]*Ibid.*, p. 60.

[155]*Ibid.*, p. 69.

[156]*Ibid.*, p. 81.

[157]*Ibid.*, p. 88.

[158]*Ibid.*, p. 89.

[159]*Ibid.*, p. 97.

[160]*Ibid.*, p. 98.

[161]*Ibid.*, p. 549.

[162]Freud (1910), *Leonardo da Vinci and A Memory of His Childhood*, p. 74.

[163]" . . . the view may be hazarded that Leonardo's development approaches Spinoza's mode of thinking," *Ibid.*, p. 75.

[164]*Ibid.*

[165]*Ibid.*, p. 76.

[166]*Ibid.*, p. 137.

[167]Lee, *Freud and Christianity*, p. 136. Eickhoff, "The Psychodynamics of Freud's Criticism of Religion," *Pastoral Psychology*, XI, No. 104 (May 1960), 35. Harry E. Meserve, "Freud's Contribution to Religion: An Editorial," *Journal of Religion and Health*, V, No. 2 (1966), 90.

[168]Lee, *Freud and Christianity*, p. 139.

[169]*Ibid.*, Lee, *Psychology and Worship*, p. 9.

"If psychoanalysis helps to clear away the rubbish that clings to Christianity and frees it to grow to its full strength and maturity, it will do it an immeasurable service. If Christianity insists on clinging to neurotic manifestations of the unconscious as true religion for full-grown men and women, it dooms itself to be cast aside in man's upward struggle towards the natural goals of freedom, power and love. It will cease to be truly 'Christian.' " Lee, *Freud and Christianity*, p. 197.

[170]Luijpens, *Phenomenology and Atheism*, p. 153.

[171]*Ibid.*, p. 158.

[172]*Ibid.*, p. 159.

[173]*Ibid.*, p. 324.

[174]*Ibid.*, p. 326.

[175]C. G. Jung, "Sigmund Freud in his Historical Setting," *Character and Personality*, I (Sept. 1932-June 1933), 51.

[176]Helen V. McLean, "A Few Comments on *Moses and Monotheism*," *Psychoanalytic Quarterly*, IX, (1940), 211.

"History gives sufficient evidence that expiation, atonement, and regression to simpler beliefs, are preferable. A monotheistic, spiritual father religion easily regresses to a son-mother religion with superstitious idolatry; democracy yields to fascism, and prejudice and dogma replace the scientific search for truth. In every individual genitality is maintained with difficulty, and in society the tendency to regress to primitive infantile social forms is always recurring." *Ibid.*

[177]David Bakan, *Sigmund Freud and the Jewish Mystical Tradition* (Princeton: Van Nostrand Co., Inc., 1958), p. vii.

[178]D. C. McClelland, "Religious Overtones in Psychoanalysis," *Theology Today*, XVI, (1959), 64.

[179]*Ibid.*, p. 44.

[180]James Collins, *God in Modern Philosophy*, p. 392.

[181]Luijpens, *Phenomenology and Atheism*, p. 91.

[182].*Ibid.*, p. 336-37.

[183]Henri de Lubac, *The Discovery of God* (New York: P. J. Kennedy & Sons), 1960), p. 24.

[184]*Ibid.*

[185]Harvey Cox, *The Secular City* (New York: The Macmillan Co., 1965), p. 258.

[186]Paul Ramsey, "Preface," in *The Death of God* by G. Vahanian, (New York: George Braziller, Inc., 1961), p. xxvii.

[187]*Ibid.*

[188]Freud, "Letter to Ludwig Binswanger," in *Sigmund Freud: Reminiscenses of a Friendship* (1 Oct. 1936), p. 96.

Bibliography

Achinstein, Peter. "Models, Analogies, and Theories," *Philosophy of Science*, 1964.

Agassi, Joseph. "Analogies as Generalization." *Philosophy of Science*, 1964.

Aldington, Hilda. *Tribute to Freud.* New York: Pantheon Books, Inc., 1956.

Alston, William P. *Philosophy of Language.* Englewood Cliffs: Prentice-Hall, Inc., 1964.

Altizer, Thomas J. J. *The Gospel of Christian Atheism.* Philadelphia: The Westminster Press, n.d.

————, and Hamilton, William. *The Death of God.* New York: Bobbs-Merrill Co., 1966.

Andreas-Salome, Lou. *The Freud Journal of Lou Andreas-Salome.* Translated and with an introduction by Stanley A. Levy. New York: Basic Books, Inc., 1964.

Arlow, Jacob A. "Psychoanalysis as a Scientific Method." *Psychoanalysis, Scientific Method and Philosophy.* Edited by Sidney Hook. New York: New York University Press, 1959.

————, and Brenner, Charles. *Psychoanalytic Concepts and the Structural Theory.* New York: International Universities Press, Inc., 1964.

Bakan, David. *Sigmund Freud and the Jewish Mystical Tradition.* Princeton, N.J.: Van Nostrand Co., Inc., 1958.

Barag, G. "The Question of Jewish Monotheism." *American Imago*, IV, 1947.

Bartemeier, Leo H. "Psychoanalysis and Religion." *Bulletin of the Menninger Clinic*, XXIX, Sept. 1965.

Beck, Lewis W. "Conscious and Unconscious Motives." *Mind*, LXXV, April 1966.

Bellak, Leopold. "The Unconscious." *American Handbook of Psychiatry*, II. New York: Basic Books, Inc., 1959.

————. "The Unconscious." *Conceptual and Methodological Problems in Psychoanalysis*. Edited by L. Bellak. Annals of the New York Academy of Sciences, LXXVI, Art. 4, Jan. 1959.

————, and Smith, M. Brewster. "An Experimental Exploration of the Psychoanalytic Process." *Psychoanalytic Quarterly*, XXV, 1956.

Benjamin, John D. "Methodological Considerations in the Validation and Elaboration of Psychoanalytical Personality Theory." *American Journal of Orthopsychiatry*, XX, Jan. 1950.

Bergmann, Gustav. "Psychoanalysis and Experimental Psychology: A Review from the Standpoint of Scientific Empiricism." *Psychological Theory*. Edited by Melvin H. Marx. New York: MacMillan Co., 1951.

Berkower, Lary. "The Enduring Effect of the Jewish Tradition Upon Freud." *American Journal of Psychiatry*, CXXV, Feb. 1969.

Bernfield, Siegfield. "Freud's Scientific Beginnings." *The American Imago*, VI, Sept. 1949.

Brathwaite, Richard B. *Scientific Explanation.* Cambridge: Cambridge University Press, 1968.

Brenner, Charles. "The Mechanism of Repression," *Psychoanalysis—A General Psychology*. New York: International Universities Press, Inc., 1966.

Brown, Norman O. *Life Against Death*. Middletown: Wesleyan University Press, 1959.

Carr, H. Wildon. "Philosophical Aspect of Freud's Theory of Dream Interpretation." *Mind* (New Series), XXIII, 1914.

Christiansen, Bjorn. "The Scientific Status of Psychoanalytical Clinical Evidence, III." *Inquiry*, VII, (Spring, 1964).

Dalbiez, Roland. *Psychoanalytical Method and the Doctrine of Freud*. Translated by T. F. Lindsay. Vols. I and II. London: Longmans, Green & Co., 1941.

Danto, Arthur C. "Meaning and Theoretical Terms in Psychoanalysis." *Psychoanalysis, Scientific Method and Philosophy*. Edited by Sidney Hook. New York: New York University Press, 1959.

Deabler, Herdis LeRoy. "Freud's View of Religion." Unpublished

Ph.D. dissertation, Department of Psychology of Religion, Boston University, 1936.

Demos, Raphael. "Psychoanalysis: Science and Philosophy." *Psychoanalysis, Scientific Method and Philosophy.* Edited by Sidney Hook. New York: New York University Press, 1959.

Dewart, Leslie. *The Future of Belief.* New York: Herder & Herder, 1966.

Edel, Abraham. "The Concept of the Unconscious: Some Analytic Preliminaries." *Philosophy of Science,* 1964.

Ellis, Albert, "An Introduction to the Principles of Scientific Psychoanalysis." *Genetic Psychology Monograph,* XLI, 1950.

————. "An Operational Reformulation of Some of the Basic Principles of Psychoanalysis." *Minnesota Studies in the Philosophy of Science.* Edited by H. Feigl and M. Scriven. Vol. I. Minneapolis: University of Minnesota Press, 1956.

Eysenck, Hans J. *Uses and Abuses of Psychology.* London: Pelican, 1953.

————. "Psychoanalysis—Myth or Science?" Inquiry, IV, (Spring, 1961).

Farrell, B. A. "The Criteria for a Psycho-analytic Interpretation." *The Aristotelian Society Supplement,* No. 36. London: Harrison and Sons, Ltd., 1962.

————. "The Status of Psychoanalytic Theory." *Inquiry,* VII, Spring, 1964.

————. "Can Psychoanalysis be Refuted?" *Inquiry,* IV (Spring, 1964).

Feldman, H. "The Id: Present, Past—and Future." *Psychoanalytic Review,* XLVII, 1960.

Fenichel, Otto. "Psychoanalysis and Metaphysics." *The Collected Papers of Otto Fenichel, I.* New York: W. W. Norton & Co., 1953.

Field, G. C. and Aneling, F., and Laird, John. "Is the Conception of the Unconscious of Value in Psychology." *Mind.* 1922.

Flew, Antony. "Motives and the Unconscious." *Minnesota Studies in the Philosophy of Science.* Edited by H. Feigl and M. Scriven. Vol. I. Minneapolis: University of Minnesota Press, 1956.

————. "Psychoanalytic Explanation." Revised edition.

Philosophy and Analysis. Edited by Margaret Macdonald. Oxford: Blackwell, 1954.

Frank, Philipp. "Psychoanalysis and Logical Positivism." *Psychoanalysis, Scientific Method and Philosophy.* Edited by Sidney Hook. New York: New York University Press, 1959.

Frankel, Charles. "The Status of Freud's Ideas." *Psychoanalysis, Scientific Method and Philosophy.* Edited by Sidney Hook. New York: New York University Press, 1959.

Frenkel-Brunswik, Else. "Meaning of Psychoanalytic Concepts and Confirmation of Psychoanalytic Theories." *Scientific Monthly,* LXXIX, 1954.

————. "Psychoanalysis and the Unity of Science." *Proceedings of the American Academy of Arts and Sciences,* LXXX.

Freud, Sigmund (1886). *The Complete Psychological Works of Sigmund Freud.* Edited and Translated by James Strachey. Vol. I-XXXIII. London: Hogarth Press, 1966.

Fromm, Erich. *Psychoanalysis and Religion.* New York: Bantam Books, 1967.

————. "The Philosophical Basis of Freud's Psychoanalysis." *Pastoral Psychology,* XIII, Feb. 1962.

Gramlich, Francis W. "On the Structure of Psychoanalysis." *Psychoanalysis, Scientific Method and Philosophy.* Edited by Sidney Hook. New York: New York University Press, 1959.

Gregor, A. J. "Psychoanalytic Disposition Terms and Reduction Sentences." *Journal of Philosophy,* 1966.

Grunbaum, Adolf. "Remarks on Dr. Kubie's Views." *Psychoanalysis, Scientific Method, and Philosophy.* Edited by Sidney Hook. New York: New York University Press, 1959.

Hartmann, Heintz. *Psychoanalysis and Moral Values.* New York: International University Press, 1960.

————. "Comments on the Scientific Aspects of Psychoanalysis." *The Psychoanalytic Study of the Child,* XIII. New York: International University Press, Inc., 1958.

————. *Essays on Ego Psychology.* London: The Hogarth Press and the Insitute of Psycho-analysis, 1964.

————. "The Application of Psychoanalytic Concepts to Social Science." *Psychoanalytic Quarterly,* 1950.

————. "Psychoanalysis as a Scientific Theory." *Psy-*

choanalysis, Scientific Method, and Philosophy. Edited by Sidney Hook. New York: New York University Press, 1959.

————, and Kris, Ernst. "The Genetic Approach in Psychoanalysis." *The Psychoanalytic Study of the Child,* I. New York: International Universities Press, 1945.

————; Kris, A.; and Loewenstein, R. "Comments of the Formation of Psychic Structure." *Psychoanalytic Study of the Child,* II. New York: International Universities Press, 1946.

Herron, William G. "The Evidence for the Unconscious." *Psychoanalytic Review,* Part I, 1962.

Hesse, Mary. "Analogy and Confirmation Theory." *Philosophy of Science,* 1964.

Higgins, J. "Some Considerations of Psychoanalytic Theory Preliminary to a Philosophical Inquiry." *Proceedings of American Catholic Philosophical Association,* XXXV, 1961.

Hoffman, Martin. "The Idea of Freedom in Psychoanalysis." *International Journal of Psychoanalysis,* XLV, 1964, Part 4.

————. "On the Relationship between Psychoanalysis and the Philosophy of Mind." *Psychoanalytic Quarterly,* XXXI, No. 1. 1962.

Homans, Peter. *Theology after Freud.* New York: Bobbs-Merrill Co., Inc., 1970.

Hook, Sidney. "Science and Mythology in Psychoanalysis." *Psychoanalysis, Scientific Method, and Philosophy.* Edited by Sidney Hook. New York: New York University Press, 1959.

Hospers, John. "Philosophy and Psychoanalysis." *Psychoanalysis, Scientific Method, and Philosophy.* Edited by Sidney Hook. New York: New York University Press, 1959.

Inkeles, Alex. "Psychoanalysis and Sociology." *Psychoanalysis, Scientific Method, and Philosophy.* Edited by Sidney Hook. New York: New York University Press, 1959.

Jones, Ernest. *The Life and Work of Sigmund Freud.* 3 vols. New York: Basic Books, 1961-65.

Jung, Carl G. *Memories, Dreams, Reflections.* Edited by A. Jaffe. Translated by R. & C. Winston. New York: Pantheon Books, 1963.

————. *Collected Works.* Translated by R. F. C. Hull. London: Routledge & Kegan Paul, 1961.

————. "Sigmund Freud in his Historical Setting." *Character and Personality*, I (Sept. 1932-June 1933).

Kardiner, Abram. *The Individual and His Society.* New York: Columbia University Press, 1955.

———— "Social and Cultural Implications of Psychoanalysis." *Psychoanalysis, Scientific Method, and Philosophy.* Edited by Sidney Hook. New York: New York University Press, 1959.

Kennedy, Gail. "Psychoanalysis: Protoscience and Metapsychology." *Psychoanalysis, Scientific Method, and Philosophy.* Edited by Sidney Hook. New York: New York University Press, 1959.

Kaplan, Abraham. "Freud and Modern Philosophy." *Freud and the Twentieth Century.* New York: The World Publishing Co., 1967.

Klingender, F. D. "Paleolithic Religion and the Principle of Social Evolution." *British Journal of Sociology*, V, June 1954.

Kris, Ernst. "The Nature of Psychoanalytic Propositions and Their Validation." *Freedom and Experience.* Edited by Sidney Hook and Milton R. Konvitz. New York: Cornell University Press, 1947.

————. "On Preconscious Mental Processes." *Psychoanalytic Quarterly*, 1950.

Kroeber, A. L. "*Totem and Taboo*: An Ethologic Psychoanalysis." American Anthropologist, XXII, Jan. 1920.

————. "*Totem and Taboo* in Retrospect." *American Journal* of Sociology, XLV (Nov. 1939).

————. *Anthropology Today.* Chicago: University of Chicago Press, 1953.

————. *Anthropology.* Revised Edition. New York: Harcourt, Brace and World, Inc., 1948.

Kubie, Lawrence S. "Problems and Techniques of Psychoanalytic Validation and Progress." *Psychoanalysis as Science.* Edited by E. Pumpian-Mindlin. New York: Basic Books, Inc., 1952.

————. "Psychoanalysis and Scientific Method." *Psychoanalysis, Scientific Method, and Philosophy.* Edited by Sidney Hook. New York: New York University Press, 1959.

Laird, J., Field, G. C., and Aveling, F. "Is the Conception of the Unconscious of Value in Psychology." *Mind*, 1922.

Lazerowitz, Morris. "The Relevance of Psychoanalysis to Philosophy." *Psychoanalysis, Scientific Method, and Philosophy.* Edited by Sidney Hook. New York: New York University Press, 1959.

Luijpen, William A. *Phenomenology and Atheism.* Pittsburgh: Duquesne University Press, 1964.

MacIntyre, Alasdair C. *The Unconscious.* London: Routledge and Kegan Paul, 1958.

MacIver, R. M. *Social Causation.* Boston: Ginn & Co., 1942.

Marcuse, Herbert, *Eros and Civilization.* Boston, Beacon Press, 1955.

Martin, M. "The Explanatory Value of the Unconscious." *Philosophy of Science,* 1964.

Martin, Michael. "The Scientific Status of Psychoanalytic Clinical Evidence." *Inquiry,* VII, Spring 1964.

Masih, Y. "Metapsychology of James and Freud." India: Journal of Bihar University, I, 1956.

McClelland, D. C. "Religious Overtones in Psycho-analysis." *Theology Today,* XVI, 1959.

Mead, Margaret. "*Totem and Taboo* Reconsidered with Respect." *Bulletin of the Menninger Clinic,* XXVII, July, 1963.

Meserve, Harry E. "Freud's Contribution to Religion: An Editorial." *Journal of Religion and Health,* V, 1966.

Miles, T. R. *Eliminating the Unconscious: A Behaviorist View of Psychoanalysis.* New York: Pergamon Press, 1966.

Nagel, Ernest. *The Structure of Science.* New York: Harcourt, Brace and World, Inc., 1961.

————. "Methodological Issues in Psychoanalytic Theory." *Psychoanalysis, Scientific Method, and Philosophy.* Edited by Sidney Hook. New York: New York University Press, 1959.

Nelson, Benjamin. "The Future of Illusions." *Man in Contemporary Society.* Edited by Contemporary Civ. Staff of Columbia College. II. New York, 1956.

Nunberg, Herman, and Federn, Ernst (eds.) *Minutes of the Vienna Psychoanalytic Society.* Vol. I (1906-1908), and Vol. II (1908-1910). New York: International Universities Press, Inc., 1962.

Ostow, Mortimer. "The Structural Model: Ego, Id and Superego." *Conceptual and Methodological Problems in Psychoanalysis.*

Edited by L. Bellak. Annals of the New York Academy of Sciences, LXXVI, Art. IV. Jan. 1959.

————. "Religion and Psychoanalysis: The Area of Common Concern." *Pastoral Psychology,* X, May, 1959.

————. "Psychoanalysis and Ethology." *Journal of American Psychoanalytic Association,* VIII, 1960.

Pap, Arthur. "On the Empirical Interpretation of Psychoanalytic Concepts." *Psychoanalysis, Scientific Method, and Philosophy.* Edited by Sidney Hook. New York: New York University Press, 1959.

Pasquarelli, B. "Psychoanalysis and Religion: A Postulated Autonomy." *Philadelphia Psychoanalytic Association,* X, March, 1960.

Popper, Karl R. "Philosophy of Science: A Personal Report." *British Philosophy in the Mid-Century.* Edited by C. A. Mace. London: Allen & Unwin, 1957.

Pumpian-Mindlin, Eugene (ed.). *Psychoanalysis as Science.* New York: Basic Books, Inc., 1952.

————. "The Position of Psychoanalysis in Relation to the Biological and Social Sciences." *Psychoanalysis As Science.* Edited by E. Pumpian-Mindlin. New York: Basic Books, Inc., 1952.

————. "Propositions Concerning Energetic-Economic Aspects of Libido Theory: Conceptual Models of Psychic Energy and Structures in Psychoanalysis." *Conceptual and Methodological Problems in Psychoanalysis.* Edited by L. Bellak. Annals of the New York Academy of Sciences, LXXVI, Art. IV (Jan. 1959).

Racker, Heinrich. "On Freud's Position Towards Religion." *American Imago,* XIII, 1956.

Ramsey, Paul. "Preface to Gabriel Vahanian *The Death of God.*" New York: George Braziller, Inc., 1961.

Rapaport, David. "Psychoanalysis and Developmental Psychology." *Perspectives in Psychological Theory.* Edited by B. Kaplan and S. Wapner. International Universities Press, 1960.

————. "The Structure of Psychoanalytic Theory: A Systematizing Attempt." *Psychological Issues Monograph,* II, 1960.

Reik, Theodore, *Freud als Kulturkritcher.* Vienna: Max Praeger, 1930.

258

————. *Dogma and Compulsion*. New York: International Universities Press, 1951.

————. *The Psychological Problems of Religion*. New York: Farrar, Straus & Co., Inc., 1946.

Reiner, Markus. "Causality and Psychoanalysis." *Psychoanalytic Quarterly*, I, 1932.

Richfield, Jerome. "On the Scientific Status of Psychoanalysis." *Scientific Monthly*, LXXIX, 1954.

Ricoeur, Paul. "The Atheism of Freudian Psychoanalysis." *Is God Dead?* Vol. XVI of *Concilium*. Edited by Johannes B. Metz. New York: The Paulist Press, 1966.

————. "Religion, Atheism, and Faith." *The Religious Significance of Atheism*. New York: Columbia University Press, 1969.

————. *Freud and Philosophy*. Translated by Denis Savage. New Haven: Yale University Press, 1970.

————. *De l'interpretation*. Paris: Editions du Sevil, 1965.

————. *Freedom and Nature: The Voluntary and the Involuntary*. Translated by E. V. Kohik. Evanston: Northwestern University Press, 1966.

Rieff, Philip. "Freud's Contribution to Political Philosphy." Unpublished Ph.D. dissertation, Department of Political Science, University of Chicago, 1954.

————. *Freud, The Mind of the Moralist*. New York: Viking Press, 1959.

————. "The Meaning of History and Religion in Freud's Thought." *The Journal of Religion*, XXXI, April, 1951.

————. *The Triumph of the Therapeutic*. New York: Harper Torchbooks. 1966.

Riese, Walther. "The Pre-Freudian Origins of Psychoanalysis." Edited by Jules H. Masserman. *Science and Psychoanalysis*. New York: Grune & Stratton, 1958.

Riesman, David. "Freud: Religion as Neurosis." *University of Chicago Round Table*, No. 638 (June, 1950).

Ritvo, Lucille B. "Darwin as the Source of Freud's Neo-Lamarckianism." *Journal of the American Psychoanalytic Association*, XIII, 1965.

Ross, Nathaniel. "Beyond the Future of an Illusion." *New Bulletin of the New York Psychoanalytic Association,* IV, Oct. 1964.

————. "Psychoanalysis and Religion." *Journal of the American Psychoanalytic Association.* Vol. VI. New York: International Universities Press, 1958.

Rubinstein, Benjamin B. "On the Inference and Confirmation of Clinical Interpretations." Presented in abbreviated form to the New York Psychoanalytic Society, May 28, 1968.

Salmon, Wesley C. "Psychoanalytic Theory and Evidence." *Psychoanalysis, Scientific Method, and Philosophy.* Edited by Sidney Hook. New York: New York University Press, 1959.

Sanders, Benjamin Gilbert. *Christianity After Freud.* London: Macmillan Co., 1949.

Schoenfeld, C. G. "Three Fallacious Attacks on Psychoanalysis as Science." *Psychoanalytic Review,* XLIX (Winter, 1962),

Schmidl, Fritz. "The Problem of Scientific Validation in Psychoanalytic Interpretations." *International Journal of Psycho-analysis,* 1955.

Schoenfeld, C. G. "God the Father and Mother: Study and Extension of Freud's Conception of God as an Exalted Father." *American Imago,* XIX, 1963.

Scriven, Michael. "The Experimental Investigation of Psychoanalysis." *Psychoanalysis, Scientific Method, and Philosophy.* Edited by Sidney Hook. New York: New York University Press, 1959.

Seaborn, James G. *Some Philosophical Implications of Psychoanalysis.* Ph.D. dissertation, University of London, 1961.

Shope, Robert, "Wish Fulfillment and Psychic Energy in Psychoanalytic Theory." Unpublished Ph.D. dissertation, Harvard University, 1966.

Silverman, Robert E. "Psychoanalysis and Scientific Method." *Psychoanalysis, Scientific Method, and Philosophy.* Edited by Sidney Hook. New York: New York University Press, 1959.

Skinner, B. F. "Critique of Psycho-analytic Concepts and Theories." *Minnesota Studies in the Philosophy of Science.* Edited by H. Feigl and M. Scriven. Vol. I. Minneapolis: University of Minnesota Press, 1956.

Southard, S. "Nineteenth Century Religion and Early Psychoanalysis." *Review and Exposition*, LII, 1955.

Stern, Karl. *The Third Revolution: A Study of Psychiatry and Religion.* New York: Harcourt, Brace & World, Inc., 1954.

Stoodley, B. H. *The Concepts of Sigmund Freud.* Glencoe, Ill.: The Free Press, 1959.

Taubes, Jacob. "Religion and the Future of Psychoanalysis." *Psychoanalysis,* IV, 1957.

Van den Haag, Ernest. "Psychoanalysis and its Discontents." *Psychoanalysis, Scientific Method, and Philosophy.* Edited by Sidney Hook. New York: New York University Press, 1959.

Waelder, Robert. *Psycho-analysis, Scientific Method and Philosophy* (Review. *Journal of the American Psychoanalytic Association*) X, 1962.

Wiegand, Dietmar. "Religions Philosophie bei S. Freud." *Z. Religions und Geistegeschite*, XII, (1960).

Williams, Donald C. "Philosophy and Psychoanalysis." *Psychoanalysis, Scientific Method, and Philosophy.* Edited by Sidney Hook. New York: New York University Press, 1959.

Wisdom, J. O. "The Criteria for a Psycho-analytic Interpretation." *The Aristotelian Society Supplement.* No. 36. London: Harrison and Sons, Ltd., 1962.

Zilboorg, Gregory. "Psychoanalysis and Religion." *Atlantic Monthly*, CLXXXIII, (1949).

————. *Freud and Religion.* Westminster: The Newman Press, 1964.

Index

The Index has been kept short, so as to provide merely references to definitions of important terms within the work. For extended treatment of the major topics, the Table of Contents should be used.

dialectic, 7, 8, 42, 43
Devil, 108-112
faith, 2
genesis, 7-9, 11, 38, 41-44, 65-79
genetic, 5, 23, 41, 56, 188
God, 2, 4, 108-112, 115, 123, 136
growth, 24, 28
Holy Communion, 177
hysteria, 102, 106, 117
identification, 72
model, 34
monotheism, 176
neurosis, 160
Oedipus Complex, 25, 62, 63
ontogeny, 19, 21
obsessions, 91, 116
oceanic feeling, 218
paranoia, 85, 116
paraphrenias, 83, 116
phobia, 117

phylogenetic, 23, 24, 38
pleasure principle, 4, 7, 11, 15, 46
psychoanalysis, 2, 3, 226
regression, 22, 26, 33, 37
reductionism, 2, 3, 5, 7, 20, 194
reality principle, 4, 7, 11, 15, 46
sublimation, 73
symbol, 133, 134, 144, 145
religion, 2-4, 6, 13, 93, 208
science, 224
taboo, 169
telos, 7-9, 41-44, 69-75, 194, 232
teleology, 2, 7, 9, 10, 12, 15, 20, 23, 28, 38, 40, 56
totemism, 173
unconscious, 65-69, 70
"Wholly Other," 1, 2, 7, 10-12, 16, 17, 82, 135, 137-142, 145-149, 195-201, 232